SELECTED ESSAYS
OF AHAD HA–'AM

SELECTED ESSAYS

OF AHAD HA–'AM

TRANSLATED FROM THE HEBREW, EDITED,
AND WITH AN INTRODUCTION

by Leon Simon

A TEMPLE BOOK

ATHENEUM 1981 NEW YORK

TO MY TEACHER
AHAD HA-'AM
AND TO MY FRIEND
ASHER GINZBERG
THIS VOLUME OF TRANSLATIONS
IS DEDICATED

Published by Atheneum
Reprinted by arrangement with
The Jewish Publication Society of America
Copyright © 1912, 1939 by
The Jewish Publication Society of America
"Preface to the 1962 Reprint" copyright © 1962 by
The Jewish Publication Society of America
All rights reserved
Library of Congress catalog card number 62-20752
ISBN 0-689-70246-9
Manufactured in the United States of America by
The Murray Printing Company
Forge Village, Massachusetts
Published in Canada by McClelland and Stewart Ltd.
First Atheneum Printing August 1970
Second Printing October 1981

PREFACE TO THE 1962 REPRINT

Over half a century has elapsed since first the Jewish Publication Society of America accepted my suggestion that it should publish a volume of Ahad Ha-'Am's Essays in English translation. At that time Zionism was a subject of acute controversy in Western Jewry, and the responsible heads of the Society thought it desirable to avoid any appearance of taking sides on so explosive an issue. Hence the Ahad Ha-'Am of *Selected Essays* is rather the Jewish scholar and thinker, the humanist with a passion for morality, than the implacable Zionist critic of political Zionism. After the end of the First World War, I produced, at the author's express request, a further volume of translations[1] designed to correct the one-sidedness of *Selected Essays* by presenting him in his more polemical aspect also; and many years after his death (which occurred in 1927) there appeared a third volume of translations,[2] in which I attempted a kind of synthesis of the other two. Both these volumes were published in England. That of 1922 includes, along with the most important of Ahad Ha-'Am's early criticisms of Herzlian Zionism, three of his best-known essays not directly connected with that subject—his exposition of the philosophy of Maimonides ("The Supremacy of Reason"), his criticism of Claude Monte-

[1] *Ten Essays on Zionism and Judaism*. London, George Routledge and Sons, 1922.

[2] *Ahad Ha-Am: Essays, Letters, Memoirs*. Oxford, East and West Library, 1946.

fiore's attitude to Christianity ("Judaism and the Gospels"), and the essay in which he assessed, from his own point of view, the achievements of Zionist work in Palestine up to the year 1912 ("Summa Summarum"). The 1946 volume contains revised translations of many of the essays in both its predecessors, some of them in a condensed form, besides a few additional essays, a selection of his published letters, and extracts from his autobiographical notes.

That Zionist polemics were excluded from the Jewish Publication Society's volume of translations does not mean that the essays chosen for inclusion in that volume are not Zionist essays. Zionism—or, to use the earlier name, the Love of Zion—was Ahad Ha-'Am's consuming passion, and everything he wrote was in one form or another an expression of his conviction that there was no salvation for the Jewish people except through its restoration to freedom and creative life in its ancient land. But the Jewish people was for him a unique phenomenon, unique not only in the sense that it has clung to life through many centuries of experience differing radically from that of any other people known to history, but also in the sense that its national cohesion and its hope of a national restoration are inseparably bound up with those specifically Jewish values and ideals which have found their highest expression in the utterances of the ancient Hebrew Prophets. Thus there was for him no real distinction between the national and the ethico-religious strands in the fabric of Jewish thought, or, in other words, between Zionism and Judaism ; and he did not write sometimes about Judaism and sometimes about Zionism, but always, or nearly always, about both at once. To take as examples two of the essays included in the present volume: "The Transvaluation of Values," though its concern is with Judaism in relation to the philosophy of Nietzsche, a subject which seems to have no connection with Zionism, was in fact a broadside in his prolonged controversy with the "angry young men" of his generation, M. J. Berdichewsky and others, who were in revolt against the traditional devotion of the Jewish people to the things of the spirit because they saw in it an obstacle to the achievement of national emancipation; and even "Moses," the finest of his essays, which appears on the face of it to be remote from current controversy, ends with a veiled but unmistakable declaration of faith in spiritual Zionism. It is not that with Ahad Ha-'Am Zionism was a sort of King Charles's head, which would obtrude itself into whatever he might write, but simply that it was for him unthinkable that the problem of the Jewish future and the historic manifestations of the characteristic Jewish attitude to life should be treated as separate and unrelated subjects.

Time has robbed Ahad Ha-'Am's more polemical essays, and in particular those directed against Herzlian Zionism, of their actuality. But his conception of the function of Palestine as the "national spiritual centre" of a still dispersed Jewish people is still—or rather is now more than ever—a live issue; and his contributions to the exposition and illumination of the distinctive ethical and religious ideas of the Jewish people are as valuable today as they were two generations ago. It is therefore not surprising that, despite the revolutionary changes in Jewish life which the past few decades have brought about, there is still some demand for this book, which, originally published in 1912, has already been twice reprinted without change (1936 and 1948); and my gratitude to the Jewish Publication Society for taking steps to satisfy that demand will, I trust, be widely shared.

The opportunity of the present reprint has been taken to make a few small corrections in the text; but substantially the translations remain as they were first printed. The translator's Introduction also has been left as it was, although there is much in it that would be modified or expressed differently if I were writing it today. For a more comprehensive account of Ahad Ha-'Am's life and work, I can now refer the reader to *Ahad Ha-Am (Asher Ginzberg): A Biography,* which the Society published for me in 1960.

LONDON, APRIL, 1962.

L. S.

PREFACE

The collected Essays of Ahad Ha-'Am [1] (Asher Ginzberg) appeared in 1904 in three volumes, under the title '*Al Parashat Derakim* (" At the Parting of the Ways "). The Essays included in the present volume are a comparatively small selection, but they will probably give an adequate idea of the author's attitude on Jewish questions.

The Essays do not appear in strict chronological order in this volume, because the first eight of them form a single series (to which the author gave the name of " Fragments," with the subtitle " Short Talks on Great Subjects " [2]), and it did not seem desirable to break up this series. Moreover, the essay " Flesh and Spirit," which is latest in date, belongs of right to the " Fragments," and has been placed immediately after them at the author's wish.

Ahad Ha-'Am has been translated into many languages, but very few of the Essays in his collected

---

[1] This pseudonym, which has been invariably used by Asher Ginzberg, since his first appearance in print, means "one of the people."

[2] It is worth mentioning that this subtitle was chosen before the author had heard of J. A. Froude's book with a very similar name.

works have appeared in English.[1] I have refrained of set purpose from consulting any other translation, desiring that my own version should be as close a reproduction of the original as I could make of it.

The translation has had the advantage of the author's revision, and my best thanks are due to him for the correction of many errors and the suggestion of many improvements. But this acknowledgment of assistance involves no transfer of responsibility.

The foot-notes which I have added are placed in square brackets: the others appear in the original.

LONDON, DECEMBER, 1911.

L. S.

[1] He has written a good deal since 1904, but the later essays have not yet appeared in book form. A translation of one of them ("Judaism and the Gospels") appeared in the Jewish Review for September 1910 (vol. i, no. 3).

CONTENTS

INTRODUCTION

BY THE TRANSLATOR

The Essays of Ahad Ha-'Am deal with a great variety of subjects; but they are all concerned more or less directly with the theoretical and the practical problems of the Jewish people. They present, in outline at least, a philosophy of Jewish history (that term being used in its widest sense, to include the development of Jewish thought) ; and at the same time they advocate certain practical steps which are the logical outcome of that philosophy. Many of them have been written on the occasion of passing events, and are mainly critical, or even polemical, in character. Essays of this kind have their value as indicating the application of the author's point of view to particular questions. But for the purpose of the present volume of translations it has been considered preferable to select those Essays which deal with the more permanent aspects of Jewish life and thought.

The aim of this Introduction is to present the author's main ideas, which are scattered through the various Essays, in a connected form, and thus place the reader at a standpoint from which each Essay can be appreciated in its relation to the general scheme of the author's thought. In performing this task, it may well be that the translator has not escaped the danger that besets any writer who attempts to state in his own way the philosophy of his teacher—the danger of putting things in a wrong perspective, of distributing the emphasis in a way which the teacher would not accept. For this reason I think it well to state that the responsibility for the presentment of " Ahad Ha-'Amism " contained in this Introduction rests with myself alone. How far it is a just presentment the Essays themselves will enable the reader to determine.

I

The history of the Hebrews (it will be convenient to use this term in speaking of the race, because " Jew " and " Jewish " have acquired a specifically religious connotation) is the history of a living organism, whose life is the outward expression of a certain fundamental character or spirit. The mode of expression varies at different times, being determined largely by external circumstances. But throughout the national " will-to-live " is asserting itself, not merely in the physical survival of the Hebrews, but in the creation of a specific type of life, and the expression of a specific outlook on human problems, without which the mere existence of the Hebrews as a race would mean nothing. This type of life and this outlook embody, in deed and in thought, the Hebrew spirit.

It will be as well to examine this word " spirit " a little more closely, because the Hebrew word of which it is the nearest English equivalent is one of very frequent occurrence in the writings of Ahad Ha-'Am, and the word " spirit " and more especially the adjective " spiritual " are apt, if used without explanation, to convey an impression foreign to the meaning of the original. To begin with, we instinctively think of " spirit " as the antithesis of " flesh " or " body: " devotion to " the things of the spirit " implies at once an attitude of hostility, or, at best, of indifference, to the things of the flesh. To read that idea into the word " spirit " as used in an English translation of Ahad Ha-'Am—inevitably used, for there is no better word—would be to misconstrue him entirely. The " spirit " is that of which " mind " and " body " are alike the expression: it is the inner or real life, the *inwardness* of a thing—what the Germans call *das Wesen*. The English use of the word approaches nearer to this sense in such a phrase as " the spirit of the age." But the case is even harder with the adjective " spiritual," which, as ordinarily used in English, has a distinct reference to religion, and to religion conceived as something essentially apart from (and above) the ordinary concerns of human life. To be " spiritual " is to be " other-worldly." But there is no such suggestion about the word as it must be used in translating or writing about Ahad Ha-'Am. That which is " spiritual " is simply that which relates to the " spirit "—the inwardness, *das Wesen*—of a thing, or a person, or an institution, or a nation. Thus the literature and the type of life in which the spirit of a people expresses itself may be spoken of as the " spiritual creations," or " spiritual possessions " of that people, without its being implied that they are of a religious as opposed to a secular character. The line of distinction is drawn not between the higher and the lower, or between the next world and this, but between the underlying idea and its outward expressions.

In saying, then, that the history of the Hebrews is the history of the working out of the Hebrew spirit, one is not, so far, implying that spirituality, in the ordinary sense of the term, is a special characteristic of the Hebrew race. A similar statement would be true of the history of any nation, be it never so materialistic in its outlook and its aims. But it is, in fact, the case that the outlook and the aims of the Hebrew genius have never been materialistic. Nay, more: the bent of the Hebrew mind has never been turned even towards the spiritualized materialism that finds its expression in beauty of form and language, but always to the discovery of fundamental truths about the universe, and the embodiment, in actual life, of fundamental principles based on those truths. Thus the Hebrew spirit is essentially religious and moral. It has expressed itself not in the building up of an empire, not in the elaboration of political institutions, not in the perfection of mechanical devices, not in the production of works of art, but in the search after God, and in the attempt to found a social order based on God's will.

It follows, then, that the typical products of the Hebrew spirit are not conquerors or inventors or artists, but prophets—men whose special gift it is to see into the heart of things, and to enunciate moral laws based on the spiritual truths which are revealed to their superior insight. The Prophets, from Moses onwards, have been regarded by the Hebrews throughout their history as the fine flower of the race; and the Prophetic writings present the Hebraic outlook on life in its supreme literary expression. The historical (or rather archeological) accuracy of the particular statements about the Prophets as individuals which are contained in the Bible does not affect their value, and the value of their writings, from this point of view. Their acceptance by the nation as the highest type which it has produced, and as the exponents of its own outlook and ideals, endows them with more than individual importance, and gives their writings a value which depends in no way on their personalities. The Prophetic books are not merely the utterances of particular men at particular epochs of history; they are the mirror of the Hebrew soul.

In the essential characteristics of the Prophet, therefore, we shall find the Hebrew ideal of character; and in the Prophetic teaching we shall find the Hebrew ideal of conduct. Thus through the Prophets we can discover the real meaning of the term "Hebrew spirit"—the quintessence, as it were, of Hebraism.

The functions of the Prophet do not necessarily include foretelling the future; he is rather a Seer than a fore-seer. Hebrew tradition finds the greatest of the Prophets in Moses, who has little claim to the title in the narrower current sense; and so it is appro-

priately in his essay on Moses that Ahad Ha-'Am sets
forth what are in his view the fundamental qualities
of the Prophetic type. " The Prophet has two fundamental qualities, which distinguish him from the rest
of mankind. First, he is *a man of truth.* He sees
life as it is, with a view unwarped by subjective feelings ; and he tells you what he sees just as he sees it,
unaffected by irrelevant considerations. He tells the
truth not because he wishes to tell the truth, not because he has convinced himself, after inquiry, that
such is his duty, but because he needs must, because
truth-telling is a special characteristic of his genius—
a characteristic of which he cannot rid himself, even
if he would. . . . Secondly, the Prophet is an *extremist.* He concentrates his whole heart and mind
on his ideal, in which he finds the goal of life, and to
which he, is determined to make the whole world do
service, without the smallest exception. . . . He can
accept no excuse, can consent to no compromise, can
never cease thundering his passionate denunciations,
even if the whole universe is against him."

From the absolute truthfulness of the Prophet, and
his absolute refusal to compromise, it follows that his
ideal is perfect Justice, which is " truth in action," or
Righteousness. The Prophet as such stands for the
ideal of a society based on absolute righteousness : a
society, that is, in which each individual does that
which is right from the point of view of the whole,
without regard to his personal interest or convenience.
And that which is right from the point of view of the

whole society is that which is right from the point of view of the whole universe: for such a society embodies in human life the principle of right on which the universe is based. It is, in religious phraseology, a society which works out the will of God on earth.

But the Prophets were not content merely to lay down in the abstract the ideal of a righteous society: they laid it down as an ideal *for their own people*. Their outlook was universal—they wished to see the sway of righteousness established over the whole earth. But it was at the same time essentially national, inasmuch as they regarded it as the peculiar function of the Hebrews to work out the ideal in their own national life and thus secure its universal acceptance. They demanded that Israel should be among the nations what they themselves were in Israel—an elemental force making for righteousness. Such a force can be thwarted, or deflected from its course, by adverse circumstances, or, in other words, by the impact of other opposing forces with which it comes into conflict; but it can never cease to be what it is, or to struggle along its own path. The nation of the Prophets can no more compromise with life than could the Prophets themselves. Other nations may rest content with something less than the absolute ideal; they may recognize that this or that, though desirable in itself, is impossible of attainment in a world such as ours, and may rest satisfied with here or there a step forward. But for the Hebrew nation—as the Prophets conceived it—there could be no acceptance of half-measures. Nothing less than the ideal of absolute righteousness could suffice.

In accepting, as they did, this conception of the Prophets, the Hebrews laid on themselves the duty of struggling forever against the world on behalf of a cause which is, in the ordinary human view, hopeless. They condemned themselves to an everlasting life of preaching in the wilderness. Only by ceasing to be a nation can they cease to be a force making for absolute righteousness, brooking no compromises and content with no half-attainments. This is what it means to them to be " a peculiar people."

II

In accepting the Prophets and their Law, the Hebrews were simply expressing their own national spirit. But the acceptance of an ideal is easier than its fulfilment. In a moment of spiritual exaltation, when we rise to our true height, we may cry " we will do and we will obey ; " but the thing is not so simple as it seems. When the moment's enthusiasm is gone, a body of ordinary mortals cannot take hold of an absolute ideal which has been enunciated without regard to the facts of everyday life. The ideal must be led down to them, as it were, through suitable channels, by which it is adapted to their requirements and their capabilities. These channels—these intermediaries between the Prophets and the people—are the Priests. The Priest is essentially what the Prophet essentially is not—a man of compromise, a man of the hour.

Aaron, making a golden calf because the people want something tangible to worship, is the typical Priest. In his anxiety to prevent a complete revolt from the Prophet by a reasonable compromise, he abandons the very principle for which the Prophet stands, and by virtue of which alone he is worth following. Thus the Priest, devoted adherent of the Prophet as he is, becomes the Prophet's worst enemy. But, the facts of ordinary life being on the side of the Priest, on the side of compromise, it follows that the Prophetic ideal would be lost entirely, did not the unquenchable spirit of the nation, which is the Prophetic spirit, ever and anon reassert itself.

The centuries that elapsed between the close of the Prophetic era and the rise of the Maccabeans were essentially a Priestly period, a period of compromise. And so, when Alexander let loose the flowing tide of Hellenism over the East, the Hebrews accepted an amalgamation of their own traditional way of life with Greek ideas and practices. It was only when Antiochus threatened the complete extinction of Hebraism that the Hebrew spirit rose again in all its strength. The success of the Maccabean rising led to a reaction against Hellenism, and to much missionary activity in the outside world, which sowed the seeds of the coming revolution. But within the Maccabean kingdom itself the victory was not complete. The Sadducees, who for the most part were favored by the royal house, were men of the Priestly type. They stood for a rigid adherence to the letter of the

Prophetic Law; but they acquiesced in the replacement of its spirit by a materialism which regarded wealth and political power as desirable ends. They secured for a time the political existence of the Hebrews, without which the Prophetic ideal could not be realized; but they preserved the body of Hebraism at the expense of its soul. And over against them there rose up another sect, the Essenes, which went to the opposite extreme, and in a life of asceticism and abnegation endeavored to preserve the soul without the body.

But the Prophetic ideal, demanding as it did the expression of the Hebrew spirit in the national life, found its heirs neither in the Sadducees nor in the Essenes. It was the Pharisees who, despite the obloquy so liberally meted out to them in the New Testament, were the true heirs of the Prophetic spirit. It was they who refused either to compromise with the materialism of the world, like the Sadducees, or to abandon the world as hopeless because it was materialistic, as the Essenes did. Their ideal was to make the Law a living tradition, developing organically in connection with the development of the society whose spirit it both reflected and moulded, and remaining true throughout to the Prophetic teaching. The national separateness of the Hebrews was no less essential to them than to the Sadducees; but they saw what it was that made that national separateness essential, and did not mistake immediate political independence for an end in itself. They could not sacrifice the substance for the shadow. Hence they acquiesced in the destruction of the last vestiges of their national liberty by the Romans, so long as they were permitted to keep the lamp of Hebrew tradition alight in their schools, to preserve their ideal intact against the day when its perfect fulfilment should be possible. And the preservation of their ideal was for them not only worth more than political independence: it was worth more even than the acceptance by the world of their ideal in a modified form. The spread of Christianity was a victory for the Hebrew spirit; but it was a Priestly victory, a victory gained at the expense of the abandonment of something funda-mental—of the idea that the spirit must be embodied in the corporate life of a definite society. It was impossible to breathe the soul of Hebraism into an alien body without distorting and corrupting the soul itself. Hence the Pharisees could not throw in their lot with the Christians; Hebrew separateness was maintained, and the ideal was kept alive, as a memory and a hope, through the centuries.

III

For the Prophets, as we have seen, the national ex-istence of the Hebrews—their existence as a corporate society of human beings, living out their own life in accordance with a law that expressed their own spirit —was something essential. Hence the Pharisees and their Rabbis, who were the heirs of the Prophets, were cheered in their exile by the hope of an early restoration of their national life. But as time went on, and the exile continued, this simple faith was inevitably weakened. The hope was not, indeed, abandoned; but it became a yearning for a " far-off divine event " rather than an active expectation of an imminent change in material circumstances. The coming of the Messiah still meant the national restoration of Israel to his ancestral land; there was no thought of a " spiritual Zion." But the exile, the *Galut*, was now a thing of indefinite duration, not simply a temporary accident; and the national way of life and thought had to be adapted to the new circumstances. The armory of the Hebrews, their *Torah*, had now to be drawn on for shields and bucklers against the forces that threatened to extinguish them, rather than for weapons with which to fight for the attainment of their ideal. The Hebrew spirit, robbed of its natural setting in a Hebrew life, and thrown on the defensive, had to express itself as best it could in those human activities which were left untouched by the demands of life in a non-Hebraic environment; and in that narrower sphere every precaution had to be taken to keep out the devastating hand of alien influences. The Hebrews, in a word, became Jews, and their Hebraism was narrowed down to Judaism, and to a Judaism which was forced, in self-defence, to express itself in an ever more stringent code of observances, to make a fence round the Law in place of the lost safeguard of a national life.

The Judaism of the Rabbis, then, is but an imperfect reproduction of the Prophetic Hebraism. It is vitally affected on its practical side, and to a less degree on its theoretical side, by the exchange of freedom for Galut. But for all that Judaism is still an expression, albeit a truncated expression, of the Hebrew spirit—of that spirit which knows no compromise with opposing forces, which demands absolute truth in thought and absolute righteousness in action. In order to realize this, we have but to examine the characteristic Jewish attitude on one or two of the fundamental problems of religion and morality.

At the outset of any inquiry into the nature and functions of man, we are faced with the apparent dualism of body and soul. For the philosopher this dualism is something illogical, and therefore unbearable: he is driven to seek for some single reality to which the two elements can be referred, be that unity matter or spirit or something which is neither. Religion, on the other hand, in its modern forms, tends not only to accept this dualism, but to regard the two elements as necessarily antagonistic. The soul is the Divine element in man, striving upwards towards its Divine source; the body is of the earth, and its evil nature must be constantly combated, lest it drag down the soul into the mire. Hence arises the distinction between " religious " and " secular," and, in the last resort, the abandonment of merely worldly concerns to the devil. Religion, fighting the battle of the soul against the body, is faced with a task that is hopeless from the outset. Hence the ideal of absolute right-doing becomes an impossible one for this life. The soul must struggle through this " vale of tears " as best it can, supporting and consoling itself by the hope of full fruition in the world to come.

To this " religious " attitude the Hebraism of the Prophets is of necessity fundamentally opposed. For them the ideal of absolute righteousness was a first postulate. It was an ideal to which the life of their own nation—the whole life, not merely a part of it—was consecrated; and the task thus set before the nation was of sufficient grandeur, the hope thus held out to it was sufficiently splendid, to remove any temptation to exalt the future life at the expense of this. Thus Hebraism knows of no antagonism between body and soul, nor of any distinction between " religious " and " secular." Nor does Hebraism trouble about personal immortality. The nation is immortal by virtue of its lofty mission ; and for the individual it is sufficient to know that he is doing his part in the work of an immortal nation.

This conception, however, could not be expected to stand the strain of a national calamity, which seemed for the time to deal the national ideal its death-blow. In hours of darkness and despair men naturally sought comfort in the thought that death might bring a consummation which seemed too much to expect from life. And if this tendency made itself felt among the Hebrews even in the time of the Babylonian captivity, it was bound to become stronger still in the protracted gloom of the second exile. Thus " other-worldliness " came to play a not inconsiderable part in Jewish thought. Men came to believe that this world, which offered them no comforting prospect of the realization of their national ideal, did not really matter—that it was nothing more than a preparation for another world, in which the sway of righteousness would be established without any effort on the part of weak human beings. Hence such sayings as this are found in the Talmud: "This world is, as it were, the entrance-hall to the world to come. Prepare thyself in the entrance-hall, that thou mayest become worthy to enter the banqueting-hall." But the influence of the Prophets was too strong to allow of a complete shifting of the centre of gravity from this world to the next. Personal immortality became an accepted idea among Jews, but its acceptance did not involve any condemnation of life on earth. And, above all, the idea of the sanctification of the whole of human life in the service of God has remained the cornerstone of Judaism throughout its history. Judaism, true to the Prophetic teaching, regards the body as an instrument of the Divine will, not as something inherently recalcitrant and bound up with sin. It accepts the fundamental facts of human life and strives to make the best of them, never resting content with any standard lower than that of absolute perfection.

It might seem at first sight that in this acceptance of facts there is something inconsistent with the "extremeness" which is characteristic of the Prophetic outlook. But to be an extremist does not necessarily involve taking a distorted view of the facts or shutting one's eyes to half the truth. That kind of " extreme- ness " is essentially opposed to the love of truth, which is another characteristic of the Prophet. The real extremist is he who, realizing the whole truth so far as he can, will rest content with nothing less than the complete embodiment of that whole truth in actual life. The truth for which he stands is certain to lie somewhere between two exaggerated conceptions, and it is just because he stands for truth and justice (which is " truth in action ") and will admit of no compro- mise, that he cannot allow any quarter to the exag- gerations, but must have the perfect mean. From this point of view we may appreciate the Jewish attitude towards asceticism as a correct interpretation of the Prophetic Hebraism. Asceticism in its true form— that is to say, asceticism practiced because the flesh and its appetites are believed to be inherently evil— is in one sense an extreme. But it does not corre- spond, in the Jewish view, to the truth, any more than does the opposite idea, that the flesh and its appetites are the only things that make life worth living. Each of these views is unjust to one side of humanity. Hence asceticism as a principle of life is as far re- moved from Judaism as is sensualism. So far as self- mortification has played a part in Jewish life, its ob- ject has been, not to punish the flesh as something evil, but to purify it and render it more worthy of **the high mission which it has in common with the soul.**

And as the false "extremism" which rests on a neglect of half the truth has no place, for Jewish thought, in regulating the economy of the individual life, so also it is debarred from exerting any influence on the determination of the correct relation between the individual and society as a whole. Judaism has no place for that extreme altruism which makes self-sacrifice an end in itself. The justice of the individual's claim is to be decided by a reference to the good of the whole; and if that criterion gives one individual a certain right, it would be positively unjust on his part (because detrimental to the interests of the whole) to waive his right. Judaism is "extreme" only in demanding that the test of the common good shall be applied with absolute impartiality. The ideal can only be attained when each individual is capable of judging his own case with as complete disinterestedness as though it were another's.

But if the individual cannot assert the claims of his individuality against the commonwealth, this does not mean that Judaism stands for the ideal of a dead level of mediocrity. That ideal is another "extreme" of the wrong kind, like that of unfettered individualism. Judaism not only has room for, but demands, the supreme personality, the Superman; but his supremacy is to lie in the development of his exceptional gifts, not at the expense of his weaker fellows, but for their good in common with his own. The Prophet is the Jewish Superman; and only through their Prophets can the Jews become what their national ideal demands that they should be—a Supernation. Thus for Judaism the Prophet is the goal as well as the source of its life; and it is the true Hebrew spirit that finds expression in the aspiration which has been the life-breath of Judaism for centuries. It is the true Hebrew spirit that demands ultimately the single supreme Prophet, in whom prophecy and fulfilment shall be united—the Messiah.

IV

If we turn from this examination of some of the fundamental conceptions of Judaism to look at the Jews of the modern world, we are struck with a painful sense of contrast. Neither the Hebraism of the Prophets nor the Judaism of the Rabbis seems to find expression in the Jew whom the world knows to-day. A burning idealism, a passionate and uncompromising pursuit of righteousness, a determination to make religion and life coextensive—these are not the characteristics that are associated with the cosmopolitan financier who too often figures in the popular mind as the typical Jew. Of the Jew who is more really typical—the Ghetto Jew, who lives the life of his forefathers, and clings to their ideas, unenlightened and untarnished by the culture and the materialism of modern civilization—the outside world knows nothing. And the growing class of assimilated Jews which lies between these extremes is so anxious—and so successfully anxious—to be like its surroundings, and to keep its differences in the background, that it can-

not be marked out as standing for a distinctive ideal:
its outlook on life, its manners and customs, are too
completely dominated by the influences of its non-
Jewish surroundings. Where, then, is the Hebrew
spirit to-day? Perhaps in the unexplored Ghetto?
But the Ghetto is breaking up before our eyes; and
in any case a spirit that can only live by shutting out
the light of modern progress might as well be dead.
Are we then to conclude that the survival of the
Jews is a meaningless freak of history? Are we to
advise them to give up a hopeless struggle against
overwhelming odds?

Before advocating such a step, we should remember
what it is that has brought about the present condition
of things. For eighteen centuries the homeless Jew
has been the butt of hatred and oppression, has been
seaman on board every ship of state but his own, has
been made the huckster of the world's spiritual and
material goods, has been alternately master in the
narrow Ghetto and slave in the larger world of an
alien culture, has been driven from the soil and the
sun into the soul-withering atmosphere of the count-
ing-house—has been forced, in a word, to live every
life imaginable except that of his own individuality.
It is this long-drawn-out tragedy of a lodger life that
has produced the apparent impotence of the Hebrew
spirit to-day, not any weakening of the spirit itself,
nor any lack of a field in which it might work. And
just because the spirit has dragged on a weary existence through all these centuries—for that very

reason a voluntary act of national suicide (even if the
world would allow it) is unthinkable. The escape
from impotence is to be found in life, not in death.
The solution of the Jewish problem lies in the " revival
of the spirit "; and when we have ascertained what
change in existing conditions is necessary to that
revival, we shall have determined the practical course
which the Jews of the present day must pursue.

V

If Hebraism is a force in the modern world only
by virtue of its expression in ancient Hebrew literature, and not by virtue of any influence exerted by
Jews at the present time, that is because neither of the
two kinds of life open to the Jews—life in the Ghetto
and life under conditions of emancipation—offers
conditions in which there is any possibility of an unfettered development of the Hebrew spirit.

In the Ghetto, indeed, the Jew is to some extent his
own master. He can lead there a kind of life which
is distinctively his own, organized in such a way as to
reflect his particular outlook and ideals. And, in fact,
it is true that the Ghetto, with its insistence on tradition, its devotion to the study of the past, and its
steadfast persistence in hoping against hope for the
realization of the Messianic dream, has been an expression and a preservative of the Hebrew spirit. But
the autonomy of the Ghetto, if such it can be called, is
too cramped and too precarious to permit of any real
progress. Pent up within the Ghetto walls, and sur-

rounded by enemies on whose "tolerance" they depended, the Jews have been cut off from all contact with the bigger problems of modern life, and with the broad movements of thought that went on outside. The life of which they were masters was a narrow one; and the concentration of their enormous mental and moral forces within an area so circumscribed led, on the one hand, indeed, to the production of a human type unsurpassed, at its best, for spirituality and moral grandeur, but, on the other hand, to the piling up of mountains of minute regulations and prescriptions, which threatened in time to stifle the underlying spirit. The Ghetto saved Hebraism from extinction, but only at the expense of a one-sided development, and finally of petrifaction. And even if Hebraism in its Ghetto form were ultimately worth preserving, the Jews could not be expected deliberately to resist the forces which, since the time of Moses Mendelssohn, have been making for the overthrow of the Ghetto walls. They must inevitably take advantage of the progress—a progress all too slow, it is true—among modern European nations of the recognition of their rights as human beings. They were and are bound to accept emancipation with the eagerness of the prisoner who is allowed to leave his dungeon for the air and the sunshine. But what are the effects of emancipation on the Hebrew spirit?

At first sight they appear to be favorable. The cramping and the spiritual inbreeding of the Ghetto are gone. The Jew is allowed to breathe the free air of European enlightenment, and even to play his part in the wide arena of European political life. He can drink freely at the well of culture from which modern nations derive their spiritual sustenance. He can stand up as a free man among free men. But there is another side to the shield. For the Jew can only win all these privileges by becoming part and parcel of the particular nation in which he happens to live; and as his own racial instinct is too strong to allow him to merge himself absolutely in his surroundings (a consummation which, in any case, modern nations are not over-ready to accept), he has to cast about for some means of preserving his own identity while becoming something else. This was the problem which confronted the earliest generation of emancipated Jews in modern times; and they could only solve it by deliberately accepting Judaism as a substitute for Hebraism—in other words, by acquiescing once for all in the restriction of that part of their lives which remained their own to the sphere of religion. The exiled Hebrews of old time submitted perforce to this restriction; it was a necessary condition of the Galut, and could only be removed by the restoration of their national life. But their emancipated descendants in modern times regarded it as a privilege that they were able to be Jews by religion only, and to become Germans or Englishmen or Frenchmen in all their ordinary relations with other men. We shall have occasion to glance later on at the results of this gymnastic feat, by which the emancipated Jew saved his Judaism for the time being.

But for the moment it is sufficient to point out that Judaism was saved at the expense of Hebraism. The Hebrew spirit can only be fully expressed in a life which it moulds and fashions from start to finish; but in the life of the emancipated Jews the area of its operations is even more restricted than in the Ghetto. For in the Ghetto life, stunted though it be, the terms " Jew " and " man " are at least coextensive; in the outside world the larger part of the man belongs irrevocably to another form of life, another social organization, in the fashioning of which the Hebrew spirit has had no hand.

Thus the Jew cannot be himself again, cannot live out his own life and develop his essential individuality, either in the Ghetto or under conditions of emancipation. What he needs for the " revival of the spirit " is the possibility of combining the unadulterated Jewishness of the Ghetto with the breadth and freedom of modern life. And this combination can only be rendered possible by the restoration of that element which has been lacking in Jewish life for so many centuries, and to the lack of which the present impotence of the Hebrew spirit is traceable. What the Jew needs is a soil of his own, a fixed centre for his national life. And that centre can be found only in the land with which the history of the Jews is inevitably bound up, which has been the goal of their most cherished aspirations since they left it for the wilderness of Galut, which is one of the fibres of their national being. Only in Palestine can the Jew become once more a Hebrew. There and only there can he take up the thread of his national history, and begin over again the eternal pursuit of his ideal. There and only there can the Hebrew spirit again find a body, and become effectively a force making for absolute righteousness.

VI

The return to Palestine, then, is essential. But this idea, though it follows inevitably from a true view of Jewish history, cannot be widely accepted without a revolution in thought. The Ghetto Jew still cherishes the hope of an eventual restoration, and of the ultimate establishment of the kingdom of righteousness; but the centuries of cramping and stunting have made him unable to realize that there can be any direct connection between the ideal and life as it is. For him the longed-for consummation must be brought about by a sudden miracle from above, not by a process of evolution in which human effort plays a part. Nay, he has even come to regard as sacrilegious any attempt on the part of mere human beings to hasten the end. The emancipated Jew, again, is losing his hold on the ancestral hope, which does not fit with ease into his scheme of things. In so far as he retains the hope, it is of a purely spiritual nature, and is even more emphatically for him than for the Ghetto Jew a thing that must be banned from the sphere of practical life, since his immediate ideals can only be those of his adopted nation. In neither case, therefore, is the idea of a return to Palestine likely to find ready acceptance. In both cases a radical change is necessary before any progress can be made.

It is not difficult to see by what means that change is to be brought about. Hebraism has expressed itself both theoretically and practically; and, while the practical rebirth of the Hebrew spirit can only take place in Palestine, it can be cultivated on the theoretical side even in the Diaspora, by a study of the literature in which it is enshrined. That literature is, of course, a literature written in Hebrew: for body and soul are one, and the Hebrew language is the natural and inevitable vesture of Hebraic thought. Hence the immediate step towards the solution of the Jewish question is the return of the Jews to their own " spiritual possessions "—to the Hebrew language and literature. Only by learning to understand and to value the ideas for which they have stood in the past can they become capable of desiring to stand for something in the present and the future. They must grasp and assimilate Hebraism as a way of thought and an outlook on life—as a " culture "—before they can attain either the will or the power to embody Hebraism in practice.

Now the study of the Hebrew language and literature is not dead, either in the Ghetto or among emancipated Jews; and its value is so generally recognized (at least in theory) by the Jewish people, that any advocacy of its claims is like forcing an open door. But what Ahad Ha-'Am demands is not the study of the Hebrew language and literature as it is pursued at present either within or without the Ghetto. In the one case, devotion to the past involves the sacrifice of the breadth and fulness of life in the present; in the other case, the study of Hebrew literature is mainly a pursuit of the antiquarian and the archeologist, and even so it tends (for a reason which we shall have occasion to mention later) gradually to lose its hold on the intellectual element of emancipated Jewry, and to be driven out of the field by non-Jewish culture. But the study that is to lead to the rebirth of the Hebrew spirit must have throughout a conscious relation to its end. Its touch must be the touch of life, not that of death. It must not kill either the present, like the Ghetto student, or the past, like the emancipated Jewish antiquarian; it must make past and present a living, organic whole in the world of ideas, in order that it may fructify in the creation of a living, organic whole in the world of fact. It was in this spirit that Ahad Ha-'Am once projected a great Hebrew Encyclopedia, which should do for the Jews something like what the French Encyclopedia did for the French people. It would be, as the Talmud was of old, a storehouse of Hebraism, restating the Hebrew point of view in terms adapted to modern ideas and methods of historical research. Such an encyclopedia would not be a collection of dead facts for the use of the antiquarian. It would be a living literary expression of the Hebrew spirit, and would impress that spirit on the minds of the rising generation of Jews.

But it must not be thought that this educating process can be satisfactorily carried on under present conditions. The return to an understanding of the Hebrew spirit, which has Palestine for its goal, cannot be attained without the help of Palestine. The ancient land of the Hebrews must play its part in the reintegration of Hebraism on the theoretical as well as on the practical side. The immediate function of Palestine is to be a " spiritual centre " of Hebraism: the seat of a small settlement of Jews, not necessarily independent in the political sense, but free from the cramping conditions of the Ghetto, and drawing inspiration for its work of learning and teaching from the life-giving touch of the native soil of Hebraism. From this centre a new life would be breathed into the dead bones of the scattered Jewish people; and the " revival of the spirit," receiving its impulse from Palestine, would result in the further strengthening of the Palestinian settlement. But without this " spiritual centre " the work of national regeneration in the Diaspora cannot make headway against the forces of assimilation. Hence the return to Palestine must precede as well as follow the restoration of Jewish culture to its proper place in the lives of Jews in other lands. It must be undertaken at once by the remnant in whom the national consciousness has been neither sublimated into a pious aspiration nor crushed by the weight of a foreign culture. It will be the work of these pioneers to make Palestine a magnet for larger sections of those yet unborn generations to whom the

" spiritual centre " will give a true conception of their birthright and their destiny.

VII

Such is, in outline, Ahad Ha-'Am's presentment of the Jewish problem, and the solution which he offers. His attitude toward the two other solutions which are advocated in modern times can be indicated briefly, as it is the natural result of his own positive standpoint.

It is not to be expected that he should show much sympathy with those who hold that not only the survival of the Jews, but their survival as a homeless and scattered people, is necessary in order that they may fulfil their " mission "—that is, in order that they may be a light to the nations, and lead them in the path of righteousness. Philosophically, this theory has a teleological basis which is repugnant to him. But his objection does not rest solely on abstract grounds. The facts of Jewish life do not square with the pretensions of the " mission " theory, whatever may be its metaphysical justification. So far as the congested masses of Jews in Eastern Europe are concerned, nobody could claim that they are or could be accepted by the nations which rob them of human rights as a pattern and an inspiration. The privilege of a " mission " is only claimed for the emancipated minority of Jews. But the very conditions of emancipation rob that minority of the power to embody Hebrew ideals in its own life so fully as to impress them by force of example on the life of the nations. Dominated as they are by the culture of their environment, emancipated Jews lack not only the opportunity, but also—what is worse—the desire to preserve their spiritual kinship with their own past. The "mission" postulates a spiritual separateness which can only be maintained if Jews are spiritually fed on the products of the Hebrew genius; but the training of the average emancipated Jew differs very little from that of his non-Jewish neighbor. And this state of things is inevitable so long as the Jew can attain fulness of life only through more or less complete assimilation. If the Jews are to perform a "mission," they must work out their ideals in their own life first of all: and for that they must have a concrete basis of their own. The "mission" theory is in fact the view of the Essenes over again: it expects the spirit to live without a body.

With the other modern solution of the problem—that which is known as Zionism—Ahad Ha-'Am is naturally in closer sympathy: for Zionism demands, no less than his own theory, the restoration of Jewish life in Palestine. It is not surprising that he went to the first Zionist Congress; but it is not surprising, either, that he came away disappointed. For he found that the similarity between his own ideal and that of the Zionist movement was only external. The Zionists seemed to be trying to save the body of the Jewish people, not its soul. Like the Sadducees, they would have the corporate national existence at all costs, without regard to the spirit which it might express. But for him body without soul was as meaningless as soul without body. This is not the place to discuss how far the more recent development of Zionism has brought it nearer to his ideal. But in its earlier years, at any rate, Herzl's movement could no more satisfy him than the "mission" theory. For him the only possible way was and is that of the Pharisees—the union of body and soul, the revival of the Hebrew spirit through the creation of a concrete Jewish life in Palestine.

SACRED AND PROFANE

(1892)

Between things sacred and profane there is this difference among others. In profane matters the instrument derives its worth from the end, and is valued for the most part only in so far as it is a means to that end; and consequently we change the instruments as the end demands, and finally, when the end is no longer pursued, the instruments automatically fall into disuse. But in sacred matters the end invests the instrument with a sanctity of its own. Consequently, there is no changing or varying of the instrument; and when the end has ceased to be pursued, the instrument does not fall out of use, but is directed towards another end. In other words: in the one case we preserve the shell for the sake of the kernel, and discard the shell when we have eaten the kernel; in the other case we raise the shell to the dignity of the kernel, and do not rob it of that dignity even if the kernel withers, but make a new kernel for it.

The ancient Egyptians were accustomed on certain festivals to use only vessels of stone. This custom was a survival from the Stone Age, when the human race did not know how to use other minerals [1]; and it survived in spite of the fact that subsequently the

[1] Lubbock.

Egyptians learned to make vessels of better material. That is to say, for ordinary purposes they had no difficulty in changing a worse instrument for a better; but on sacred days they did not dare to drive out the old before the new, because here the instrument itself had become sacred. No doubt the Egyptian priests sought and found weighty esoteric reasons for this custom; that is, they sought and found a new end for an outworn instrument, a new kernel for an empty shell.

Take an instance nearer home. Why do we Jews continue to write the Law only on parchment, in manuscript, and in scroll form? Wherefore all this trouble four hundred years after Gutenberg? It is because our ancestors, in common with the rest of the human race, used to make all their books in this fashion in the days when the Temple stood, and when the world knew no better means than this. For our ordinary books, of course, we use the improved modern methods; but in the case of books devoted to sacred purposes, everything, even the mode of writing, is sacred.

We find the same distinction within the sphere of books itself. Profane books (except poetry, the whole essence of which lies in its beautiful shell) are nothing but instruments for imparting knowledge of a certain subject-matter, nothing but shells of the ideas contained in them. Hence, as knowledge of the subject-matter grows and spreads, so does the book itself sink more and more into oblivion. Thus the books of most importance in the history of man's intellectual development, books whose content has become common property for all time, lie on remote shelves in our libraries, and are but seldom opened. The theories of Copernicus, Kepler, and Newton are imparted to the young students in our schools; but even among trained physicists there are few who have drawn their knowledge of these theories from the original sources. Plato's works, again, that mighty river of whose waters we drink even to-day through so many channels— how many are there now who read them, or even know their names? Maybe we grieve to see that even the children of the spirit are not immortal, that in the fulness of days each is forgotten when its work is done; and one might well believe that if the authors of these books had had the choice, they would have asked that their teachings should not spread so widely as to enable their books to be forgotten. But they had not the choice, and, though the heart may grieve, stern logic finds that thus it must be: when we have eaten the kernel, we have no more use for the shell.

Thus it is with profane books; but with sacred books it is otherwise. Here the content sanctifies the book, and subsequently the book becomes the essential, and the content the accident. The book remains unchanged forever; the content changes ceaselessly with the progress of life and culture. What is there that men have not found in our sacred books, from Philo's day to this? In Alexandria they found Plato in them; in Spain, Aristotle; the Cabbalists found their own teaching, and the followers of other religions theirs;

nay, some pious scholars have even found in them
Copernicus and Darwin.   All these men sought in
Scripture only the truth—each one his own truth—and
all found that which they sought.   They found it because they had to find it: because if they had not found
it, then truth would not have been truth, or the Scriptures would not have been holy.

And yet we have among us " Reformers " who
think that we can strip the shell of practical observance from our religion, and retain only the kernel, the
abstract beliefs; or, again, that we can strip our sacred
writings of their original language, and retain only
their kernel in translations.   Both fail alike to see that
it is just the ancient cask with its ancient form that is
holy, and sanctifies all that is in it, though it may be
emptied and filled with new wine from time to time;
whereas, if once the cask is broken or remoulded, the
wine will lose its taste, though it be never so old.

The Reformers fail to see this; but the people
as a whole has always acted as though it felt this
truth by some natural instinct.   The people has not
violently attacked those of its teachers who have filled
its cask with new wine from foreign vintages, like
Maimonides and his school; on the contrary, it has
never ceased to honor and reverence them.   But the
Karaites and such, who dared to lay a hand on the
holy cask, and change its form according to their own
ideas—these have had but short shrift, despite all
protests and assurances that their wine was the real
old wine, which had lain long years in the cellar,
untouched.

Laugh who will at this zealous regard for the cask;
the history of those who have treasured the wine will
give him pause.[1]

[1] [An allusion to a Talmudic legend (Baba Batra, 16[1]) according to which, when God told Satan that he might do what
he liked with Job, but must spare his life, Satan replied that he
might as well have been told to break a cask without spilling
its contents.]

JUSTICE AND MERCY

(1892)

The difference between Justice and Mercy is only this, that Justice measures the cause by the effect, Mercy the effect by the cause. That is to say, Justice regards only the character of the deed, and judges the doer accordingly; Mercy considers first the character of the doer at the moment of the deed, and judges the deed accordingly.

For instance: the Law says, " Thou shalt not steal." If a man transgresses and steals, " he shall surely pay." So far all will agree. But what if he has not the wherewithal? Justice answers, " If he have nothing, then he shall be sold for his theft;" Mercy says, " Men do not despise a thief, if he steal to satisfy his soul when he is hungry." Justice judges the theft, Mercy the thief.

Or again: it is a well-known fact that parents generally transmit their moral characteristics to their children. But while Justice drew from this fact the inference that the sins of the fathers should be visited on the children, Mercy in our time has extracted a teaching of opposite import: that the sins of the children may be forgiven if they are an inheritance from the fathers. Justice seeks to exterminate sin; Mercy regards only the sinner.

According to an ancient legend, the Creator intended at first to create His world by the attribute of Justice alone, and it was only afterwards that He repented Him, and joined with it the attribute of Mercy. In truth, we find that the attribute of Justice precedes that of Mercy in the process of moral development, both in individuals and in nations. Children, and nations in their childhood, distinguish only between deeds, not between doers. They exterminate evil by rooting out the evil-doers and all that is connected with them; they do not discriminate between the sin of error and the sin of presumption, between the sin of compulsion and the sin of freewill, between the sin committed with knowledge and that committed in ignorance. The angry child breaks the thing over which he has stumbled; nations in the stage of childhood kill the beast " through which hurt hath come to a man." It is only at a later stage and by a gradual process that Mercy finds its way first into the human head, to refine our moral ideas, and then also into the human heart, to purify and to soften the feelings.

First we have the judicial pronouncement: " Whoso sheddeth man's blood " (whether in error or of evil intent), " his blood shall be shed." The deed itself, the blood that has been shed, demands recompense from the doer; and " the land cannot be cleansed . . . . but by the blood of him that shed it." In the fulness of time man comes to understand that the unintentional homicide is " not worthy of death; " but even when that stage has been reached, it is long before he can restrain the feelings of his untamed heart, which demands vengeance for blood. It is at this stage that nations set aside cities of refuge for the benefit of the homicide, " lest the avenger of the blood pursue the slayer, *while his heart is hot.*"

" The Law exonerates him who acts under compulsion: " [1] for us this is axiomatic. But there was a time when this principle needed proofs and examples to secure its acceptance, and so we read: " But unto the damsel thou shalt do nothing; there is in the damsel no sin worthy of death: for as when a man riseth against his neighbor, and slayeth him, even so is this matter: for he found her in the field, and the betrothed damsel cried, and there was none to save her." The Law does not usually give reasons for its ordinances in this fashion; but it was recognized that here was a great innovation, opposed to popular ideas.

The legend quoted above says that the Creator *joined* the attribute of Mercy with that of Justice, not that He *substituted* the one for the other. In truth, Mercy is of value only when it is combined with Justice. Mercy stands high on the ladder of moral development; but Justice is the moral foundation on which the ladder stands.

There can be no doubt that mankind would not have struggled hard to climb the moral ladder, if not for the fear of that inward monitor, which tells a man of his sin in the secret recesses of his soul, and gnaws his heart, and says, " Climb upwards: cleanse thy-

[1] [Baba Kamma, 29 [2].]

self." This inward voice, which we call "conscience," or (in more mystical phrase) "the voice of God moving in the heart of man," is in reality nothing but the echo of a man's own pronouncement on the sins of others: so it has been well explained by Adam Smith and his followers. Every man is accustomed from his earliest years to see his parents and his teachers pronouncing condemnation on every act of wrong-doing; and so he learns to do the same himself. In time habit becomes second nature, and when he meets an act of wrong-doing, he not merely condemns it with his lips, but actually experiences a feeling of moral indignation or loathing. This feeling, accompanying the phenomenon of sin, becomes ever (as is the way of all feelings) more and more closely connected with the phenomenon that gives rise to it; until at last the tie becomes so strong that the two can no longer be severed, even if both the phenomenon and the feeling are predicable of the same person. So, when a man's conscience pricks him, he is, for the moment, a double personality; it is as though the conscience (that is, the feeling that accompanies the phenomenon) were a separate being, hurling reproaches at its possessor, and saying: "Wretch! What would you have said, if you had seen others acting thus?"

The moral ideas that flourish in the atmosphere of society, and become implanted in the mind of each individual through education and social intercourse— these, then, are the real source of the inward moral voice. Thus, so long as the feeling of Justice predominates, men become accustomed from their youth to hate abstract evil as such, and to loathe evil-doers, without much inquiry into the distant causes that have led to the evil act; and, by a further development, they learn to gauge their own actions also by the measure with which they gauge the actions of others. It is not so when the atmosphere is one of Mercy only. Then it is not the evil deed, but the evil *will* that awakens the moral feeling; then a man is absolved from Justice, if he can be excused by an appeal to the hidden facts of his spiritual life. Such an atmosphere as this does not encourage the utterance of " man's pronouncement on the sins of others; " and therefore the inward echo of this voice—conscience—is also silent.

Yet in every generation Mercy has its apostles—the men who climb the moral ladder till they reach the level of absolute Mercy. They believe, in their simplicity, that if all mankind mounted with them to this height, the world would become a Garden of Eden; and so they teach their followers, " Judge every man favorably." [1] The pupils argue, rightly enough, that they, too, are men; and so they apply this teaching to themselves first of all. It is for the most part difficult to find excuses for another man, to penetrate into his spiritual life, and seek there the psychological cause of his transgression; but it is all too easy for a man to be always finding excuses for himself, seeing that in reality even our " free " actions are bound and knit

[1] [Pirke Abot, i. 6.]

by thousands of slender threads, seen and unseen, to various causes that precede them in the inner life. It may be that a man cannot always find these chains, cannot always understand how the sin came to be committed, why he chose evil; but he always *feels* that some hidden hand influenced his choice, that some " spirit of folly " entered into him at that moment. And so the fault is not his; the hidden cause is to blame.

When our apostles of Mercy see that the only result of their teaching is to enable men to justify *themselves,* they attempt to put matters right by carrying their original error a stage further, and adding another precept, " Judge not thy fellow until thou hast come into his place." [1] That is to say, if you cannot judge another man favorably, do not judge him at all until you have been in his position: then, when it is your own soul instead of his, you will understand his feelings, and it will not be difficult for you to excuse him as you would excuse yourself.

Here, then, Mercy has reached its uttermost limit: the abolition of all judgments, a general pardon to all men for all actions. But how has it reached this point? Its path has been exactly the opposite of that pursued by the moral sentiment in its natural development. The moral sentiment finds the criterion of morality in the social atmosphere, and by this criterion measures first others, and then itself; whereas Mercy allows a man first of all to measure himself by any criterion

[1] [Pirke Abot, ii. 5.]

that he may choose, only on condition that he proceed next to apply the same standard to others.

This doctrine, if it were universally followed, might well reduce the world to a condition of moral chaos. The moral sentiment, robbed of all external assistance and support, would gradually be uprooted from the human heart. But, happily for mankind, the multitude is not large-hearted enough for this doctrine of Mercy, which, despite all the honor lavished upon it, will never be more than a beautiful phrase of the moralists. It is not such phrases that stir the moral atmosphere, but the needs of life, individual and social. Our individual needs do, indeed, whisper to us sometimes, " Judge thy fellow unfavorably, in order that thou mayest come into his place "—that is, gain esteem from his disgrace, and benefit by his downfall. But, on the other side, the needs of society tell us, " In righteousness shalt thou judge thy neighbor: " judge him, yes; but in righteousness: and so learn to judge yourself also, when you find yourself in his place.

There are in every generation a few righteous men who arrive at this middle position—not beloved of the apostles of Mercy—after a hard struggle with that whisper of the Self; who by dint of habit come to make Righteousness a need of the individual Ego. These are the men who bear the banner of moral progress, the end of which is to make peace between the individual needs and the social, and to impose on both one single law—the law of Righteousness.

POSITIVE AND NEGATIVE

(1892)

Even when the world as a whole is at peace, there is no rest or peace for its inhabitants. Penetrate to the real life, be it of worms or of men, and beneath the veil of peace you will find an incessant struggle for existence, a constant round of aggression and spoliation, in which every victory involves a defeat and a death.

Yet we do distinguish between time of war and time of peace. We reserve the term "war" for a visible struggle between two camps, such as occurs but seldom—a struggle that we can observe, whose causes and effects we can trace, from beginning to end. But to all the continual petty wars between man and man, of which we know in a general way that they are in progress, but of which we cannot envisage all the details and particulars, we give the name of "peace," because such is the normal condition of things.

In the spiritual world also there is war and peace; and here also "peace" means nothing but a number of continual petty wars that we cannot see—wars of idea against idea, of demand against demand, of custom against custom. The very slightest change in any department of life—as, for instance, the substitution of one letter for another in the spelling of a word—

can only be brought about by a battle and a victory; but these tiny events happen silently, and escape observation at the time. It is only afterwards, when the sum total of all the changes has become a considerable quantity, that men of intelligence look backwards, and find to their astonishment that everything—opinions, modes of life, speech, pronunciation—has undergone vast changes. These changes appear to have taken place automatically; we do not know in detail when they came about, or through whose agency.

Peace, then, is the name that we give to a continuous, gradual development. But in the spiritual world, as in the material, there is sometimes a state of war; that is, a visible struggle between two spiritual camps, two complete systems, the one new, the other old. The preparations for such a war are made under cover, deep down in the process of continuous development. It is only when all is in readiness that the war breaks out openly, with all its drums and tramplings; and then a short space of time sees the most far-reaching changes.

The character of these changes, as well as the general course of the war, depends chiefly on the character of the new system of thought that raises the storm. They differ according as the system is wholly positive, wholly negative, or partly positive and partly negative.

A new *positive* system comes into existence when the process of continuous development produces in the minds of a select few some new positive concept. This may be either a belief in some new truth not hitherto accepted by society, or the consciousness of some new need not hitherto felt by society; generally the two go together. This new conception, in accordance with a well-known psychological law, gives rise to other conceptions of a like nature, all of which strengthen one another, and become knit together, till at last they form a complete system. The centre-point of the system is the new positive principle; and round this centre are grouped a number of different beliefs, feelings, impulses, needs, and so forth, which depend on it and derive their unity from it.

A new system such as this, though essentially and originally it is wholly positive, cannot help including unconsciously some element of negation. That is to say, it cannot help coming into contact, on one side or another, with some existing system that covers the same ground. It may not damage the essential feature, the centre, of the old system; but it will certainly damage one of the conceptions on its circumference, or, at the very least, it will lessen the strength of men's attachment to the old principles. When, therefore, the reformers begin to put their system into practice, to strive for the attainment of what they need by the methods in which they believe, their action necessarily arouses opposition on the part of the more devoted adherents of the old system, with which the reformers have unwittingly come into conflict. The result of this opposition is that the new system spreads, and attracts to its ranks all those who are adapted to receive it. As their number increases, the animosity of their opponents grows in intensity; and so the opposition waxes stronger and stronger, until it becomes war to the knife.

At first the disciples of the new teaching are astounded at the accusations hurled at them. They find themselves charged with attempting to overthrow established principles; and they protest bitterly that no such thought ever entered their minds. They protest with truth: for, indeed, their whole aim is to add, not to take away. Intent on their task of addition, they overlook the negation that follows at its heels; even when the negation has been made plain by their opponents, they strive to keep it hidden from others, and to ignore its existence themselves, and they do not recognize the artificiality of the means by which they attain this end.

The older school, on the other hand, who derive all their inspiration from the old doctrine, are quick to see or feel the danger threatened by the new teaching; and they strive, therefore, to uproot the young plant while it is still tender. But as a rule they do not succeed. Despite their efforts, the new system finds its proper place; gradually the two systems, the new and the old, lose some of their more sharply opposed characteristics, share the forces of society between them in proportion to their relative strength, and ultimately come to terms and live at peace. By this process society has been enriched; its tree of life has gained a new branch; its spiritual equipment has received a positive addition.

It was by such a process as this that philosophy found its way into Jewish thought in the Middle Ages. First of all a new positive system came to birth in a few minds. Their need was for the understanding of natural phenomena and human life; their belief, that they could attain this end by means of Arabic philosophy. There followed the diffusion of this system; the opposition of the Rabbis, who saw in the new teaching a source of danger to another, older, positive system—the Law and religious observance; then the apologetic treatises of the Reformers, who denied the existence of the danger; finally, a compromise between the Bible and philosophy, resulting on the one hand in " rationalized faith," on the other in " religious philosophy."

The birth and development of Hasidism in modern times followed similar lines. First there was a new positive system: the *need* for spiritual exaltation and enthusiasm, the *belief* in the possibility of their attainment through the service of God as a joyful performance of duty. Then the system spread; it was attacked by the Talmudists; the new sect defended themselves; finally, Hasidim study the Talmud, Talmudists adopt Hasidism. If the first Hasidim could hear the great designs attributed to them in our generation, as though it had been their set purpose to oppose Rabbinic teaching, they would be at a loss to understand them; just as in their own day they could not understand why they were persecuted. They did not feel that in their teaching and in their practice there was an element opposed to any tenet accepted and held sacred by the nation as a whole. On the contrary, they called their persecutors Mitnaggedim (opposers) : unlike Luther's disciples, who chose the name of Protestants for themselves.

Just as the continuous process of development gives birth to new positive elements, so also it destroys old positive elements in individual minds, and undermines some of the needs and the beliefs on which the social fabric is built. The result is that these individuals find in some department of life, each one in the sphere nearest to himself, certain excrescences or superfluities, the removal of which would, in their opinion, be of benefit to the world. Then these negatives find each other, on the principle of " like to like ; " they stimulate and strengthen one another, until they, too, become united at last in a single complete system, with a fundamental and universal negative as its centre-point. This negative attracts to its banner many of the individuals whose attitude is negative on particular points of belief. Hitherto they have been but scattered units, agreeing (or sometimes disagreeing) with one another as regards certain particulars, without being conscious of their inner unity; henceforth they form a single camp, which wages war against an existing positive system—war in the name of negation and destruction.

The result of such a war is usually neither a decisive victory for one side nor the establishment of peace and intercourse between the two opponents. The result is absolute and eternal separation. Weary and spent with the stress of battle, the two enemies leave the field to rest. Those who believe in the positive doctrine return to their former system of life; the unbelievers go their own way, and form a separate sect with a new system. This negative sect represents a step backwards, not a step forwards; it rubs one inscription from the slate without substituting another. All that it can do is to rewrite what it has left in larger letters, until the gap left by the erasure is filled: that is to say, it emphasizes some other, older, positive belief, and strives to unite under this banner all the spiritual forces that were attached to the positive belief which it has destroyed, and are now left without a rallying-point. This method is satisfactory so long as the new sect has to continue fighting its enemies. The very negation, gathering all its forces to conquer, becomes by this means a source of warmth and life, and adds strength to the positive element, which was left untouched. But when the external war is at an end, and the negation sinks back into what it really is, mere nothingness, then its internal life also comes to a standstill. The positive content of its creed shrinks to its proper proportions; and the spiritual life, half emptied of its content, becomes withered and impoverished.

The sect of the Karaites is an excellent example of such a negative movement. Even before the time of Anan there were men whose attitude was negative on particular points, who could not find satisfaction in the disputations of the Talmudic schools of Babylon, or in this or that new-fangled legal pronouncement. But they were not united in a single sect, so long as these particular negatives did not group themselves as a system round about some fundamental negation. Anan found a common ground for them all in the destruction of the belief in the existence of the Oral Law, and the denial of the need for that Law. Immediately large numbers trooped to enlist under this banner, and became a single army, a negative sect. So long as this sect persecuted and was persecuted, it lived and felt: felt a burning hatred for the Talmud, and a boundless love for the Bible, in which it still believed. But so soon as it separated itself altogether from the body of the people, and its hatred and its love no longer found sustenance in the spirit of opposition, it ceased to move, and so lay like a stone, which none has turned to this day.

But a purely negative movement, like Karaism, is as a matter of fact extremely rare. Most men are unable to uproot that which is firmly implanted in their hearts, even after the plant has withered. Even if a certain doctrine no longer appeals to them for its own sake, yet they cannot dispense with other beliefs and spiritual needs which depend on it, either as its immediate results, or as having been subsequently combined with it. Such men anticipate from the beginning the spiritual void that will be left by the process of uprooting, and so they shrink back. They stand and wait, these moderates of the party of negation, until some new positive belief comes in their way, capable of filling up this void, and of becoming a new centre for all those feelings, impulses, and so forth, hitherto centred on the old positive belief, which they now wish to destroy. The first apostles of this new positive belief are persecuted by the conservatives, who reveal the hidden negation that it contains; and then those who consciously stand for a negation have a new lease of life. They have found something on which to anchor: they stand forth at once to assist the persecuted, and accept the new positive belief, and all that it involves, with extravagant enthusiasm. They accept it without overmuch examination or inquiry, because the important thing for them is not the positive belief, but the possibility, which they obtain at the same time, of holding to their negation. In proportion as they scrutinize the old doctrine in all its details, and find in it the tiniest and subtlest flaws and shortcomings, so do they shut their eyes to all that is bad in the new creed. On this they lavish a far more exaggerated admiration than did its first propounders, because, whereas for the latter it is but a part, an addition to the old doctrine, for these it is all in all, and they must needs find everything in it. The originators of the new movement are at first opposed to this alliance, thrust on them by men whose sole creed is a negation. But the persecution meted out to both alike by the conservatives, which forces them to fight for life together on the same field of battle, gradually accustoms them to this alliance; until at length they become in fact a single army, devoted to a single system. This system is a combination of positive and negative; but the one party accepts the positive for the sake of the negative, while the other accepts the negative for the sake of the positive.

A war of this kind extends over many years, or even over many generations. As a rule the innovators have at first the upper hand, for two reasons. On the one side, it is difficult to restrain the force of skepticism, or negation, when once it has been aroused; on the other side, the new positive belief is stronger than the old, being a product of the present, and therefore more in accord with the spirit of the time than the belief inherited from past ages. But then a change comes. The innovators believe that victory is at hand; they cease to concentrate all their forces on the battle against the old doctrine; and many of them begin instead to scrutinize the new system with the same penetrating gaze to which hitherto they have subjected only the old. Naturally, they find in the new system also withered shoots that need uprooting. Nay, more: when they take stock of the old shoots that have been weeded out, they find that many of them are sound and healthy, that skepticism has uprooted them unnecessarily, in the heat of opposition to the received beliefs. Thus their scrutiny enlightens them in two ways: they see that the change has not been a complete deliverance, and that in many respects their loss has exceeded their gain. Too much of the old has been removed; and the gap cannot wholly be filled by the new.

At this stage the camp of the new movement is full

of sects and small parties of all conceivable kinds. Those who feel dissatisfied pursue some ideal, look for some means of satisfying their souls; and as they wander this way and that, they move away from the main body, some forwards, others backwards. But neither party finds the rest that it seeks. Artificial ideals cannot long satisfy a natural need. Thus in the end many of them despair; they become accustomed to a life of spiritual emptiness, and seek no further.

When the conservatives see the trouble in the reform camp, they have a new lease of strength. Their despair is again turned to hope. A little longer, and the world will turn back to the point at which it stood in the good old days. But as a rule they are out in their reckoning. For the most part such movements as these, progressive or retrogressive, do not move society either forwards or backwards. They simply show that society needs some third system, intermediate between the other two, which shall stand in between the new and the old, uprooting from the new that which needs uprooting, and restoring to the old that which has been uprooted in ignorance. Thus the old and the new will be clothed in a single new form, suited to the spirit of the age, which will set up an equilibrium between the spiritual inheritance from the past, and those elements of the new teaching which have already fastened their roots firmly in the life of the community. A system such as this comes forward of itself in course of time, as a result of the movements that we have described. But sometimes it comes sooner, sometimes later: this depends on a number of complex causes and a variety of circumstances.

A combined movement of this sort began in Jewish history a hundred years ago, and is still pursuing its course. Judging by its progress in recent years, we may conclude that it is no longer far from the right path.

Even before the modern Haskalah [1] movement, there were among Western Jews certain " moderates of the party of negation "; but they did not declare war on the existing order of things, because they had nothing wherewith to fill the gap. At last a new positive creed developed in a few minds: the need for the rights of citizenship, coupled with the belief in their attainment through European culture. At once the forces of negation attached themselves to the new positive cause (whose adherents, be it remarked, may really have been at first " seekers after goodness and wisdom," [2] and did not know that subsequently negation would fasten on to their creed and count its years from the time of Mendelssohn's German translation of

[1][The Hebrew word Haskalah, translated "enlightenment" for want of a more adequate equivalent, is used to denote modern European culture, as distinguished from the purely Hebraic studies to which the Jewish mind was confined during some centuries of Ghetto life. It includes not only the pursuit of "general " (*i. e.* non-Jewish) subjects of knowledge, but also the application of modern methods of research to Hebrew literature and Jewish history.]

[2][" The Society of Seekers after Goodness and Wisdom " was the name that Mendelssohn's disciples gave to themselves.]

the Bible). The two parties became one, and proceeded mercilessly, exultantly, amid triumphant blowing of trumpets, to overthrow all the strongholds of their nation. But when the victory was won, or seemed to be won, the new doctrine was subjected to the scrutiny of criticism, which discovered shortcomings in its positive element, and still greater shortcomings on its negative side. The process of overthrowing had gone too far. It had not stopped short at primitive beliefs and outworn customs, but had affected the very essentials of national life and national unity. So the critics became conscious of a gap, and cast about for means to fill it. And not in vain, as they believed. Some of them thought to fill the gap by building magnificent synagogues and preaching sermons full of " water, water everywhere "; others again—and these were the bigger men—by that new creation of theirs, to which they gave a high-sounding title, commensurate with the loftiness of its mission: to wit, Jewish Science.[1]

The literature of Jewish Science sometimes presents a strange phenomenon. One finds a preface full of reverent devotion to Israel, to Jewish nationality, and Jewish literature; while the body of the book—the " science " in whose honor the preface was written— consists of minute investigations and discussions of

[1] ["Jewish Science" is a mistranslation of the German term *Jüdische Wissenschaft*, which has unfortunately obtained currency. The term denotes the application of modern, so-called "scientific" methods of investigation and research to Jewish history and the problems of Judaism.]

commentators and punctuators and lifeless liturgical compositions, without which the world would have been no whit the poorer. This is a striking proof of the need that these writers feel for some positive national conception, to justify their love for their people to themselves, and so enable them to devote themselves to the service of the national spirit. But alas! their quest is vain; they must needs be content with tombstones and synagogue chants. Others, too, have sought in vain, and have retraced their steps to the camp of conservatism. Others, again, are left unsatisfied, or else depart, never to return.

In later years a movement of an almost identical character was set on foot among the Jews of Northern Europe. But in Russia circumstances have brought about, as though automatically, that " middle system " for which the *savants* of Germany sought in vain—a system capable of restoring equilibrium between the old and the new, by clothing both in a single new form. We stand and gaze at this " form," so simple, so natural, so easily intelligible to the plainest mind, and we wonder that it was so long in coming.

Is it necessary to name this movement? Or is it enough to point eastwards, to the land of our ancestors?

ANTICIPATIONS AND SURVIVALS

(1892)

Students of jurisprudence know (and who knows so well as the Jew?) that the laws and statutes of every nation are not all observed and obeyed at all times in the same degree; that in all countries and in all ages there are certain laws, be they new or old, which are perfectly valid according to the statute book, and are yet disregarded by those who administer justice, and are wholly or largely ineffective in practice.

If one examines a law of this kind, one will always find that its spirit is opposed to the spirit that prevails at the time in the moral and political life of society. If it is a new law, it will be found to have come into existence before its time, to have been the work of lawgivers whose spiritual development was in advance of that of the general body of society. If it is an old law, we shall find that its day is past, that society in its spiritual development has left behind it the spirit of those old lawgivers. In either case, this particular law, being out of harmony with the spirit that governs the progress of life in that particular age, may be valued and honored like all the other laws, but has no power to make itself felt in practice.

And yet reformers act quite rightly when they anticipate the course of events, and put laws on the statute book before the time has come when they can be practically effective; and conservatives also act rightly when they secure the survival in the statute book of laws whose time has gone by. Both parties know that they are doing good service, each for its own cause. They both understand that the spirit of society moves in a circle, now forwards, now backwards, and that in this circular movement it may arrive, sooner or later, at the stage of development that these laws represent. When that time comes, it will be a matter of importance whether the laws are there in readiness or not. If they are, the spirit of society will quickly enter into them, as a soul enters into a body, and will inform them with life, and make them active forces, while they will be for the spirit a definite, material form, through which its pre-eminence will be secured. But if there is not this material form waiting for the spirit to enter into it; if the spirit is compelled to wander bodiless until it can create for itself a new corporeal vesture, then there is danger that, before the spirit can gain a firm footing where it desires to stay, the wheel may turn again, and the favorable moment be lost.

This is true not only of written laws and statutes, but also of the unwritten ideas and judgments of the human mind. In every age you will find certain isolated beliefs and opinions, out of all relation to the ruling principles on which the life of that age is built. They lie hidden in a water-tight compartment of the mind, and have no effect whatever on the course of practical life. Ideas such as these are mostly survivals, inherited from earlier generations. In their own time they were founded on current conceptions and actual needs of life; but gradually the spirit of society has changed: the foundations on which these ideas rested have been removed, and the ideas stand by a miracle. Their appearance of life is illusory: it is no real life of motion and activity, but the passive life of an old man whose " moisture is gone, and his natural force abated." Anthropologists (such as Tylor and many after him) have found aged creatures of this description in every branch of life; and they live sometimes to a remarkable age.

So much for the survivals. But there are here also anticipations, children who have not reached their full strength—ideas born in the minds of a few men of finer mould, who stand above their generation, and whom favoring circumstances have enabled to disseminate their ideas, and to win acceptance for them, before their time: that is, before the age is fully able to understand and assimilate them. These ideas, being only learned parrot-wise, and being out of harmony with the prevailing spirit, are left, like the survivals, outside the sphere of active forces. Their life is that of the babe and the suckling. Grown men fondle them, take pleasure in their childish prattle, sometimes play with them; but never ask their advice on a practical question.

And yet, so long as the breath of life remains in them, there is hope both for the anticipations and for the survivals: for the one in the forward march of the spirit, for the other in its backward trend. And so here also we must say that philosophers have done well to work for the dissemination of their new opinions, or the strengthening of the old opinions to which they have been attached, without caring whether the age was fit to receive them, whether it received them for their own sake or for the sake of something else, whether it could find in them a mode of life and a guide in practice. These philosophers know that a live weakling is better than a dead Hercules; that so long as an idea lives in the human mind, be it but in a strange and distorted form, be its life but a passive life confined to some dim, narrow chamber of the mind —so long it may hope in the fulness of time to find its true embodiment; so long it may hope, when the right day dawns, to fill the souls of men, to become the living spirit that informs all thoughts and all actions.

For an instance of an anticipation, take the idea of the Unity of God among the Jews in the period of the Judges and the Kings, until the Babylonian Exile.

Hume and his followers have proved conclusively that what first aroused man to a recognition of his Creator was not his wonder at the beauty of nature and her marvels, but his dread of the untoward accidents of life. Primitive man, wandering about the earth in search of food, without shelter from the rain or protection against the cold, persecuted unsparingly by the tricks of nature and by wild beasts, was not in a position to take note of the laws of creation, to gaze awe-struck at the beauty of the world, and to ponder the question " whether such a world could be without a guide." [1]   All his impulses, feelings, and thoughts were concentrated on a single desire, the desire for life; in the light of that desire he saw but two things in all nature—good and evil: that which helped and that which hindered in his struggle for existence. As for the good, he strove to extract from it all possible benefit, without much preliminary thought about its source. But evil was more common and more readily perceptible than good: and how escape from evil?   This question gave his mind no rest; it was this question that first awoke in him, almost unconsciously, the great idea that every natural phenomenon has a lord, who can be appeased by words and won over by gifts to hold evil in check.   Yes, and also—the idea developed of itself—to bestow good.   Thus all the common phenomena of nature became gods, in more or less close contact with human life and happiness; the earth became as full of deities as nature of good things and evil.

But it was not only from nature and her blind forces that primitive man had to suffer. The hand of his fellow-man too was against him.   In those days there were no states or kingdoms, no fixed rules of life or ordinances of justice.   The human race was divided into families, each living its own life, and each engaged in an endless war of extinction with its neighbor.   The evil caused by man to man was some-

[1] [Midrash, Lek Leka, 39.]

times even more terrible than the hostility of nature. And here also man sought and found help in a divine power; only in this case he did not turn to the gods of nature, who were common to himself and his enemies. Each family looked for help to its own special god, a god who had no care in the world but itself, no purpose but to protect it from its enemies. Thus, when in course of time these families grew into nations living a settled life, and the war of man against man took on a more general form; when the individual man was able to sit at peace with his household in the midst of his people, and the process of merciless destruction was carried on by nation against nation, not by family against family: then the family gods disappeared, or sank to the level of household spirits; but their place was filled by national gods, one god for each nation, whose function it was to watch over it in time of peace, and to punish its enemies in time of war.

This double polytheism, natural and national, has its source, therefore, not in an accidental error of judgment, but in the real needs of the human soul and the conditions of human life in primitive ages. Since these needs and these conditions did not differ materially in different countries, it is no matter for wonder that among all ancient peoples we find the same faith (though names and external forms vary): a faith in nature-gods, who help man in his war with nature, and in national gods, who help the nation in its war with other nations. But in some cases the belief in the nature-gods is more prominent, in others the belief in the national gods; this is determined by the character and history of the particular nation, by its relation to nature and its status among other peoples.

Hence, when the abstract idea of the Unity of God arose and spread among the Israelites in early days, it could not possibly be anything but an anticipation. Only a select few had a true and living comprehension of the idea, compelling the heart to feel and the will to follow. The masses, although they heard the idea preached times without number by their Prophets, and thought that they believed in it, had only an external knowledge of it; and their belief was an isolated belief, not linked with actual life, and without influence in practice. It was in vain that the Prophets labored to breathe the spirit of life into this belief. It was so far removed from the contemporary current of ideas and feelings, that it could not possibly root itself firmly in the heart, or find a spiritual thread by which to link itself with actual life.

The author of the Book of Judges has a way of complaining of the fickleness of our ancestors in those days. In time of trouble they always turned to the God of their forefathers; but when he had saved them from their enemies, they regularly returned to the service of other gods, "and remembered not the Lord their God who had delivered them from all their enemies round about." But, in fact, our ancestors were not so fickle as to change their faith like a coat, and alternate between two opposed religions. They had always one faith—the early double polytheism. Hence, in time of national trouble, of war and persecution at the hands of other nations, " the children of Israel cried unto the Lord their God." It was not that they *repented,* in the Prophetic sense, and resolved to live henceforth as believers in absolute Unity. They turned to *the God of their ancestors,* to their own special *national* God, and prayed Him to fight their enemies. When the external danger was over, and the national trouble gave way to the individual troubles of each man and each household, they returned to the everyday gods of nature.

It was only after the destruction of the Temple, when the spirit of the exiled people had changed sufficiently to admit of a belief in the Unity, that the Prophets of the time found it easy to uproot the popular faith, and to make the idea of the Unity supreme throughout the whole range of the people's life. It was not that the people suddenly looked upwards and was struck with the force of the " argument from design ; " but the national disaster had strengthened the national feeling, and raised it to such a pitch that individual sorrows vanished before the national trouble. The people, with all its thoughts and feelings concentrated on this one sorrow, was compelled to hold fast to its one remaining hope: its faith in its national God and in the greatness of His power to save His people, not merely in its own country but also on foreign soil. But this hope could subsist only on condition that the victory of the Babylonian king was not regarded as the victory of the Babylonian gods. Not they, but the God of Israel, who was also the God of the world, had given all countries over to the king of Babylon; and He who had given would take away. For all the earth was His: "He created it, and gave it to whoso seemed right in His eyes."[1] Thus at length the people understood and felt the sublime teaching, which hitherto it had known from afar, with mere lip-knowledge. The seed which the earlier Prophets had sown on the barren rock burst into fruit now that its time had come. When the Prophet of the Exile cried in the name of the Lord, " To whom will ye liken Me and make Me equal? . . . I am God, and there is none else," his words were in accord with the wishes of the people and its national hope; and so they sank into the heart of the people, and wiped out every trace of the earlier outlook and manner of life.

This national hope, as embodied in the idea of the return to Palestine, affords, in a much later age, an instance of a " survival."

It is a phenomenon of constant occurrence, that an object pursued first as a means comes afterwards to be pursued as an end. Originally it is sought after not for its own sake, but because of its connection with some other object of desire; but in course of time the habit of pursuing and esteeming the first object, though only for the sake of the second, creates

[1][Rashi on Gen. i. 1.]

a feeling of affection for the first, which is quite independent of any ulterior aim; and this affection sometimes becomes so strong that the ulterior aim, which was its original justification, is sacrificed for its sake. Thus it is with the miser. He begins by loving money for the enjoyment that its use affords; he ends by forgetting his original object, and develops an insatiable thirst for money as such, which will not allow him even to make use of it for purposes of enjoyment.

Similarly, the great religious idea, which, at the time of its revival, after the destruction of the first Temple, was meant to be only a foundation and support for the national hope, grew and developed in the period of the second Temple, until it became the whole content of the nation's spiritual life, and rose superior even to that national ideal from which it drew its being. Religion occupied the first place, and everything else became secondary; the Jews demanded scarcely anything except to be allowed to serve God in peace and quiet. When this was conceded, they were content to bear a foreign yoke silently and patiently; when it was not, they fought with the strength of lions, and knew no rest until they were again free to devote themselves uninterruptedly to the service of their Heavenly Father, whom they loved now not for the sake of any national reward, but with a whole-hearted affection, beside which life itself was of no account.

Thus it came about that, after the destruction of the second Temple, what the Jews felt most keenly was not the ruin of their country and their national life, but " the destruction of the House [of God] : " the loss of their religious centre, of the power to serve God in His holy sanctuary, and to offer sacrifices at their appointed times. Their loss was spiritual, and the gap was to be filled by spiritual means. Prayers stood for sacrifices, the Synagogue for the Temple, the heavenly Jerusalem for the earthly, study of the Law for everything. Thus armed, the Jewish people set out on its long and arduous journey, on its wanderings " from nation to nation." It was a long exile of much study and much prayer, in which the national hope for the return to Zion was never forgotten. But this hope was not now, as in the days of the Babylonian exile, a hope that materialized in action, and produced a Zerubbabel, an Ezra, a Nehemiah; it was merely a source of spiritual consolation, enervating its possessor, and lulling him into a sleep of sweet dreams. For now that the religious ideal had conquered the national, the nation could no longer be satisfied with little, or be content to see in the return to Zion merely its own national salvation. " The land of Israel " must be " spread over all the lands," in order " to set the world right by the kingdom of the Eternal," in order that " all that have breath in their nostrils might say, The Lord God of Israel is King." And so, hoping for more than it could possibly achieve, the nation ceased gradually to do even what it could achieve ; and the idea of the return to Zion, wrapped in a cloud of phantasies and visions, withdrew from the world of action, and could no longer be a direct stimulus to practical effort. Yet, even so, it never ceased to live and to exert a spiritual influence; and hence it had sometimes an effect even on practical life, although insensibly and indirectly. At first our ancestors asked in all sincerity and simplicity, " May not the Messiah come to-day or to-morrow? " and ordered their lives accordingly. Afterwards their courage drooped; their belief in imminent salvation became weaker and weaker, and no longer dictated their every-day conduct; but even then it could occasionally be blown into flame by some visionary, and become embodied in a material form, as witness the so-called " Messianic " movements, in which the nation strove to attain its hope by practical methods, which were as spiritual and religious as the hope itself. But from the day when the last " Messiah " (Sabbatai Zebi) came to a bad end, and the spread of education made it impossible for any dreamer to capture thousands of followers, the bond between life and the national hope was broken; the hope ceased to exert even a spiritual influence on the people, to be even a source of comfort in time of trouble, and became an aged, doddering creature—a survival.

It had almost become unthinkable that this outworn hope could renew its youth, and become again the mainspring of a new movement, least of all of a rational and spontaneous movement. And yet that is what has happened. The revolutions of life's wheel have carried the spirit of our people from point to point on the circle, until now it begins to approach once more the healthy and natural condition of two thousand years ago. This ancient spirit, roused once more to life, has breathed life into the ancient ideal, has found in that ideal its fitting external form, and become to it as soul to body.

But it is not for us, who see " the love of Zion " in its new form, full of life and youthful hope, to treat with disrespect the aged survival of past generations. It is not for us to forget what the new spirit owes to this neglected and forgotten survival, which our ancestors hid away in a dim, narrow chamber of their hearts, to live its death-in-life until the present day. For, but for this survival, the new spirit would not have found straightway a suitable body with which to clothe itself ; and then, perhaps, it might have gone as it came, and passed away without leaving any abiding trace in history.

PAST AND FUTURE

(1892)

Adam was unconsciously a great philosopher when he first uttered the word " I." Think how subsequent philosophers have labored, how they have created " mountains " of argument " hanging on a hair," in order to explain this little word; and yet they have never arrived at a full understanding and a clear definition. What is the " self "? This question is asked again and again in every age, and in every age finds a different answer, according to the position of science and philosophy at that particular time. Thus philosophers believed a generation ago that the existence of the " self " as a complete and fundamental reality was an obvious fact, a universal intuition that needed no proof; whereas contemporary philosophy speaks of the " division of the self," of " a double self," and so forth.

But without following the philosophers into the deep waters of metaphysics, we may say in the speech of ordinary men that the " self " of every individual is the result of the combination of his memory and his will—that is, the union of the past and the future. When a man says " I," he is not thinking of his hair and his nails, which are here to-day and tossed on the dust-heap to-morrow; nor of his hands and feet, or the other parts of his anatomy of flesh and blood, which is constantly changing. He is thinking of that inner spirit, or force, which in some hidden manner unites all the impressions and memories of the past with all his desires and hopes for the future, and makes of the whole one single, complete, organic entity.

This spiritual entity grows and develops concurrently with the physical, external man; but its growth is in the reverse direction—from the future to the past. "When a man is young,"—so the ancient sages said of King Solomon—" he writes songs; grown up, he speaks in proverbs; in old age he preaches pessimism." So in truth it is. The " self " of the young man is poor in memories, but rich in hopes and desires. Wholly intent on the boundless future, he is inspired to lyric song and to action. When he reaches middle age, and has grown rich in experiences and memories, while he has still strength to desire and to work for the attainment of his desires, an equilibrium is established between the two parts of his self: the future arouses his will to activity, but this activity is curbed and guided by the past. At this stage he speaks in proverbs—that is, he lays down general principles for the future on the basis of the past. Finally, when he grows old, and has no more strength to work for the future, his self is inevitably emptied of desires and hopes; there is nothing left for him but to dive into the sea of the past, to confine himself to the analysis of those impressions and memories which he has acquired in his lifetime: and so at last, if he is as wise as Solomon, he " preaches pessimism," and gets him comfort.

But not all old men are as wise as Solomon. Most
men have not the strength or the aptitude for finding
comfort in " vanity of vanities," and so dying in
peace. Old age in its distress calls Faith to its aid,
and Faith gives to the self the future that it lacks:
a future adapted to the character of old age, a future
which does not demand strength and activity, but
gives everything without effort. The self takes hold
of this future, though it has no warrant in experience,
and links it firmly with the past, till they become a
single whole. The future will supply all that was
lacking in the past ; the future will be as sweet as the
past was bitter. Nay, more : jealousy, as well as the
desire for pleasure, takes toll of the future for the
debt of the past ; and the poor are not satisfied till they
have said that the kingdom of Heaven is for them
alone.

The " national self," also, has been made the subject of subtle inquiry and profound reasoning. But
here, too, some philosophers (John Stuart Mill and
Renan) have come to recognize that in essence and
principle this idea is nothing but a combination of past
and future—a combination, that is, of memories and
impressions with hopes and desires, all closely inter-
woven, and common to all the individual members of
the nation.

As in the individual, so in the nation, if we consider the proportion of the two component parts to
each other in the complex self, we find three stages.

A nation has its childhood, the time of the Song of Songs, in which it looks more especially at the future, and its life is a medley of desires and hopes, expressed in speech and in action, without limit, system, or measure. It has no experience, no reasoned memories of the past, to serve as canon or criterion; on the contrary, even the little that it does inherit from the past is affected by its aspirations, and becomes poetry. But gradually the nation is taught by events to look backwards with a clearer vision, to understand itself, its character, and the conditions of its existence in the light of its past experience. Thus it becomes a wise and enlightened nation, knowing " whence it hath come and whither it goeth "; past and future are united in the self in the true proportion, and in a way calculated to further its happiness and development. Such good times as these endure for a longer or a shorter period, at the end of which the nation enters, sometimes prematurely, on its old age. Then, seeing that its strength is dwindling, and it can no longer work for the objects of its desire, it ceases even to desire, and confines itself to memories of the past. This period of degeneracy (as in the case of the Greeks) is the golden age of the antiquarian, of the manuscript collector and the bibliophile, of the critic and the commentator and the supercommentator. At last the members of the nation gradually attain to the wisdom of Solomon: they say " vanity of vanities," and disappear one by one.

But in this case also it sometimes happens that, in spite of all the external symptoms of old age and weakness, the feeling of self is still strong in the heart of the nation, which neither will nor can accept the verdict of history, and be content to have its last moments sweetened by pleasant memories. It demands a future; it desires life, come what may. Then, in this case also, Faith comes on the wings of Fancy, and gives the nation what it seeks without trouble or effort, and in liberal measure, proportioned to the bitterness of the past. " According to the sorrow shall be the reward." [1] But at this stage there is an important difference between the individual and the nation. The individual dies: die he must: all his hopes for the future cannot save him from death. But the nation has a spiritual thread of life, and physical laws do not set a limit to its years or its strength. And so, let it but make the future an integral part of its self, though it be only in the form of a fanciful hope, it has found the spring of life, the proper spiritual food which will preserve and sustain it for many a long year, despite all its ailments and diseases. And, since it lives, it is always possible that in course of time circumstances will enable it to live and regain strength among healthy and powerful nations, and derive sustenance from its intercourse with them: until at last, with the healthy blood of youth in its veins, the nation, conscious of its new strength, will become conscious also of new desires, impelling it to work actively, with body and spirit, for the future.

The historical books of the Bible were written or

[1] [Pirke Abot, v. 26.]

arranged, as is well known, in the period of the Babylonian exile. Israel was old at that time, and the decay of its powers had gone so far that all the people were conscious of it, and cried in bitterness of soul, " Our bones are dried, and our hope is lost ; we are cut off for our parts." So there arose wise men who tried to save the national self by strengthening the element of the past. It is very doubtful whether they could have attained their object by this means alone. But, fortunately for itself, the nation did not look to the wise men for a solution of the question of its existence, but to the Prophets ; and the Prophets gave the solution required. They made the future live again, and so completed the self. The future of Prophecy was at first a future close at hand : it was afterwards, when the second Temple had been built and the great promises were not fulfilled, that the future was postponed, as a consequence, from generation to generation. This postponement was carried on and on, until and after the destruction of the second Temple. Sometimes the future loomed unduly large, sometimes it sank far into the background, according to the conditions and the needs of different generations ; but throughout the whole course of history, almost till our own time, it never ceased to be an important and fundamental part of the national self. It was the future that enabled our ancestors to live on, despite their weakness and their heavy burden, while other nations, with a more brilliant past, perished and disappeared.

We are, indeed, in the habit of thinking that Israel was kept alive by the Law alone. But our remote ancestors, who handed down the Law to us, admitted that the Law itself only lived in our keeping for the sake of the future, and that, if not for the future, there would have been no real reason for its preservation. " Though I banish you from the land, yet be ye observant of my commandments, so that, when ye return, they will not be new to you." [1]

It was because they regarded the Law in this way that they compiled whole treatises on the minutiæ of the laws of sacrifices and offerings, of the garments and service of the priests, and so forth. They had no love of antiquarian research; but they firmly believed that all these matters would again become living questions: and, as they could not observe these commandments in practice, they endeavored at least to know them perfectly, " in order that when they returned, they should not be new to them." These treatises, on which the youth of Israel was subsequently trained generation after generation, did a great deal to implant the hope for a future in the nation's heart. Those who studied them grew accustomed to regard the future for which they hoped as a tangible thing. They must be prepared for it, and must spend their time in discussing questions connected with it. Thus the " commandments depending on the Land " helped to preserve the race perhaps more than those which applied in exile also.

[1] Sifre, 'Ekeb.

Even in the twelfth century c. e., more than a thousand years after the destruction of the Temple, the greatest sage of the exile [1] spared himself no labor in collecting and arranging the " laws for the time of the Messiah." [2] The author of the " Letter to the Jews of Yemen " was fully aware of the importance of the future for the preservation of the people ; and therefore he gave it a place among the principles of the Jewish religion. His acutely logical mind did not fail to see the objections that were brought against this proceeding after his death by the pupils of his pupils (like the author of the *Principles*)[3]; but he understood what they failed to understand—that a people cannot live on logic, that without a hope for the future even the Law, with all its logical principles, would sink into oblivion, and that all the signs of history and all the proofs of scholasticism would not avail to save the Law—and its people—from death.

In Babylon, then, when the nation was beginning, under the stress of a sudden disaster, to despair of the future, the wise men saved what they could of the national Ego, and the Prophets completed their work, and saved the whole. But in more recent days we observe a different phenomenon, which is without a parallel since the dispersion. The nation does not

[1] [Maimonides, who formulated thirteen articles of the Jewish faith, and included belief in the Messiah. Some of his followers opposed him on this point.]

[2] [That is, laws which cannot be observed until the Messiah comes.]

[3] [Rabbi Joseph Albo.]

despair of the future: on the contrary, the future is ever on its lips, as of old: but in its heart it has *forgotten* the future, first through overwhelming troubles, afterwards through excess of prosperity. And in this latter time, when the condition of the people has vastly improved, and it has been able to regain strength among strong and healthy nations; when its newborn strength might have enabled it to work actively for the future, and nothing was needed but to awake the dormant hope: just at this auspicious time the wise men have set about to uproot the sleeping hope and banish its very name even from the *lips* of the people. Nirvana is the new ideal preached by our latter-day sages, in place of the national future. Even Nirvana, however, cannot be reached by a single step, but only through a long series of metempsychoses. What shall the people do meantime? For answer, we find that just in proportion as the Future sinks into insignificance as an element in the national Ego, so, under the influence of these same sages, at the same time and in the same place, the Past grows in importance. Between the new Prayer Book without a reference to the Future, and the new literature dealing with the history of the Past, there is an internal, psychological bond of relation, the strength of which is not fully recognized by the Reformers themselves. The aged people, whose hope they have killed, asks for consolation and recompense for the loss. They point to the past, and tell the people that it must find there its pleasure and delight, until at length it will recognize that a Past without a Future needs no individual Ego to support it; that even if that Past is worthy of a permanent place in human memory, it can hold its place independently of its former guardians; and a mere aristocratic pride (as who should say, " My ancestors saved Rome ")[1] does not make it worth while to live and to suffer.

Those who desire the completion of the national Ego will not agree with these apostles of the past as to their aim; but they will approve their methods and find them useful. By all means let the sages strengthen the Past at the expense of the Future. The " Prophets " will follow, and will build a strong Future on the foundations of the Past. From this combination the national Ego will derive fulness and strength.

Far more dangerous, therefore, is that other section, which seeks salvation in a Future not connected with our Past, and believes that after a history extending over thousands of years a people can begin all over again, like a newborn child, and create for itself a new national land, a new national life and aims. This section forgets that it is the nation—that is, the national Ego in the form given to it by history—that desires to live: not some other nation, but just *this* one, with all its essentials, and all its memories, and all its hopes. If this nation could have become another, it would long since have found many ways to its salvation. There is, indeed, another Ego, the particular

[1] [i. e., the geese on the Capitol, which saved Rome from the Gauls].

temporary Ego of each individual Jew. The individual
whose existence is endangered is certainly at liberty
to seek an escape by any means, and to find a refuge
in any place; and whoever saves a large number of
such individuals, by whatever means and in whatever
place, confers a temporary benefit on the whole people,
of which these individuals are parts. But the *national*
Ego, the eternal Ego of the Jewish people, is another
matter; and they err who think it possible to lead
this also along the path of their own choice. The path
of the national Ego is already marked and laid out by
its essential character, and that character has its
foundation in the Past, and its completion in the
Future.[1]

[1] [This essay was written in the early days of the Argentine
colonies, when Baron Hirsch and many others still dreamt of
saving *the Jewish people* by means of such colonies.]

TWO DOMAINS

(1894)

Familiar as we now are with the phenomena of hypnotism, we know that under certain conditions it is possible to induce a peculiar kind of sleep in a human being, and that, if the hypnotic subject is commanded to perform at a certain time after his awakening some action foreign to his character and his wishes, he will obey the order at the appointed time. He will not know, however, that he is compelled to do so by the will and behest of another. He will firmly believe (according to the evidence of expert investigators) that he is doing what he does of his own freewill and because he likes to do so, for various reasons which his imagination will create, in order to satisfy his own mind.

The phenomenon in this form excites surprise, as something extraordinary; but we find a parallel in the experience of every man and every age, though the phenomenon is not ordinarily thrown into such strong relief, and therefore does not excite surprise or attract attention. Every civilized man who is born and bred in an orderly state of society lives all his life in the condition of the hypnotic subject, unconsciously subservient to the will of others. The social environment produces the hypnotic sleep in him from his earliest years. In the form of education, it imposes on him a load of various commands, which from the outset limit his movements, and give a definite character to his intelligence, his feelings, his impulses, and his desires. In later life this activity of the social environment is ceaselessly continued in various ways. Language and literature, religion and morality, laws and customs—all these and their like are the media through which society puts the individual to sleep, and constantly repeats to him its commandments, until he can no longer help rendering them obedience.

Society, however, which thus influences the individual, is not a thing apart, external to the individual. Its whole existence and activity are in and through individuals, who transmit its commands one to another, and influence one another, by word and deed, in ways determined by the spirit of society. It may, therefore, be said with justice that every individual member of society carries in his own being thousands of hidden hypnotic agents, whose commands are stern and peremptory. " Such and such shall be your opinions; such and such your actions." The individual obeys, unconsciously. His opinions and his actions are framed to order. At the same time, he finds cogent arguments in favor of his opinions, and sound reasons for his actions. He is not conscious that it is the spirit of other men that thinks in his brain and actuates his hand, while his own essential spirit, his inner Ego, is sometimes utterly at variance with the resulting ideas and actions, but cannot make its voice heard because of the thousand tongues of the external Ego (what a French philosopher, Bergson, calls the " verbal Ego ") in which society enfolds him.

We may go further. Society does not create its spiritual stock-in-trade and its way of life afresh in every generation. These things come to birth in the earliest stages of society, being a product of the conditions of life, then proceed through a long course of development till they attain a form that suits that particular society, and then, finally, are handed down from generation to generation without any fundamental change. Thus society in any given generation is nothing but the instrument of the will of earlier generations. The arch-hypnotizers, the all-powerful masters of the individual and of society alike, are the men of the distant past. The grass has grown on their graves for hundreds of years, it may be for thousands; but their voice is still obeyed, their commandments are still observed, and no man or generation can tell where lies the dividing line between himself and them, between his and theirs.

When, therefore, we hear people talking loudly about their " inner consciousness," by which they pronounce judgment on truth and falsehood, good and evil, beauty and ugliness, we have a right to remember what we should find if we could analyze this " consciousness." We should find that the elements of which it was compounded were almost entirely the different commands of different hypnotic agents in different ages, which, through a complex chain of causes, had become united in this particular body of men, and had found its manifestation in their peculiar Ego. For example: when Mortara, the well-known priest, hurls his thunders from the pulpit at the enemies of the Catholic faith, and strives out of the depths of his " inner consciousness " to prove the righteousness and truth of that faith, we have a right to remember that if the Catholic priests had not snatched him in childhood from the arms of his Jewish mother, and had not brought him perforce under the sway of certain hypnotic agents, ancient and modern, his " inner consciousness " would now have been composed of far other elements, and other hypnotic agents, of a very different character, would now have been speaking through his lips, with precisely the same warmth of conviction.

In normal periods—that is, when society is proceeding in all matters along the path marked out by preceding generations—past and present join forces in a single task: they repeat the tale of social commands to the individual in the same language and the same words. At such a time, therefore, the individual is able to live in peace and quiet in his condition of hypnotic slumber; he can move all his life long in the narrow circle described around him by the past and the present, and yet consider himself a free man, knowing and feeling nothing of the iron chains by which he is bound.

But times are not always normal. Occasionally (it does not matter here from what cause) the social atmosphere is suddenly disturbed by the breath of a new spirit, which brings with it new ideas, new desires, of which earlier generations had no conception. These spiritual aliens knock at the door, and seek admission into the heart of society. The old ideas, already in possession, come out to meet the strangers, and examine them critically, to see whether they bring peace or war. Finding that they possess no disqualification except their strangeness, they admit the newcomers, and allot them a quiet corner for themselves, on condition that they do not interfere with the work and the sovereign power of the natives. For a time the aliens observe this condition; they keep to their quiet corner, and take no part in the administration. But gradually they extend their domain, take firmer root, and spread their ramifications abroad: until at last they also have power, they rule and command, they are now the citizens of the present. And then they come out of their obscurity, and stand revealed in all their strength. In this their new position they meet once more with the citizens of earlier days.

This meeting of the old and the new sometimes leads to unity and amity. This happens when they are useful to each other: thus the doctrine of hypnotism and the belief in spiritualism have come to terms in the systems of certain thinkers. But more usually the result is hatred and contention. There is suddenly revealed an inner contradiction between the characteristics and the tendencies of the old and of the new, a contradiction unseen at the time of their first meeting, when the new idea was young, and its characteristics insufficiently developed.

Fortunately for mankind, this contradiction is only revealed when it has already been adjusted under the surface: that is to say, when the present has not merely found a firm foothold for itself, but has also succeeded, silently and unobserved, in tunnelling under the foundations of its enemy, the past. It is only when the old fortress is wholly overthrown that men open their eyes, and notice what has already been done without their knowledge. They see a tottering ruin in place of what they thought a solid building; and, though the sight may grieve them, they are bound to admit that what is done cannot be undone. So they must needs find consolation, and the wound is soon healed.

Phenomena of this kind are of frequent occurrence in the history of enlightened nations, and it is to such phenomena that historians generally refer when they speak of " the spirit of the age," which they regard as the justification and the cause of various social changes. This spirit is always the result of a number of small changes, which at first do not seem to trench on the domain of the past, and therefore make headway easily enough. But when once they have won an assured place, and become as it were at home, they never turn back again, even if their path is beset with hostile survivals from the past. Gradually they suck the strength out of such survivals, and leave them mere dry bones: and when that is done it needs but a very small breeze to blow these antiques once for all out of existence.

Such is the course of events where development proceeds naturally, without any sudden and artificial stimulus. But it sometimes happens, especially in connection with questions of great importance, that men of wisdom and foresight observe and proclaim the contradiction between the old and the new before the new has succeeded in secretly undermining the strength of the old. These tale-tellers are always extremists: that is to say, men whose life has been such that their " inner consciousness," in relation to the particular question at issue, is composed only of elements of the old, or only of elements of the new. In either case they draw inferences from their own state of mind to that of society, and see there only half the truth—either the power of the old alone, or that of the new alone. And just as they themselves have found it easy to expel the one before the other, so they believe that it will not be difficult to expel the object of their aversion (whether that is the old or the new) from society by revealing the contradiction between it and the other element.

Whether this movement is initiated by those who believe in the old or by those who believe in the new, it causes serious trouble, because it forces society to seek an answer to the question, Which is to go? at a time when society is still bound by ties of affection to each of the opposing forces, and cannot drive out either the one or the other. Sometimes, indeed, society attempts to silence, by forcible measures, one of the two voices, though each voice is its own, and to be guided for a time by one alone; but the other voice is soon heard again, and society is compelled to listen, cannot be deaf. Then the great question, the question that must have an answer, is this: How is it possible to serve both these masters, who are at war with each other?

There are no limits to the power of Necessity; and it finds an answer even to so hard a question as this. The thinking members of the community begin to find a compromise, a *via media,* between the old and the new. Either they clothe the one in a new guise, or they cast a veil over the other: anything rather than that the two should confront each other in their true forms. The new guise may be but an imperfect and ill-fitting cloak, and the veil may be full of holes; but as a temporary expedient it is enough. Society finds peace for a time, and can become gradually accustomed to serving the two masters at once; until at last the hour arrives when there is no need for a *modus vivendi* between them. Men become habituated to an extraordinary state of mind, in which two conflicting ideas are not fused, but are kept separate in water-tight compartments. Each idea works itself out in its own compartment, without interfering with the other or trespassing on its domain.

"In our day," says an American philosopher (John Fiske), "it is hard to realize the startling effect of the discovery that man does not dwell at the centre of things, but is the denizen of an obscure and tiny speck of cosmical matter quite invisible amid the innumerable throng of flaming suns that make up our galaxy. To the contemporaries of Copernicus the new doctrine seemed to strike at the very foundations of Christian theology. In a universe where so much had been made without discernible reference to man, what became of that elaborate scheme of salvation which seemed to rest upon the assumption that the career of Humanity was the sole object of God's creative forethought and fostering care? When we bear this in mind, we see how natural and inevitable it was that the Church should persecute such men as Galileo and Bruno. At the same time it is instructive to observe that, while the Copernican astronomy has become firmly established in spite of priestly opposition, the foundations of Christian theology have not been shaken thereby. It is not that the question which once so sorely puzzled men has ever been settled, but that it has been outgrown."

At first, that is, when the priests revealed the awful contradiction between the old and the new, and these two forces stood opposed to each other, society was compelled to seek some answer to a question by which the peace of mankind was disturbed. So volumes were written with the object of concealing the weakness of the old belief, or casting a veil over the new theory. But in course of time the human mind became accustomed to the coexistence of these two powers; and by dint of habit the contradiction between them ceased to be a cause of trouble or disturbance of the peace. It was no longer necessary, therefore, to combine the two by artificial means. A definite sphere of influence was conceded to each, in which it might hold undisputed sway, without trenching on the dominion of the other.

The result of the change is seen in its most complete form in such men as the Italian Secchi, who was at the same time a distinguished astronomer and a devout priest. When he was asked how he combined the two opposites, he used to reply, "When I study astronomy I forget my priesthood, and when I perform my priestly duties I forget astronomy."

We meet with a similar state of mind constantly in the affairs of every day, only it passes unobserved. How common it is to find one of the parties to a discussion adducing arguments to show that some received opinion, or some established custom, cannot hold ground against "the spirit of the age," and being met, not with a refutation of his arguments, but with the curt reply, "That is an old objection." Men of healthy intelligence regard this answer with surprise and contempt, and return to the charge with the question, "If the objection is old, does it follow that it has no force?" Logically they are doubtless right. But the human mind has laws of its own, which are not always consonant with those of logic; and from the point of view of these psychological laws the victory is with the defendant, though he is generally ignorant himself of the inner meaning of his defence.

The inner meaning is this: the contradiction between the old and the new has long been matter of common knowledge, and yet they both live and flourish. This proves that the human mind has by now become accustomed to their coexistence, in spite of the opposition between them; and therefore no harm can result to either from their meeting.

Thus the priests in the times of Copernicus and Galileo, opposing the new as they did only out of regard for the safety of the old, adopted a wise course in hastening to bring the two into open conflict, while the old belief was yet strong. They did not succeed in driving out the new teaching, as they wished; but they attained their real object. The old remained, its strength undiminished, side by side with the new, in spite of the contradiction between them.

There is a lesson here for the extremists on the other side, the apostles of reform. It should be their business to put off the open conflict until their new doctrine has done its work in secret, and the weakening of the old belief has proceeded so far as to render possible its complete overthrow. If they do not follow that course, but precipitate matters, and disclose the gulf in the mind of society before it has widened to its utmost limits, hoping by this means to hasten the death of the old belief and dethrone it prematurely, then their action is ill-advised, and their hopes will not be fulfilled. More than that: they will actually prolong the life of the old belief, and their own hands will build its defences against the new doctrine, by habituating society to the conflict, and making men regard the contradiction between the two as " an old objection."

This lesson in tactics has proved a stumbling-block to the best spirits of our people in the past; and to this day they have not mastered it, and a stumbling-block it remains.

Hatred of the Jews is one of the best-established commands of the past to the nations of Europe, among whom its roots are firm and deep. Jerusalem and Rome—religion and life—combined to cast a hypnotic sleep on the " barbarians " who conquered Europe, by imposing on them laws and ordinances innumerable; and this law also, that of Jew-hatred, they promulgated in concert, and handed it down through many different channels to these their heirs. Later generations strengthened the law, and repeated it to their children, until it became in very truth a spiritual disease transmitted from father to son.[1] Not that it was a disease at first. On the contrary: until the end of the Middle Ages it might well be reckoned a sign of health in the peoples of Europe, because it was in complete accord with all the other prevailing opinions and sentiments: and what is the health of society but the perfect harmony of all its ways of thought? But in modern times, since opinions and sentiments founded on the conception of humanity have come into being, and developed, and gained a commanding influence on the life of society, Jew-hatred really deserves the name of

[1] Leo Pinsker, Auto-Emancipation, p. 5.

a disease, inasmuch as it is opposed to the foundations on which society is based.

Yet, call it what you will, the fact remains that this hatred, this behest of past ages, remains in its full strength, with all its practical consequences, even now, when the Present has attained strength and a large measure of development, and in many departments of life the shadows of the Past have vanished. This proves that in this case the Past had struck its roots very deep, so deep that the developing Present has not yet reached them, nor been able to weaken them beneath the surface.

If our leaders, who fought the battle of emancipation at the beginning of the nineteenth century, had paid heed to this warning, they would have armed themselves with patience (ever the armor of our people), and would have waited for the Present to develop and strengthen itself yet further. Then, without the alarums of war, this relic of the Past would have been undermined; its practical consequences would have become " dry bones "; and then would have been the time to make an open attack on the remnant, in order to sweep it out of existence. But our leaders in those days saw nothing but the Present, and judged society by themselves. In *their* " inner consciousness " there was no longer any place for religious zealotry or national hatred; and so they believed that the forces of the Past were equally weak in society as a whole. If society was yet the slave of the Past in relation to the Jews, this, they thought, could only be due to an error of logic, to the failure to recognize the contradiction between this relic of the Past and the spirit of the age. All that was necessary, therefore, was to disclose this contradiction: the shadows would vanish immediately, and the sun of emancipation would shine on the Jews.

It is quite true that society was taken aback at first, and could find no answer to the complaints and the demands of the Jews, who suddenly came forth from the Ghetto to appeal to that humanity of which society is so proud. And so society made an honest attempt to silence the Past by main force, and resolved, perhaps with a half-stifled sigh, to include even the hated Jew in the great ideal of "liberty, equality, fraternity." But this artificial state of things could not endure. The Past was still too strong; its voice rose in spite of forcible attempts to silence it, and made itself heard first in the inner consciousness of men, then publicly as an avowed doctrine.

But even now we fail to appreciate the significance of this warning. In our distress we still appeal to "the spirit of the age," still insist on the discrepancy between that spirit and our own condition. By such open and continuous insistence we compel society, not to tear out the Past by its roots (that it could no longer do, even if it wished), but to seek some artificial means of restoring the inner harmony; to find some excuse for amplifying the accepted ideal of the Present by a small addition, which the Past demands: to wit, "except the Jews." Such an artificial means is found in those monstrous and amazing accusations which are periodically revived, although convincing proofs of their falsehood have been published times without number. These accusations, like the speculations of Galileo and his followers on the relation of religion to the Copernican system, are merely the result of the psychological necessity of combining, by any possible means, two powerful spiritual forces which are in opposition to each other. So long, therefore, as society is compelled, in relation to the Jewish question, to seek peace of soul by such means as this, the accusations in question will always come up again, and nothing can suppress them.

Perhaps—indeed, it is a fair conclusion from what precedes—this need for an artificial means of harmonizing contradictions is only temporary. Perhaps the continual conflict of Past and Present, in which we ourselves are engaged, will gradually accustom society to the coexistence of these two powers; and one day the contradiction will cease to be a disturbing force, even without the aid of a harmonizing middle term.

Should this be so, it is not outside the bounds of possibility that in course of time the gospel of Humanity will grow and spread, until it really embraces the whole human race, white, black, and yellow, and until its wings shelter even the worst criminals, to the satisfaction of certain well-known criminologists. Then our world will be a world of righteousness and justice, mercy and pity, in relation to every living thing: its mercy will extend even to the bird in its nest: but always—" except the Jews." If any man arise in that day and ask, " How can this be? Surely, the contradiction is obvious and glaring," he will receive two answers. Thinking men will say, with Secchi, " When we are occupied with Humanity, we forget the Jews, and when we are occupied with the Jews, we forget Humanity." But simple men will give a simple answer: " That is an old objection."

IMITATION AND ASSIMILATION

(1894)

We use the term Imitation, generally in a depre-
ciatory sense, to indicate that which a man says, does,
thinks, or feels, not out of his own inner life, as an inevitable consequence of his spiritual condition and his
relation to the external world, but by virtue of his in-
grained tendency to make himself like others, and to
be this or that because others are this or that.

If we accept the doctrine that moral good is good
in itself, and evil evil in itself, and that we distinguish
between the two not by syllogisms, but by a particular
" moral sense " implanted in our being, then we are
certainly justified in regarding Imitation as a moral
shortcoming. The moral sense does not approve this
habit of the ape. But if we agree with another school
of thought, that the distinction between good and evil
rests on a balancing of gains and losses from the point
of view of the happiness and development of human
society, then we may doubt whether the judgment of
the moral sense in this case is just. There may be a
certain amount of exaggeration and one-sidedness in the
doctrine of the French thinker Tarde, who holds that
all history is but the fruit of Imitation, acting in
accordance with certain laws. But as to the essential
point, a cursory examination of history is sufficient

to convince us that this not entirely praiseworthy habit is in truth one of the foundations of society, without which its birth and development would have been impossible. For, consider: had men been by nature not inclined in any way to follow one another, had each one thought his thoughts, and done his deeds, out of his own inner world alone, without yielding obedience to the force of any other personality, could men like these have attained, by common consent, to such social possessions as established laws and customs, and common ideas about religion and morality, possessions which are, indeed, in their general aspect, natural results of general causes, but which, regarded in detail, depend wholly on causes of a particular and individual character? Above all, how could language have been created and developed in any society, if no man had imitated his neighbor, but each had waited until he reached the spiritual condition in which he would be impelled to call each thing by the particular name by which his neighbor called it? Without language, no knowledge: and so man would never have risen above the beast.

But even Imitation would not have been enough to secure the spreading of these common possessions among all the individual members of society, if each individual had imitated all the rest in an equal degree. In that case the number of the objects of imitation would have been equal to that of the imitators; each man would have chosen one object of imitation out of many, according to his " spiritual condition "; and so the same difficulty would confront us again. If society is to be moulded into one single form, there must be some centre towards which all the forces of Imitation are attracted, directly or indirectly, and which thus becomes the single or the chief object of universal imitation.

Such a centre was, indeed, found in every society in the earliest stages of its development, and especially in that primitive period in which the human spirit was struggling to emerge from the depths of beast-hood and attain to a human and social form of life. At that low stage, in which savage tribes remain to this day, when man was constantly threatened by dangers from all sides, he set an exaggerated value on brute force, and reverenced the stronger as an angel of Heaven. Every family or tribe looked with reverence on its head and protector, " the prince of God in its midst." The individuality of each man, with all its particular characteristics and qualities, was completely suppressed before the majestic dignity of this their ideal. Thus he became the centre towards which the imitative instinct of all his fellow-tribesmen directed itself automatically; and it is no wonder if, not of design or set purpose, but merely through the effacement of the lower personality before the higher, his words and his actions and his habits became the common possession of the whole tribe. This common possession was handed down as an inheritance from father to son; and in each succeeding generation there was another " prince of God," who was faithful to tradition, but also amplified it where it no longer satisfied the needs of a more developed life; and so his addition became, through imitation, common property. Thus, by an easy process, certain fixed habits of life became general in that particular society, until, in course of time, its individual members were like so many reproductions of a single type.

There is no nation or society, not even the most modern, that did not originally pass through this or a similar stage: the stage of becoming, or growth, in which scattered elements are welded together into a single social body around certain central figures, by means of self-effacing Imitation. But in more modern times, when the human spirit has progressed somewhat, there is this difference, that the cause of self-effacement, and thus of imitation and of the welding process, is not necessarily a purely physical force, but may equally well be some great force of a spiritual character.

Imitation of this kind, however, which has for its central object some living, active individual, inevitably grows rarer and rarer from one generation to another. Each new generation inherits from its predecessors the results of Imitation up to that time, that is, the things that have become common property; and as these things increase in number, so does the society approach the perfection of its form: until at last that form is complete and rounded on all sides, and the best men of the living generation have no opportunity of adding anything essential to it. From that time onwards, therefore, the central object of imitation lies wholly in the past, in those " mighty men of re- nown " who in their day impressed their own image on the form of society. Just as the results of Imita- tion during all the generations of growth have been combined into a single form of life, so, too, those who made that form in those earlier generations are now combined, under the name of " ancestors " or " predecessors," into a single abstract being, which is the central object of imitation. Before this model the men of later generations, great and small alike, efface their own particular individuality ; on this they gaze with reverence and say, " If our predecessors were as men, then are we but as asses." [1]

At the same time, the imitation of one man by another within the living generation does not cease ; but it is confined to unimportant details, it lacks a single common centre, and, as a rule, it arises from quite a different cause. That self-effacement, which is the result of reverent awe, no longer finds a suitable ob- ject in the present, which is living entirely on the past ; and so the impulse to imitation of the living by the living is now given by competition, the roots of which lie in jealousy and self-love. There are many who succeed even then in attracting the attention of society, and rising above their fellows, through some new discovery in matters of detail, whether theoretical or practical. Their success impels others to follow in their footsteps, not by way of self-effacement, but, on

[1] [Shabbat, 112².]

the contrary, out of jealousy for their own individuality, and a desire to rise to the same level as others.

This kind of Imitation differs from the other in its character as in its cause. At the stage that we have called self-effacement the imitator wishes to copy the spirit or personality of the model, as it is manifested in his actions; he therefore imitates these actions in every detail, faithful to the impress stamped upon them by the personality by which he is attracted. But at the stage of competition, the whole desire of the imitator is to reveal *his own* spirit or personality in those ways in which the model revealed *his*. He therefore endeavors to change the original impress, according as his personality or his position differs from that of his model.

This kind of Imitation, also, is of benefit to society. The self-effacing imitation of the past secures stability and solidity; the competitive imitation of one individual by another makes for progress, not by means of noisy and sudden revolutions, but by means of continual small additions, which have in time a cumulative effect, and carry society beyond the limits laid down by the " predecessors."

But Imitation is not always confined to the sphere of a single society. Progress gradually brings different societies into closer intimacy and fuller acquaintance with one another; and then Imitation widens its scope, and becomes intersocial or international.

The character of this Imitation will be determined by the character of the communities that are brought into contact. If they are more or less equal in strength and on much the same level of culture, then there will immediately be "competitive imitation" on both sides. Either will learn from the other new ways of expressing its spirit, and will strive to surpass the other in those ways. But it will be different if one of the two societies concerned is so much smaller and weaker than the other in physical or spiritual strength as to feel its own lack of vitality and individuality when brought face to face with the superior community. In that case the result will be a self-effacing imitation on the part of the weaker, arising not from a desire to express its own spirit, but from respect and submission. This imitation will be complete and slavish. It will not stop at those qualities which have impelled the weaker community to efface its own individuality, and in which the imitated community really excels; it will extend also to those qualities which, in the superior community itself, are only the result of subservience to the distant past, and which, accordingly, would never have forced themselves, of their own strength, on any community which had not itself inherited that past.

No community can sink to such a position as this without danger to its very existence. The new subservience to a foreign community gradually replaces the old subservience to its own past, and the centre to which the forces of imitation are directed shifts more and more from the latter to the former. The national or communal self-consciousness loses its foundation, and gradually fades away, until at last the community reaches an unnatural condition, which is neither life nor death. " The soul is burnt out, yet the body remains." [1] Then the individual members find a way of escape from this death-in-life by complete assimilation with the foreign community.

When the cause of this self-effacement is physical or material strength, and the weaker community cannot hope to strengthen itself on the material side, then, indeed, there is nothing for it but assimilation. It was in this way that the smaller nations of ancient times disappeared when their territories were conquered by more powerful nations. The strong arm—the highest ideal of those days—always brought about the self-effacement of the conquered nation before the conqueror; and after long years of slavery and humiliation, with no possibility of self-help, the survivors lost their reverence for their own past, and one by one left the fold to become swallowed up in the stronger enemy.

But such is not the usual development when the self-effacement is due to some great spiritual force. An external, material force is clearly discernible in its effects, and it is impossible for the weaker community to belittle its importance, or to stem the tide of its progress. But the advent of a foreign *spiritual* force is not so obvious; and means can be found by which its importance can be made to appear less, and its progress can be hindered, among a people to which it

[1] [Sanhedrin, 52 [1].]

is foreign. When, therefore, a community finds its individuality endangered by an alien spiritual force, and men begin to imitate the foreign mode of life in which that force is embodied, there will always be a party of patriots, who strive to belittle the external force in the estimation of their own people, and to cut off their people entirely from all contact with the foreign life, so that it may have no attraction for them. These patriots generally succeed at first in staying the progress of the external force, and thus prevent imitation. But this prevention is not a complete cure. The community remains always in danger; it may be that the conditions of life will break down the barriers erected by force, and then contact will lead to self-effacement, self-effacement to imitation, and imitation to assimilation. Nay, more: the very separation sometimes has the opposite effect to that which is intended: for there are many who catch glimpses of the foreign life from afar, and admire it without being able to approach, until at last they leap over the barrier once for all, and escape to the enemy's camp.

As a result of this experiment in restriction, the leaders of the community generally learn—and it is fortunate for them and for the community if they learn in time—that it is not Imitation as such that leads to Assimilation. The real cause is the original self-effacement, which leads to Assimilation through the medium of Imitation. Their task, therefore, is not to check Imitation, but to abolish self-effacement. This abolition, too, must be effected by means of Imitation, but of the competitive kind. That is to say, they must appropriate for their community that spiritual force which is the cause of the self-effacement, so that the community will no longer look with distant awe on the foreign life in which that force is embodied, but, on the contrary, will turn that force to its own uses, in order, as we said, " to reveal *its own* spirit or personality in those ways in which the model revealed *his.*" When once the community is started on this path of Imitation, self-love will make it believe in its own strength, and value the imitative actions peculiar to itself more than those developed by its model. The further imitation proceeds on these lines, the more it reveals the spirit of the imitators, and the less it remains faithful to the original type. Thus the self-consciousness of the imitating community becomes ever stronger, and the danger of Assimilation disappears.

Examples of this kind of imitation are found both in ancient and in modern history. Such was the relation of the Romans to Greek culture; such the relation of the Russians to the culture of Western Europe. Both began with self-effacement before a foreign spiritual force, and therefore with slavish imitation of a foreign kind of life, in thought, speech, and action. Patriots like Cato, who tried to shut out the stream of imitation altogether, succeeded only partially and temporarily. Patriots of clearer vision began subsequently to lead Imitation along the road of competition, of a striving to embody the spiritual force—the cause of self-effacement—in the particular type of life of their own people. The result was that the self-effacement ceased, and the Imitation produced a strengthening of the national self-consciousness.

This will explain why the Jewish race has persisted in exile, and has not become lost in the nations, in spite of its inveterate tendency to Imitation.

As early as the time of the Prophets, our ancestors learned to despise physical strength, and to honor only the power of the spirit. For this reason, they never allowed their own individuality to be effaced because of the superior physical strength of the persecutor. It was only in the face of some great *spiritual* force in the life of a foreign people that they could sink their own individuality and give themselves up entirely to that life. Knowing this, their leaders endeavored to cut them off entirely from the spiritual life of other nations, and not to allow the smallest opening for imitation. This policy of separation, apart from the fact that it caused many to leap over the barrier once for all, could not, in view of the position of our people among the nations, be carried out consistently. When the era of contact set in, and continued unbroken, there were constant proofs that the apprehensions of the patriots had been groundless, and their efforts at restriction unnecessary. The Jews have not merely a tendency to Imitation, but a genius for it. Whatever they imitate, they imitate well. Before long they succeed in appropriating for themselves the foreign spiritual force to which they have become subservient. Then their teachers show them how to use this force for their own ends, in order to reveal their own spirit; and so the self-effacement ceases, and the Imitation, turned into the channel of competition, gives added strength to the Hebrew self-consciousness.

Long before the Hellenists in Palestine tried to substitute Greek culture for Judaism, the Jews in Egypt had come into close contact with the Greeks, with their life, their spirit, and their philosophy: yet we do not find among them any pronounced movement towards Assimilation. On the contrary, they employed their Greek knowledge as an instrument for revealing the essential spirit of Judaism, for showing the world its beauty, and vindicating it against the proud philosophy of Greece. That is to say, starting from an Imitation which had its source in self-effacement before an alien spiritual force, they succeeded, by means of that Imitation, in making the force their own, and in passing from self-effacement to competition.

If those Elders, who translated the Bible into Greek for the benefit of the Egyptian Jews, had also translated Plato into Hebrew for the benefit of the Jews in Palestine, in order to make the spiritual power of the Greeks a possession of our people on its own land and in its own language, then, we may well believe, the same process—the transition from self-effacement to competition—would have taken place in Palestine also; but in a still higher degree, and with consequences yet more important for the development of the inner spirit of Judaism. As a result there would have been no " traitorous enemies of the covenant " among our people, and perhaps there would have been no need of the Maccabees and all the spiritual history which had its ultimate cause in that period. Perhaps—who knows?—the whole history of the human race would have taken a totally different course.

But the Elders did not translate Plato into Hebrew. It was only at a much later date, in the period of Arabic culture, that the Greek spirit became a possession of our people in their own language—but not on their own land. And yet even then, though on foreign soil, self-effacement soon gave place to competition, and this form of Imitation had the most astonishing results. Language, literature, and religion, all renewed their youth ; and each helped to reveal the inner spirit of Judaism through the medium of the new spiritual possession. To such an extent did this new spirit become identified with the Hebrew individuality that the thinkers of the period could not believe that it was foreign to them, and that Israel could ever have existed without it. They could not rest satisfied until they found an ancient legend to the effect that Socrates and Plato learned their philosophy from the Prophets, and that the whole of Greek philosophy was stolen from Jewish books which perished in the destruction of the Temple.

Since that time our history has again divided itself into two periods—a long period of complete separation, and a short period of complete self-effacement. But once more we are nearing the conviction that safety lies on neither of these ways, but on a third, which is midway between them: that is, the perfection of the national individuality by means of competitive Imitation.

Signs of this conviction are to be found not alone in the most recent years, since the day when Nationalism became the watchword of a party in Israel, but also much earlier. We find them on the theoretical side in the production of a literature, in European languages, dealing with the spirit of Judaism and its value; on the practical side, in a movement towards the reform of the externals of Judaism. This practical movement is, indeed, held by many, including some of the reformers themselves, to be a long step towards Assimilation. But they are wrong. When self-effacement has proceeded so far that those who practice it no longer feel any inner bond uniting them with their own past, and really wish to emancipate the community by means of complete assimilation with a foreign body, then they no longer feel even the necessity of raising their inheritance to that degree of perfection which, according to their ideas, it demands. On the contrary, they tend rather to leave it alone and allow it to perish of itself. Until that day comes, they imitate the customs of their ancestors to an extent determined by accident. It is a sort of artificial, momentary self-effacement, as though it were not they themselves who acted so, but the spirit of their ancestors had entered into them at that moment, and had acted as it had been accustomed to act of old.

Geiger expresses the opinion that a writer who writes in Hebrew at the present day does not express his own inner spirit, but lives for the time being in another world, the world of the Talmud and the Rabbis, and adopts their mode of thinking. This is true of most of our Western scholars, as is evident from their style, because in their case the link between their ancestral language and their own being is broken. But with the Hebrew writers of Northern Europe and Palestine, for whom Hebrew is still a part of their being, the case is just the reverse. When they write, the necessity of writing Hebrew springs from their innermost being; and they therefore strive to improve the language and bring it to a stage of perfection that will enable them to express their thoughts in it with freedom, just as their ancestors did.

When, therefore, we find Geiger and his school giving their whole lives and all their powers to the reform of another part of their inheritance, according to their own ideas; when we find them content to accept the language as it is, but not content to accept the religion as it is: we have here a decisive proof that it is on the religious side that their Hebrew individuality still lives. That individuality is not dead in them, but only stunted; and their real and true desire, whether or not they admit this to themselves and to others, is just this: " To reveal *their own* spirit or personality in those ways in which their model reveals *his*."

Assimilation, then, is not a danger that the Jewish

people must dread for the future. What it has to fear is being split up into fragments. The manner in which the Jews work for the perfection of their individuality depends everywhere on the character of that foreign spiritual force which is at work in their surroundings, and which arouses them to what we have called " competitive imitation." One cannot but fear, therefore, that their efforts may be dissipated in various directions, according as the " spiritual force " varies in different countries; so that in the end Israel will be no longer one people, but a number of separate tribes, as at the beginning of its history.

Such an apprehension may derive support from experience. The Jews of Northern Europe, for example, received their first lessons in Western culture from the Jews of Germany. Thus their central object of Imitation, before which they sank their own individuality, was not the " foreign spiritual force " at work in their surroundings, but that which they saw at work among their own people in Germany. They therefore imitated the German Jews slavishly, without regard to differences of place and condition, as though they also had been perfect Germans in every respect. But in course of time, when the Jews of Northern Europe had made " enlightenment " their own to a certain extent, and became conscious of their new-won strength, they passed from the stage of self-effacement to that of competition in relation to the Jews of Germany, and began to depart from their prototype, being influenced by the different character of the " spiritual force " in the countries in which they lived. Similarly, the Jews of France are even now a model for Imitation to the Jews in the East; but even in their case this state of things is only temporary, and will disappear when the Eastern Jews become conscious of their new strength. Thus, the more any section of our people adds to its spiritual strength, the more completely it becomes emancipated from the influence of that other section which it formerly imitated; and so the danger of being split up into fragments grows ever more serious.

But there is one escape—and one only—from this danger. Just as in the stage of growth the members of the community were welded into a single whole, despite their different individual characteristics, through the agency of one central individual; so also in the stage of dissipation the different sections of the people can be welded together, in spite of their different local characteristics, through the agency of a local centre, which will possess a strong attraction for all of them, not because of some accidental or temporary relation, but by virtue of its own right. Such a centre will claim a certain allegiance from each scattered section of the people. Each section will develop its own individuality along lines determined by imitation of its own surroundings; but all will find in this centre at once a purifying fire and a connecting link.

In the childhood of the Jewish people, when it was split up into separate tribes, the military prowess of

David and the wise statesmanship of Solomon succeeded in creating for it a centre such as this, " whither
the tribes went up, the tribes of the Lord." But to-day,
in its old age, neither strength nor wisdom nor even
wealth will avail to create such a centre anew. And
so all those who desire to see the nation reunited will
be compelled, in spite of themselves, to bow before
historical necessity, and to turn eastwards, to the land
which was our centre and our pattern in ancient days.[1]

[1] [Here also, as in "Past and Future" (pp. 80-90), there is
an allusion to the attempt of Baron Hirsch to create a Jewish
national centre in the Argentine—an attempt which at that
time made a deep impression on the Jewish communities in
Russia, and was regarded by many as the beginning of the
national redemption.]

PRIEST AND PROPHET

(1894)

We learn from the science of mechanics that the impact of two forces moving in different directions— one eastward, for example, and one northward—will produce a movement in an intermediate direction. At a time when men were accustomed to attribute all motion to a guiding will, they may have explained this phenomenon by supposing that the two original forces made a compromise, and agreed that each should be satisfied with a little, so as to leave something for the other. Nowadays, when we distinguish between volitional and mechanical motion, we know that this "compromise" is not the result of a conscious assent on the part of the two forces; that, on the contrary, each of them plays for its own hand, and endeavors not to be turned from its course even a hair's breadth; and that it is just this struggle between them that produces the intermediate movement, which takes a direction not identical with either of the other two.

The motions of the heavenly bodies are determined, as is well known, not only by the relation of each one to the sun, but also by their influence on one another, by which each is compelled to swerve to some extent from the course that it would have pursued if left to itself. If, therefore, we were privileged, as Socrates was, to hear the " heavenly harmony," it may be that we should hear nothing but continual wrangling among the worlds above. We should find each one striving with all its might to make for itself a path according to its own particular bent, and unwilling to budge a single inch for the convenience of the others. But it is just because the stars do behave thus that no single one has its own way; and so the external harmony is produced by the agency of all the stars, and without the consent of a single one. Nay, more: if, by some miracle, a few of the stars were suddenly smitten with what we call " generosity," and were enabled to get outside their own narrow point of view, and to understand and allow for the ambitions of their fellow-stars, and consequently made way for one another of their own accord, then the whole cosmic order would be destroyed at once, and chaos would reign once more.

Similarly, if it were possible to observe what happens in the microcosm of the human soul, we should see the same phenomenon there.

The ancient Jewish sages, who looked at the world through the glass of morality, saw only two primal forces at work in the spiritual life: the impulse to good and the impulse to evil. The conflict between these two opposing forces was as long as life itself: they fought unceasingly, unwearyingly, without possibility of peace, each striving for the complete fulfilment of its own end, even to the uttermost. The impulse to evil (so they held) was absolutely evil, redeemed by no single spark of goodness. They pictured it lying in wait for every man to the end of his days, tempting him to evil deeds and arousing in him base desires, ever tending mercilessly to drag him down to the lowest depths of sin and infamy. And, on the other side, they beheld the impulse to good as something absolutely good; intolerant of evil in any form, in any degree, for any purpose; abominating all " the vanities of this world," even such as are necessary, because of their essential inferiority; striving ever to uplift a man higher and higher, to make him wholly spiritual. Each of the two principles is absolutely uncompromising; but it is just for this reason that their struggle results in a compromise and a certain balance of power. Neither of them is allowed to destroy the world by holding undivided sway. It happened once—so a charming Talmudic story [1] relates —that the Righteous captured the impulse to evil, and clapped it in prison. For three whole days the impulse to good was sole ruler: " and they sought for a new-laid egg, and none was found."

Modern European scholars, who investigate the soul from a very different point of view, find in it many more than two forces; but they describe the workings of those forces in much the same way. A French thinker, Paulhan, regards the human soul as a large community, containing innumerable individuals: that is to say, impressions, ideas, feelings, impulses, and so forth. Each of these individuals lives a

[1] [Yoma, 69[2].]

life of its own, and struggles to widen the sphere of its influence, associating with itself all that is akin to its own character, and repelling all that is opposed to it. Each strives, in short, to set its own impress on the whole life of the soul. There is no mutual accommodation among them, no regard for one another. The triumph of one is the defeat of another; and the defeated idea or impulse never acquiesces in its defeat, but remains ever on the alert, waiting for a favorable opportunity to reassert itself and extend its dominion. And it is just through this action of the individual members of the spiritual community, with their mutual hatred and envy, that human life attains complexity and breadth, many-sidedness and variety. It may happen in course of time, after much tossing about in different directions, that the soul reaches a condition of equilibrium; in other words, the spiritual life takes a definite middle course, from which it cannot be diverted by the sudden revolt of any of its powers, each of which is forcibly kept within bounds. This is the condition of " moral harmony," outwardly so beautiful, which the Greek philosophers—those apostles of the beautiful—regarded as the summit of human perfection.

It may be taken, then, as a general principle, that whenever we see a complex whole which captivates us by its many-sided beauty, we see the result of a struggle between certain primal forces, which are themselves simple and one-sided; and it is just this one-sidedness of the elements, each of which strives solely for its own end, but never attains it, that produces the complex unity, the established harmony of the whole.

This principle applies to social life, with all its many sides; and not least to its intellectual and moral aspects.

In the early history of any epoch-making idea there have aways been men who have devoted to that idea, and to it alone, all their powers, both physical and spiritual. Such men as these look at the world exclusively from the point of view of their idea, and wish to save society by it alone. They take no account of all the other forces at work that are pulling in other directions; and they even disregard the limits that Nature herself sets to their activities. They refuse to compromise; and, although conflicting forces and natural laws do not bow down before them, and they do not get their own way, yet their efforts are not wasted. They make the new idea a *primal force,* which drives the current of life in its own particular direction, as other forces in theirs; and the harmony of social life, being a product of the struggle between all the forces, is, therefore, bound to be affected more or less by the advent of this new force. But just as no one force ever obtains a complete and absolute victory, so there is no original idea that can hold its own unless it is carefully guarded by its adherents. If, as often happens, after the new idea has produced a certain effect, its adherents become " broad-minded," admit that things cannot go wholly one way, and acquiesce gladly in the enforced compromise produced by the conflict of forces: then they may, indeed, rise in the estimation of the masses, on whom the harmony of the community depends ; but at the same time their idea will cease to be a primal force in its own right.   Its influence will accordingly be further and further diminished by the action of other forces, old and new, in their constantly watchful and internecine struggle —a struggle in which our idea will have no special body of adherents to guard it and widen the sphere of its influence.

There are thus two ways of doing service in the cause of an idea; and the difference between them is that which in ancient days distinguished the Priest from the Prophet.

The Prophet is essentially a one-sided man. A certain moral idea fills his whole being, masters his every feeling and sensation, engrosses his whole attention. He can only see the world through the mirror of his idea; he desires nothing, strives for nothing, except to make every phase of the life around him an embodiment of that idea in its perfect form.   His whole life is spent in fighting for this ideal with all his strength ; for its sake he lays waste his powers, unsparing of himself, regardless of the conditions of life and the demands of the general harmony.   His gaze is fixed always on what *ought* to be in accordance with his own convictions; never on what *can* be consistently with the general condition of things outside himself. The Prophet is thus a primal force.   His action affects the character of the general harmony, while he himself does not become a part of that harmony, but remains always a man apart, a narrow-minded extremist, zealous for his own ideal, and intolerant of every other. And since he cannot have all that he would, he is in a perpetual state of anger and grief; he remains all his life " a man of strife and a man of contention to the whole earth." Not only this: the other members of society, those many-sided dwarfs, creatures of the general harmony, cry out after him, " The Prophet is a fool, the spiritual man is mad "; and they look with lofty contempt on his narrowness and extremeness. They do not see that they themselves and their own many-sided lives are but as the soil which depends for its fertility on these narrow-minded giants.

It is otherwise with the Priest. He appears on the scene at a time when Prophecy has already succeeded in hewing out a path for its Idea; when that Idea has already had a certain effect on the trend of society, and has brought about a new harmony or balance between the different forces at work. The Priest also fosters the Idea, and desires to perpetuate it; but he is not of the race of giants. He has not the strength to fight continually against necessity and actuality; his tendency is rather to bow to the one and come to terms with the other. Instead of clinging to the narrowness of the Prophet, and demanding of reality what it cannot give, he broadens his outlook, and takes a wider view of the relation between his Idea and the facts of life. Not what *ought* to be, but what *can* be, is what he seeks. His watchword is not the Idea, the whole Idea, and nothing but the Idea; he accepts the complex " harmony " which has resulted from the conflict of that Idea with other forces. His battle is no longer a battle against actuality, but a battle in the name of actuality against its enemies. The Idea of the Priest is not, therefore, a primal force; it is an accidental complex of various forces, among which there is no essential connection. Their temporary union is due simply to the fact that they have happened to come into conflict in actual life, and have been compelled to compromise and join hands. The living, absolute Idea, which strove to make itself all-powerful, and changed the external form of life while remaining itself unchanged—this elemental Idea has died and passed away together with its Prophets. Nothing remains but its effects—the superficial impress that it has been able to leave on the complex form of life. It is this form of life, already outworn, that the Priests strive to perpetuate, for the sake of the Prophetic impress that it bears.

Other nations have at various times had their Prophets, men whose life was the life of an embodied Idea; who had their effect, smaller or greater, on their people's history, and left the results of their work in charge of Priests till the end of time. But it is pre-eminently among the ancient Hebrews that Prophecy is found, not as an accidental or temporary phenomenon, but continuously through many generations. Prophecy is, as it were, the hall-mark of the Hebrew national spirit.

The fundamental idea of the Hebrew Prophets was the universal dominion of absolute justice. In Heaven it rules through the eternally Righteous, "who holds in His right hand the attribute of judgment," and righteously judges all His creatures; and on earth through man, on whom, created in God's image, lies the duty of cherishing the attribute of his Maker, and helping Him, to the best of his meagre power, to guide His world in the path of Righteousness. This Idea, with all its religious and moral corollaries, was the breath of life to the Hebrew Prophets. It was their all in all, beyond which there was nothing of any importance. Righteousness for them is beauty, it is goodness, wisdom, truth: without it all these are naught. When the Prophet saw injustice, either on the part of men or on the part of Providence, he did not inquire closely into its causes, nor bend the knee to necessity, and judge the evil-doers leniently; nor again did he give himself up to despair, or doubt the strength of Righteousness, or the possibility of its victory. He simply complained, pouring out his soul in words of fire; then went his way again, fighting for his ideal, and full of hope that in time—perhaps even "at the end of time"—Righteousness would be lord over all the earth. "Thou art Righteous, O Lord,"—this the Prophet cannot doubt, although his eyes tell him that "the way of the wicked prospereth": he feels it as a moral necessity to set Righteousness on the throne, and this feeling is strong enough to conquer the evidence of his eyes. "But I will speak

judgments with thee ": this is the fearless challenge
of Righteousness on earth to Righteousness in Heaven.
These "judgments" relieve his pain; and he returns
to his life's work, and lives on by the faith that is in
him.

These Prophets of Righteousness transcended in
spirit political and national boundaries, and preached
the gospel of justice and charity for the whole human
race. Yet they remained true to their people Israel;
they, too, saw in it the *chosen* people; and from their
words it might appear that Israel is their whole world.
But their devotion to the universal ideal had its effect
on their national feeling. Their nationalism became
a kind of corollary to their fundamental Idea. Firmly
as they believed in the victory of absolute Righteousness, yet the fact that they turn their gaze time after
time to "the end of days" proves that they knew—as
by a whisper from the "spirit of holiness" within them
—how great and how arduous was the work that mankind must do before that consummation could be
reached. They knew, also, that such work as this
could not be done by scattered individuals, approaching
it sporadically, each man for himself, at different times
and in different places; but that it needed a whole
community, which should be continuously, throughout
all generations, the standard-bearer of the force of
Righteousness against all the other forces that rule
the world: which should assume of its own freewill
the yoke of eternal obedience to the absolute dominion
of a single Idea, and for the sake of that Idea should

wage incessant war against the way of the world. This task, grand and lofty, indeed, but not attractive or highly-esteemed, the Prophets, whose habit was to see their innermost desire as though it were already realized in the external world, saw placed on the shoulders of their own small nation, because they loved it so well. Their national ideal was not " a kingdom of Priests," but " would that all the people of the Lord were Prophets." They wished the whole people to be a primal force, a force making for Righteousness, in the general life of humanity, just as they were themselves in its own particular national life.

But this double Prophetic idea, at once universal and national, was met in actual life, like every primal force, by other forces, which hindered its progress, and did not allow it free development. And in this case also the result of the conflict was to weld together the effects of all these forces into a new, complex organism; and so the idea of the Prophets produced the teaching of the Priests.

In the early stages, while Prophecy had not ceased altogether, the Prophets were accordingly more hostile to the Priests than to the general body of the people. The authors of the living Idea, which they had drawn from their innermost being, and by which they believed that they could conquer the whole world, they could not be content with seeing its image stamped, as it were, on the surface of an organism moulded out of many elements, and so fixed and stereotyped forever. Nay, more: in the very fact that their Idea had thus become a part of the social organism, they saw a kind of barrier between it and the people. But the opposition between the Prophets and the Priests died out gradually with the decay of Prophecy: and then the guidance of the people was left in the hands of the Priests (though they were not always called by that name), as sole heirs of the Prophetic Idea. The independence of this Idea, and the growth of its special influence, were at an end, because it had no longer a standard-bearer of its own.

When, therefore, the time came for this Idea—that is to say, its universal element—to cross the borders of Palestine, and become an active force throughout the world, the Priestly Judaism of those days was unable to guide it aright, and to preserve it in its pristine purity amid the host of different forces with which it came into conflict. Thus it was only for a moment that it remained a primal force; after that its influence became but as a single current, mingling and uniting with the myriad other currents in the great ocean of life. And since the number of alien influences at work was far greater here than it had been in the birthplace of the Idea, it followed that its visible effects were now even less than they had been before.

If, then, the Hebrew Prophets were to arise from their graves to-day, and observe the results of their work through the length and breadth of the world, they would have small cause for satisfaction or pæans of triumph. Now, after a long experience of thousands of years, they would recognize still more strongly the need of a " standard-bearer " to uphold their universal Idea; and for this reason they would be strengthened in their devotion to their national Idea. With even more fervor than before they would exclaim, " Would that all the people of the Lord were Prophets."

We do, indeed, occasionally hear some such exclamation from the lips of Jewish scholars and preachers in Western Europe, who uphold the doctrine of the " mission of Israel." But it follows from what has been said that the Prophetic mission is distinguished from theirs in three essentials.

In the first place, the mission in the Prophetic sense is not the revelation of some new theoretical truth, and its promulgation throughout the world, until its universal acceptance brings about the fulfilment of the mission. The ideal of the Prophets is to influence practical life in the direction of absolute Righteousness—an ideal for which there can never be a complete victory.

Secondly, this influence, being practical and not theoretical, demands, as a necessary condition of its possibility, not the complete dispersion of Israel among the nations, but, on the contrary, a union and concentration, at least partial, of all its forces, in the place where it will be possible for the nation to direct its life in accordance with its own character.

Thirdly, since this influence can never hope for a complete victory over the other influences at work on human society, which draw it in other directions, it follows that there can be no end either to the mission or to those to whom it is entrusted. The end can come, if at all, only when men cease to be men, and their life to be human life: in that great day of the Jewish dream, when " the *righteous* sit crowned in glory, and drink in the radiance of the Divine Presence."

FLESH AND SPIRIT

(1904)

Asceticism may be defined as the psychological tendency, frequently manifested both in individuals and in whole societies, to turn from the pleasures of the world with hatred and contempt, and to regard every material good thing of life as something evil and degraded, to be avoided by him who cares for his soul's health.

Asceticism, so defined, is not a descriptive term for certain outward practices, but a name for the inner spring of conduct which prompts those practices; and thus we exclude all those phenomena which have an external similarity to asceticism, but are of an essentially different character. A man may renounce pleasure, or even mortify his flesh of set purpose, and yet not deserve the name of ascetic, because, so far from despising the life of the body, he actually sets store by it, and only refrains from pleasure in order to avoid danger to his health, or physical pain: as when a man avoids wine and other luxuries by order of his doctor, for the sake of his health; or when, in anticipation of a long and difficult journey, a man reduces his allowance of food and sleep, so as to be able to bear privation in time of need without detriment to his health or undue suffering; and so forth. Further, even when abstinence and self-denial are prompted by religious motives, they are not always due to asceticism in the strict sense. In almost all primitive religions fasting and similar " afflictions of the soul " were considered an important part of the service of God, and the priests were accustomed, when performing their sacred duties, " to cut themselves with swords and knives till the blood flowed." But there is here no asceticism, because the motive is not hatred of the body, but excessive love of the body. Primitive man had a rooted belief that his god, like the head of his tribe, could be propitiated by a costly offering of his most valuable possession, and especially of flesh and fat and blood, which are the dainties most palatable to the savage. Now, the greater the value of the offering in the opinion of the bringer, the greater, clearly, would be his confidence in its acceptability to the god as a proof of his true service and fidelity. It was, then, by this process of reasoning, which followed inevitably from the fundamental belief just mentioned, that men were led to sacrifice even their offspring to their gods in time of trouble; and the same reasoning was responsible for the unnatural idea of sacrificing part of a man's own body, his fat and blood, as the most precious of his possessions. Thus religion produced, together with the idea of sacrifices in general, that of fasting and mortification, not from a desire to turn men away from the flesh, but because fasting and mortification seemed to be the greatest sacrifice of which flesh and blood was capable, and therefore the most certain means of propitiating God and gaining His grace. Hence it is that in all ages this method has been most used in times of acutest distress, when it was necessary "to cry mightily unto God," and avert His anger by every possible means.

But true asceticism, as I have said, is that which has its source in hatred and contempt for the flesh. It makes war on the flesh not for the sake of some further end, but because the flesh in itself is unworthy and despicable, and degrades man, who is the flower of creation. For asceticism there is no more important concern in life than this eternal war on the flesh, with all its desires and its pleasures; there is no higher victory for man than the killing of the flesh, the extinction of its desires, and the refusal of its pleasures.

Isolated instances of such asceticism are found at all times and in all places; but as a constant phenomenon, as a sovereign rule of life governing large masses of men for generation after generation, we meet with it first of all in India, among the Buddhists, and much later among Christian nations also. The history of European culture, especially from the fourth century till the end of the Middle Ages, is full of strange and almost incredible stories, which show with abundant clearness how this revolt against the flesh, this desire to wage a ruthless war of extermination on the flesh, can gain ascendancy over the human mind, and how this revolt can spread, like an epidemic, from place to place, from man to man, without limit to its growth.

We stand aghast at this phenomenon, utterly opposed

as it is to those general principles which are accepted in our day as laws of history. The whole of civilization, according to these principles, is simply a result of the ineradicable desire, which man shares with the rest of the animal world, to prolong life, to lighten its hardships, to make it smooth and pleasant. The ceaseless warfare, now physical, now spiritual, between man and man, between nation and nation, has its real cause in the desire of every man or nation to add to the number of his and its possessions, material or spiritual, so as to secure the greatest possible fulness and completeness of life, by reducing pain to the minimum and increasing pleasure to the maximum. So far the laws of history. And now, in the very heart of this all-devouring ocean of selfishness, behold one solitary stream making its lonely way *against* the flowing tide. The current of the whole world is set towards the broadening of life; every living thing struggles to drink its fill from every spring of enjoyment and happiness: and here are these mortals deliberately narrowing their lives, and running away from enjoyment and natural happiness as from the plague. Whence and in what way can a man get this unnatural impulse, so utterly opposed to the universal law of life?

This is no new problem, and I am not here concerned primarily with its solution. I will only indicate briefly the solution that seems to me most satisfactory, confining myself to what is necessary to my present purpose.

Since man emerged from the darkness of barbarism,

and became a civilized being, striving after self-knowl-
edge and knowledge of the outside world, he has developed two fundamental demands: the demand for
the *cause* and the demand for the *end*. Turn where he
will, he meets with perplexing phenomena, which force
him to stop and ask himself: Whence and whither?
What is the cause that produced these things? and
what is the end, the object, of their existence? But
there is a great difference between these two demands.
The problem of the cause is a logical one, and the demand for its solution is therefore absolute and common
to all human beings; whereas the problem of the end
is a moral one, and the demand for its solution is
accordingly relative, varying with the degree of moral
development in the individual. The laws of knowledge, which govern our reason, require absolutely
that every fact shall have a cause; anything without
a precedent cause is inconceivable. We might, however, conceive the whole world as simply the inevitable
result of certain causes, without reference to any particular end, were it not that our moral sense is up in
arms against this conception, and a world without any
end is in our view mere vanity and emptiness, as
though it had reeled back into chaos. And the demand
for an end is especially strong in the case of the individual's own life. For the most part life is a hard and
bitter thing, full of troubles and sufferings that have no
compensation; and, however clearly we recognize the
causes, natural and social, that produce this result, we
are still not satisfied or relieved. The moral sense still
complains and still questions: To what end?

No doubt there are men who are driven to despair by their failure to find an answer to this question, and bitterly resolve that " the superiority of man over the beasts is nothing," and that the whole aim and object of our being is to " eat and drink, for to-morrow we die." For man, as for all the animals, there is nothing more. Have you had the luck to feast well at life's table? Then rejoice in your good fortune, and die in peace. Have you failed of this happiness? Then suffer in silence. There is no right, no purpose, no end in the government of the world; it is just a chain of cause and effect.

But most men cannot be satisfied with this philosophy of despair, which robs life of its glamor. Their desire for existence will not let them find comfort for to-day's troubles in the thought of to-morrow's death. On the contrary, it forces them to seek consolation not only against the sufferings of the life that is theirs to-day, but also against the bitterness of the death that to-morrow will bring. Not finding what they want in the real world, they arrive finally at the idea of a world beyond nature, and transfer the centre of gravity of their Ego from the body to the soul. This flesh, condemned to suffer and finally to rot, is but a temporary external garment of the real, eternal Ego, that spiritual essence which lives independently of the body, and does not die with the body; this spiritual self alone is the real man, with a future and a lofty purpose in a world where all is good. This fleeting life in the vale of tears, bound up with the mortal flesh, is nothing but a shadow, and like a shadow it will pass, with all its sufferings. Now, when once a man has got so far as to divide himself into two, and regard his body as something external, which is not himself, he has no difficulty in going further. He follows out this idea till he regards the body as the *enemy* of his eternal Ego, keeping him from his true life by its constant demands and numerous ailments. So it follows that my Ego is bound to fight this enemy, to subdue it and weaken it as far as possible, so that it may not be a hindrance to my real life, and may not drag me at its heels into the morass of its own degraded existence, with all its bestiality and its utter worthlessness.

Since this philosophy is essentially intended as a consolation for those who are harassed by life's troubles, it is no wonder that, as these troubles grow, the hatred of the flesh grows also, and the desire to destroy it root and branch becomes more strong. It is a matter of everyday experience that when a man is troubled by pain in some part of his body which is not vital, say a tooth, he is seized with violent hatred of the particular member, and wants to have his revenge on it. The same thing happens in regard to the body as a whole. Once let a man look on his body as an external garment, on which his real life in no way depends, and he will come to hate these undesirable earthy wrappings in proportion as they cause him trouble. Hence we find the tendency to asceticism and mortification of the flesh increasing most markedly in dark and unhappy periods, when misery stalks abroad, and men suffer without knowing how to find relief. Then it is that they fall savagely on their tortured flesh as the seat of all the pain.

Thus the troubles of this life have given rise to two sharply opposed theories. On the one side there is the materialist view, which makes the flesh supreme, and sees no aim for human life but to enjoy the pleasure of the moment, until death shall come and put a stop to the silly game. On the other side we have the spiritual theory, which aims at killing the flesh, so that the spirit may be freed from its foe, and man may be brought nearer to his eternal goal.

But Judaism in its original form held equally aloof from either extreme, and solved the problem of life and its aim in quite a different way.

In the period of the first Temple we find no trace of the idea that man is divisible into body and soul. Man, as a living and thinking creature, is one whole of many parts. The word *Nefesh* (translated " soul ") includes everything, body and soul and all the life-processes that depend on them. The *Nefesh,* that is, the individual man, lives its life and dies its death. There is no question of survival. And yet primitive Judaism was not troubled by the question of life and death, and did not arrive at that stage of utter despair which produced among other nations the materialist idea of the supremacy of the flesh and the filling of life's void by the intoxication of the senses. Judaism did not turn heavenwards, and create in Heaven an eternal habitation of souls. It found " eternal life " on earth, by strengthening the social feeling in the individual, by making him regard himself not as an isolated being, with an existence bounded by birth and death, but as part of a larger whole, as a limb of the social body. This conception shifts the centre of gravity of the Ego not from the flesh to the spirit, but from the individual to the community; and, concurrently with this shifting, the problem of life becomes a problem not of individual but of social life. I live for the sake of the perpetuation and the happiness of the community of which I am a member; I die to make room for new individuals, who will mould the community afresh and not allow it to stagnate and remain forever in one position. When the individual thus values the community as his own life, and strives after its happiness as though it were his individual well-being, he finds satisfaction, and no longer feels so keenly the bitterness of his individual existence, because he sees the end for which he lives and suffers. But this can only be so when the life of the community has an end of such importance as to outweigh, in the judgment of the individual, all possible hardships. For otherwise the old question remains, only that it is shifted from the individual to the community. I bear with life in order that the community may live: but why does the community live? What value has its existence, that I should bear my sufferings cheerfully for its sake? Thus Judaism, having shifted the centre of gravity from the individual to the community, was forced to find an answer to the problem of the communal life. It had to find for that life some aim of sufficient grandeur and importance to uplift the individual, and to give him satisfaction at a time when his own particular life was unpleasant. So it was that Israel as a community became " a kingdom of priests and a holy nation," a nation consecrated from its birth to the service of setting the whole of mankind an example by its Law.

Thus Judaism solved the problem of life, and had no place for the two extreme views. Man is one and indivisible; all his limbs, his feelings, his emotions, his thoughts make up a single whole. And his life is not wasted, because he is an Israelite, a member of the nation which exists for a lofty end. Since, further, the community is only the sum of its individual members, it follows that every Israelite is entitled to regard himself as the cause of his people's existence, and to believe that he too is lifted above oblivion by his share in the nation's imperishable life. Hence in this early period of Jewish history we do not find any tendency to real asceticism, that is to say, to hatred and annihilation of the flesh. That tendency can only arise when life can find no aim in this world, and has to seek its aim in another. There were no doubt Nazarites in Israel in those days, who observed the outward habits of the ascetic; but all this, as I have said, was simply part and parcel of the practice of sacrifice. How far the Nazarites were removed from hatred of the flesh we may see from the fact that even Samson was regarded as a Nazarite.

This philosophy of life, which raises the individual

above all feelings of self-love, and teaches him to find the aim of his life in the perpetuation and well-being of the community, has been condemned by many non-Jewish scholars as being too materialistic, and has been regarded as a proof of the inferiority of Judaism, which does not promise immortality to every individual, and a reward to the righteous after death, as other religions do. So great is the power of hatred to blind the eyes and pervert the judgment!

But a change came after the destruction of the first Temple, when the national disaster weakened the nation's belief in its future, and the national instinct could no longer supply a basis for life. Then, indeed, Judaism was forced to seek a solution for the problem of life in the dualism which distinguishes between body and soul. But the deep-rooted partiality to the body and material life was so strong that even the new theory could not transform it entirely. Hence, unlike other nations, the Jews of that period did not eliminate the body even from the future life, but left it a place beyond the grave by their belief in the " resurrection of the dead." The end of man's life was now, no doubt, the uplifting of the spirit, and the bringing it near to " the God of spirits "; but the body was regarded not as the enemy of the spirit, but as its helper and ally. The body was associated with the spirit in order to serve it, and enable it to achieve perfection by good actions. And therefore, even in this period, Judaism did not arrive at the idea of the annihilation of the flesh. It regarded such annihilation not as righteousness, but as a sin. The two elements in man, the physical and the spiritual, can and must live in perfect accord, not as enemies; and this accord is not a truce between two opposing forces, based on a compromise and mutual accommodation, but a real inner union. The spiritual element is to penetrate into the very heart of the material life, to purify it and cleanse it, to make all its complex fulness a part of the spiritual life. Such union does not degrade the spirit, but uplifts the flesh, which is irradiated by the spirit's sanctity; and their joint life, each linked with and completing the other, brings man to his true goal.

Talmudic literature is full of utterances which confirm the view here put forward. It is sufficient to mention, by way of example, Hillel's saying about the importance of the body,[1] and the repeated condemnations of those who mortify the flesh, especially the familiar saying: " Every man will have to give an account of himself for every good thing which he would have liked to eat, but did not." [2]

Even the two non-conformist sects, the Sadducees and the Essenes, which might seem at first sight to have stood for the two extreme views, really based themselves on Jewish teaching, and developed no extravagant theories about the life of the individual. The Sadducees did not incline towards the sovereignty of the flesh, nor the Essenes towards its annihilation. The truth is that the Sadducees, who endeavored in

[1] Vayikra Rabba, 34.
[2] Jerusalem Talmud, end of Kiddushin.

all things to revive the older Judaism, held to the Scriptural view in this matter as in others, that is, that the individual has only his life on earth, and eternal life belongs solely to the nation as a whole, to which the individual must subordinate his existence. The Essenes, on the other side, starting from the eternity of the individual spirit as the most fundamental of all principles, endeavored to hold aloof from everything that distracts attention from the spiritual life. But they never despised or hated the flesh; and Philo says of them that " they avoided luxuries, because they saw in them injury to health *of body and soul*."

In the Middle Ages, no doubt, Judaism did not escape the infection of alien theories based on hatred of the flesh; but the best Jewish thinkers, such as Maimonides, tried to stem the tide of foreign influence. They remained true to the traditional Jewish standpoint, and taught the people to honor the body, to set store by its life and satisfy its legitimate demands, not to set body and spirit at odds. It was only after the expulsion from Spain, when the Jews were persecuted in most countries of the Diaspora, that the Cabbalists, especially those of Palestine, succeeded in obscuring the light, and won many converts to asceticism in its grimmest form. But their dominance was not of long duration; it was overthrown by a movement from within, first by the sect of Sabbatai Zebi and later by Hasidism. The ground was cut from under their asceticism, and material life was restored to its former esteem and importance.

And yet we do find even in Jewish history traces of these two extreme views—the sovereignty of the flesh and its annihilation. But that characteristic tendency, which we have already noticed, to transfer the centre of gravity from the individual to the national life, is evident here also ; and so the Jews applied to the national life those ideas which other nations applied to the life of the individual.

In the very earliest times there was in Israel a considerable party which adopted the materialistic view of the national life. The whole aim of this party was to make the body politic dominant above all other interests, to win for the Jewish State a position of honor among its neighbors, and to secure it against external aggression. They neither sought nor desired any other end for the national life. This party was that of the aristocrats, the *entourage* of the king, the military leaders, and most of the priests : in a word, all those whose private lives were far removed from human misery, which demands consolation. The spiritual aspect of the national life had no meaning for them. They were almost always ready to desert the spiritual heritage of the nation, " to serve other gods," if only they thought that there was some political advantage to be gained. Against this political materialism the Prophets stood forward in all their spiritual grandeur, and fought it incessantly ; until at last it vanished automatically with the overthrow of the State. But certain modern historians are quite wrong when they assert that the Prophets hated the State as such, and desired its destruction, because they regarded its very existence as essentially inconsistent with that spiritual life which was their aim. This political asceticism, this desire for the annihilation of the flesh of the national organism as a means to the strengthening of its spirit, was in reality quite repugnant to the view of the Prophets. We have only to read those passages in which the Prophets rejoice in the victories of the State—in the time of Sennacherib, for instance— or bewail its defeats, to see at once how they valued the State, and how essential political freedom was, in their view, to the advancement of the very ideals for which they preached and fought. But at the same time they did not forget that only the spirit can exalt life, whether individual or national, and give it a meaning and an aim. Hence they demanded emphatically that the aim should not be subordinated to the means, that the flesh should not be made sovereign over the spirit. The Prophets, then, simply applied to the national life that principle which Judaism had established for the life of the individual: the unity of flesh and spirit, in the sense which I have explained.

The real ascetic view was applied to the national life only in the time of the second Temple, and then not by the Pharisees,[1] but by the Essenes. So far as the

[1] [The word "Pharisee" is derived from the root *parosh*, which means "to separate," and is therefore usually regarded as meaning a man "separated" from the concerns of everyday life, i. e., a sort of hermit or ascetic. The author seems to accept this explanation. Others, however, regard the Pharisees as having stood for *national* separateness ; others, again, derive

individual was concerned, the Essenes, as I have said, had no leaning towards hatred of the flesh. But they did adopt that attitude as regards the body politic. These spiritually-minded men saw corruption eating at the very heart of the Jewish State; they saw its rulers, as in the time of the first Temple, exalting the flesh and disregarding all but physical force; they saw the best minds of the nation spending their strength in a vain effort to uplift the body politic from its internal decay, and once more to breathe the spirit of true Judaism into this corrupt flesh, now abandoned as a prey to the dogs. Seeing all this, they gave way to despair, turned their backs on political life altogether, and fled to the wilderness, there to live out their individual lives in holiness and purity, far from this incurable corruption. And in this lonely existence, removed from society and its turmoil, their hatred of the State grew stronger and stronger, until even in its last moments, when it was hovering betwixt life and death, some of them actually did not conceal their joy at its impending destruction.

But these political ascetics had no great influence over the popular mind. It was not they, but another sect, called Pharisees, although they had no vestige of real asceticism,[1] who were the teachers and guides of the people, and who upheld the Jewish view which

the name from a secondary sense of the same root, "to explain, expound," and make the Pharisees the "expounders of the Law."]

[1] [See the previous foot-note.]

was handed down from the Prophets: that is, the combination of flesh and spirit. They did not run away from life, and did not wish to demolish the State. On the contrary, they stood at their post in the very thick of life's battle, and tried with all their might to save the State from moral decay, and to mould it according to the spirit of Judaism. They knew full well that spirit without flesh is but an unsubstantial shade, and that the spirit of Judaism could not develop and attain its end without a political body, in which it could find concrete expression. For this reason the Pharisees were always fighting a twofold battle: on the one hand, they opposed the political materialists within, for whom the State was only a body without an essential spirit, and, on the other side, they fought together with these opponents against the enemy without, in order to save the State from destruction. Only at the very last, when the imminent death of the body politic was beyond all doubt, did the root difference between the two kinds of patriots, who stood shoulder to shoulder, necessarily reveal itself; and then the separation was complete. The political materialists, for whom the existence of the State was everything, had nothing to live for after the political catastrophe; and so they fought desperately, and did not budge until they fell dead among the ruins that they loved. But the Pharisees remembered, even in that awful moment, that the political body had a claim on their affections only because of the national spirit which found expression in it, and needed its help. Hence they never entertained the strange idea that the destruction of the State involved the death of the people, and that life was no longer worth living. On the contrary: now, now they felt it absolutely necessary to find some temporary means of preserving the nation and its spirit even without a State, until such time as God should have mercy on His people and restore it to its land and freedom. So the bond was broken: the political Zealots remained sword in hand on the walls of Jerusalem, while the Pharisees took the scroll of the Law and went to Jabneh.[1]

And the work of the Pharisees bore fruit. They succeeded in creating a national body which hung in mid-air, without any foundation on the solid earth, and in this body the Hebrew national spirit has had its abode and lived its life for two thousand years. The organization of the Ghetto, the foundations of which were laid in the generations that followed the destruction of Jerusalem, is a thing marvellous and quite unique. It was based on the idea that the aim of life is the perfection of the spirit, but that the spirit needs a body to serve as its instrument. The Pharisees thought at that time that, until the nation could again find an abode for its spirit in a single complete and free political body, the gap must be filled artificially by the concentration of that spirit in a number of

[1] [Rabbi Johanan ben Zakkai obtained permission from the victorious Romans to retire with his disciples to Jabneh, where he kept alight the lamp of Jewish study, and thus secured the continuance of Judaism despite the overthrow of the Jewish State.]

small and scattered social bodies, all formed in its image, all living one form of life, and all united, despite their local separateness, by a common recognition of their original unity and their striving after a single aim and perfect union in the future.

But this artificial building stood too long. It was erected only to serve for a short time, in the days when men firmly believed that to-day or to-morrow Messiah would come; but at last its foundations decayed, and its walls cracked and gaped ever more and more.

Then there came again spiritually-minded men, who revived the political asceticism of the Essenes. They saw at its very worst the scattered and enslaved condition of the dispossessed nation; they saw no hope of a return to the land; they saw, too, the organization of the Ghetto, in which there was at least some shadow of a concrete national life, breaking up before their eyes. Despair took hold of them, and made them absolutely deny bodily life to their nation, made them regard its existence as purely spiritual. Israel, they said, is a spirit without a body; the spirit is not only the aim of Jewish life, it is the whole life; the flesh is not merely something subsidiary, it is actually a dangerous enemy, a hindrance to the development of the spirit and its conquest of the world.

We need not be surprised that this extreme view produced its opposite, as extreme views always do, and that we have seen a recrudescence of that political materialism which confines the life of Israel to the body, to the Jewish State.

This phenomenon is still recent, and has not yet reached its full development. But past experience justifies the belief that both these extreme views, having no root and basis in the heart of the nation, will disappear, and give place to the only view that really has its source in Judaism, the view of the Prophets in the days of the first State, and that of the Pharisees in the days of the second. If, as we hope, the future holds for Israel yet a third national existence, we may believe that the fundamental principle of individual as of national life will be neither the sovereignty of the flesh over the spirit, nor the annihilation of the flesh for the spirit's sake, but the uplifting of the flesh by the spirit.

MANY INVENTIONS

(1890)

Lo, this only have I found, that God hath made man upright; but they have sought out many inventions (Eccl. 7 : 29). Be not righteous over much; neither make thyself over wise (*ib*. 16).

The progress of human beliefs and opinions offers an instructive subject of contemplation to one who has faith in the sovereign power of truth and reason. Let him consider attentively the important changes which each school of thought has undergone in the course of a development shaped by temporary and local influences; let him think of the disputes, the disquisitions, the books without number, by which each school has fondly thought to demonstrate the correctness of its own view, and to crush the opposing theory once for all, but which have almost always had the result of widening the gulf and rousing the obstinate conflict to fresh fury: and his faith, despite himself, will weaken. He will begin to see that the human mind is not guided by reason alone in pronouncing on any question which affects, in a greater or less degree, the material or moral welfare of the individual. We think, indeed, that we are seeking the truth, and nothing but the truth; and we try to establish our opinions, for ourselves as well as for others, by reasoned arguments. But in fact there is another force at work below the surface, a force which quietly assumes control of the mind's movements, and directs them whither it will, giving to its commands the semblance of reason and truth. This all-powerful force disguises itself in innumerable changes of shape and form; but a penetrating eye will recognize it, beneath them all, as *the desire for life and well-being*. This desire, which is implanted in us by nature, forces every living thing to pursue at all times that which brings life and pleasure, and to shun that which leads to destruction or pain. For every living thing this desire is the motive and the goal of every single action. In the case of human beings, it is the supreme force which influences, recognized or unrecognized, consciously or unconsciously, not only their actions and their schemes, but also their beliefs and their opinions.

For man's struggle for life and well-being has a distinct quality of its own. In the case of all other living things, the struggle is purely external: it is a struggle against hostile natural forces, against an environment inimical to life and well-being. But man has to go through a further, internal struggle, a struggle against himself, against his own thoughts and feelings, which interfere more or less with his mental peace and quiet, and thus with his general well-being. Every mishap, every wound which he gets in the external struggle, produces feelings of pain and distress, which impair his vitality for some time afterwards; the impression left by every painful experience remains long after its cause has vanished: and these memories of the past cause him painful apprehensions as to the future, and thus embitter his existence in the present, and do not allow him to enjoy whole-heartedly even such little fruit as he has been able to pluck from the tree of life. The will-to-live cannot tolerate such a condition of things: for without spiritual rest there is no life and no well-being. So man must needs endeavor, without desiring or feeling it, to transform in thought these disquieting experiences and accidents of his external struggle; he must seek explanations for them which are in harmony with his innermost desire, and can bring him satisfaction.

In the early days of the human race, when man had not laid hold of the tree of knowledge, nor searched deeply into the mysteries of life and the universe; when, with eyes closed, he followed his natural impulses, which guided spontaneously his physical and spiritual powers, and satisfied his simple wants without undue exertion: in those days his two battles were waged by two different forces—by Reason and by Imagination; and his will-to-live controlled these two forces, and made them work for his well-being. Reason discovered the chain of causation in things, and thus taught him how to obtain his desires and remove external obstacles. Imagination fulfilled its function in the inner life: it brought him comfort in trouble, and the strength that is born of hope; it kept him from faltering, and prevented a despairing flight from the battlefield. Reason was the general, directing his forces in their work; Imagination was the priest who accompanied the army, strengthening the weak and the wounded, and administering sweet comfort to their souls. Whenever Reason was unable to lead the way to victory, Imagination could lead the way to rest, by refashioning the chain of cause and effect, and could shed a cheerful light on every circumstance and every event, good and evil alike. When the thunder peals, and the blinding lightning-flashes play, and terror lays hold on all living things, man, too, leaves his work in field or forest, and hastens, quaking with fear, to hide in some rocky cavern from the anger of a hidden God: when lo! Imagination comes to his aid, and shows him Jupiter sitting on the top of Olympus, and hurling his lightnings and his thunders upon the heads of his enemies who have sinned against him. So man calls on his God, appeases Him with an offering from his flock or herd or the fruit of his land, and returns to his work with a tranquil mind, to struggle for his existence against his external enemies, under the generalship of Reason. Even in the face of death, when he sees that fell destroyer, the all-devouring, all-consuming, and knows that upon him, too, must come the end of all flesh, even then his desire for existence does not desert him; even then he does not succumb to despair and hatred of life. Imagination has power to open the gates of hell before him, to show him life and well-being even there, under the earth. And it is not a different life, of a strange, spiritual kind, that he sees there, but just a simple human life of body and soul, wherein every man lives as he did on earth; wherein the small remains small, and the great is still great; wherein the master is master, and the slave is not free. This marvellous faith, traces of which are found even among the cultured nations of the ancient world,[1] and which scientific research has discovered to-day among various tribes in the stage of childhood, is a result of the will-to-live, and dates from that distant age when man, not yet finding his natural state a burden, wished for nothing better in his eternal home. And this faith not only freed him from the fear of death, but also strengthened his hands in the battle of life, because he always remembered that he would remain forever and ever in the condition in which death overtook him, and every upward step on the ladder of well-being in this life would mean an increase of his happiness after death.

Thus, turn where we will, we find Reason and Imagination, work and hope, walking hand-in-hand in the life of the natural man, and helping each other in the internal as in the external struggle. He has not yet come to regard hatred of life as righteousness or as wisdom; and so he pursues well-being openly and without shame. It never occurs to him to look for any object in life except this single, natural object— to be, and to live a life of well-being. For this object he fights unweariedly with all his might, and with all the means which Reason can devise; while Imagination stands by the side of Reason, ready to remove every idea or feeling that might disturb its work.

[1] Comp. De Coulanges, La cité antique, bk. i.

But as society develops and grows more complex, new wants and new cares are born, which had no existence in earlier ages. The path of life is strewn with artificial obstacles, which call for deliberation and resource, demand knowledge and efficiency. The struggle for existence becomes inevitably a hard and bitter war-in-peace; and thousands are beaten for one who wins. In this period the more intelligent begin to realize that all is not right with the world. The simple dreams of childhood no longer satisfy their developed intellects. Their hope for well-being, in life or after death, is destroyed; and with it they lose the feeling of joy in life, and the strength of will to act. Finally, weary of toil and trouble, despairing of happiness, they turn away from the corpse-strewn field of battle against external forces, and concentrate their powers on their inner life, on the effort to find rest and comfort for themselves and their like. And now their world becomes a chaos; their spiritual equilibrium is upset. Imagination and Reason invade each other's provinces, and every man, according to his temperament and his education, lays hold of the one or the other, or passes from the one to the other, finding no satisfaction. For in this extremity he turns to both of them at once, seeking an answer to the question which overshadows his whole being—the question of life or death, good or evil; and each of them answers in its own way. Thus they produce two new views on the nature and the function of life. These views also have their roots in the desire for life and well-being:

but it is a stern and a terrible well-being that they
bring, and a life how different from that healthy
natural life of willing and acting and achieving!

The one view soars aloft on the wings of Imagination, up above the boundaries of nature and human
life, into the upper world of wonders, the spiritual
and eternal world. Dazzled by the lightning gleam of
such a world, the human mind turns back and regards its fortune on earth, and sighs, " Vanity of vanities, all is vanity!" There is no good and no evil, no
life and no death, in this vale of tears; all is but an
enforced preparation for the life yonder, but a series
of snares and pitfalls and hard struggles, out of which
one in a thousand may win safely through to happiness
in a world where all is good. This view, soaring as
it does beyond the bounds of nature, leaves Reason
and experience behind; it neither relies on them
nor fears them, but simply disregards them. Hence
it satisfies those who can wing their flight freely into
the upper world.

But there are men who are bound by the chains of
Reason, which judges only by what the eye can see;
and for such men there is no aerial soaring. Seeking
an answer to life's great question, they look right and
left, and find no help save in cold Reason, with its
judgments and its proofs, which promise so much and
give so little. Yet rest they must have at all costs;
their desire for life will not be stifled. So they are
forced to take up with another view, a philosophical
view, which also tells them that " all is vanity," but

in a very different sense. For whereas the first view denied death, this one does not believe in life. The first view sought tangible well-being and happiness, and found them in another world; the second seeks only perfect rest, and finds it by crushing out every disturbing feeling and desire—by deciding, like the fox in the old fable, that the unattainable grapes are sour. All human pleasures are but fleeting shadows, baits for fools, at whose stupidity the wise can laugh. Man is pure Reason; his happiness lies in a lonely life of contemplation, beyond the hurtful reach of accident.

So long as these views were widely held, they both turned the attention of men entirely away from the natural life. The one view, according to which hatred of life is *righteousness,* produced hermits and anchorites, who fled from the turmoil of life into forests and deserts, and spent all their days there with folded arms, enveloped in a cloud of dreams and fancies; the second, regarding hatred of life as *wisdom,* filled Greece and Rome with philosophizing beggars, mouths without hands, who looked on their surroundings with haughty contempt, hating and hated by all men. To the first class belonged that ancient saint of whom it is recorded that he thus rebuked the man who brought him news of his father's death: " Silence, thou blasphemer! Man is immortal! " And the second class is represented by the Greek philosopher who received the tidings of his son's death calmly, with the remark, " Even while he was alive I knew that my son was not immortal." [1]

[1] Comp. Lecky, European Morals, i, p. 191.

The course of human thought on life generally, as applied to the individual, is paralleled by that of Hebrew thought on the life of the Hebrew nation; and the one process may fitly serve to illustrate the other. After what has been said, a brief adumbration will be sufficient to indicate my meaning.

In the early days of Jewish history, when the people was full of youthful vigor, and had had no experience of misfortune, the national will-to-live was healthy and natural, and its biddings were followed spontaneously, without sophisticated questionings. Wisely and skilfully the nation fought for life against its external enemies; and at home the Prophets encouraged and incited to action, by painting in brilliant and alluring colors that national happiness which was the nation's goal—a happiness not to be sought in Heaven or outside nature, but very near to each man's heart; a happiness to be sought in the present, to be fought for every day.

But those good old times were not of long duration. East and west, on Israel's borders, mighty empires grew up; his tiny land was a stepping-stone on their way to foreign conquests; and their proud heel trod upon the poor, small nation which dwelt there alone in the midst of these encircling giants. Time after time the Jews tried to throw off the yoke, but in vain; and at last they gave up the struggle in despair. But now, when they could no longer hope to regain life and liberty by their own strength, they ceased to carry on the external struggle, and began to think about the internal, spiritual life; to find a medicine for the broken heart and bind up the wounds of the spirit. The national hopes of the earlier Prophetic visions unconsciously assumed a new form; they became etherealized, supernatural, outside time. On the foundation of these hopes the will-to-live built a castle in the air, which reached as high as the heavens. As the actual position of the nation sunk lower and lower, so its spirit soared heavenwards, leaving the concrete, present life of will and action for a visionary life in the bosom of a boundless future. The nation soon became a slave to this spiritual disease, which was an inevitable outcome of its condition and its history; it could no longer turn back and look down from Heaven upon earth, no longer feel the beauty of life, the sweetness of freedom, or the wretchedness of its own condition. It understood, as by a natural intuition, that such feelings were fraught with danger to its inward peace, perhaps even to its very existence.

For centuries this idea was supreme in Israel—its comfort in misery, its happiness in misfortune. But a new age came, when the spirit of philosophy walked the earth, and laid waste the castles of Imagination throughout the world. The Jewish castle, too, was not spared; the new spirit breathed upon it, and its foundations shook. Then among our people also there arose the second theory, the fox-and-grapes philosophy. A new generation has arisen in Israel, which believes no more than its fathers did in the possibility of achieving the national well-being by natural means, but has abandoned, in conformity with the spirit of the age, even that belief in which they found consolation. But this generation, too, is imbued, despite itself, with the national will-to-live, which cannot be crushed; and so it can find spiritual peace only by striving with all its might to transform this troublesome and disquieting feeling, by endeavoring to believe, or even to prove, that to love one's own nation means to hate mankind; that national unity is a piece of youthful folly, and a disgrace to a nation grown wise with years; that the Hebrew people can be—nay, is morally bound to be—happy without the sour grapes; that a kind Providence has given this people a mission different from that of any other people, a spiritual, intellectual mission, which demands no practical service, but only preachers and divines.

As with the human spirit in general, so with the spirit of our nation: " God hath made them aright, but *they* have sought out many inventions." But these inventions, whether they take the guise of faith or of philosophy, are not the fruit of free speculation or of the search after truth for truth's sake: they are spiritual diseases, with which the human race (or the nation) has become infected as a result of certain historical causes. The diseases are different in character, but alike in their effects. The one seeks life in death, the other death in life; but both alike prevent the human race (or the nation) from attending to this world, and lead it away from the plain, natural course which lies before every living thing—to seek life in life, and to defend its existence to the last gasp.

What does Nature say to these two extremes of human and of Jewish thought? To the one: " Be not righteous over much " ; and to the other: " Make not thyself over wise."

SLAVERY IN FREEDOM [1]

(1891)

The opponents of the Hoveve Zion in the Russian Jewish press think that they have need of no more formidable weapons than those which they used to employ when they fought the battle of "culture" against the "obscurantists." That is to say, instead of examining our views and proving us in the wrong by arguments based on reason and facts, they think that they can put us out of court by an array of distinguished names; they think that they can frighten us by pointing out how widely we differ from the Jewish thinkers of Western Europe. They forget that their new opponents include many who are no strangers to Western culture, and who are therefore quite aware that even professors sometimes sin against the light, that even members of Academies have been known to cling to obsolete beliefs.

Thus, these opponents of ours try to make us see, for our own good, to what a pitch of spiritual exalta-

[1] [This essay, published in Ha-Meliz (1891), was a reply to an article entitled "Eternal Ideals," which had appeared in the Russian Voschod, from the pen of a prominent Jewish writer. The Voschod was a Russian Jewish monthly, since defunct. It will be observed that this essay was written some years before the Dreyfus case, which first revealed to the world the strength of anti-Semitic feeling in France.]

tion our people have risen in France, where even anti-Semitism has not made them " narrow." Anti-Semitism! To the French Jews, with their " breadth of view," it is as though it did not exist: they go securely and calmly on their way towards those " eternal ideals " which their predecessors, the Jewish scholars of the last generation, set before them. But we, the small of soul, we have lost the way and turned back. Such, at least, is the opinion of our opponents : and for evidence they bring an array of distinguished names, in the face of which who so bold as to doubt that they are right ?

And yet I for one am bold enough to doubt the " calmness " of the Jews of France in the face of anti-Semitism; to doubt even their " spiritual exaltation," and the value of those " eternal ideals " which they pursue. And, indeed, I find ground for these doubts in the very words of those " distinguished " people who are held up to us *in terrorem.*

Four years ago, at a meeting of the Société des Études Juives in Paris, Theodore Reinach, the secretary of the society, drew the attention of his hearers to the danger which threatened the Jews in France through the growth of anti-Semitism. " Ah ! " he cried, " anti-Semitism, which was thought dead in this *beautiful France* of ours, is trying to raise its head. A single pamphleteer [1] beat his drum, and now he is surprised at his wonderful success. This success—*so I would fain believe*—is only temporary; but for all that it is

---

[1] [Drumont.]

a bad sign." M. Reinach thinks, all the same, that there is no smoke without fire, that there must be a grain of truth in the charges of the anti-Semites. " Being, as we are, the smallest religious sect ; being, as we are, strangers newly arrived in the French household, we are especially subject to jealousy and criticism." Even our abilities and our successes in every field are no protection for us. On the contrary, " it is just these that inflame jealousy." There is, therefore, but one remedy for us. We must be very circumspect in all our actions, so as not to give an opening to our enemies. " Our merchants must all be honest, our rich men all unassuming and charitable, our scholars all modest, our writers all disinterested patriots." Then, naturally, such angels will please even the French.[1]

It is unnecessary to say that this excellent advice of M. Reinach has never been followed, and never will be. Since then things have not become better, but the reverse. Instead of the " single pamphleteer " we find now many pamphleteers, none of whom need grumble, for " beautiful France " listens to them with keen pleasure, takes their words to heart, and is roused to increased jealousy and more inflamed hatred every day. Our brethren in France endeavor, indeed, to believe, with M. Reinach, that " this success is only temporary." But there are not many who feel, like him, and not all those who so feel proclaim it as he did,

[1] Comp. Actes et conférences de la société des études juives, 1887, p. cxxxii.

that this belief is without foundation, but is only what " they *would fain* believe," or, rather, what they *must* believe, if they are not willing to give up in despair the struggle of a hundred years. And yet, if you listen carefully to their quavering voices, when all their talk is of belief and hope, you will hear the stifled sigh, and the voice of a secret doubt, which would make themselves heard, but that they are forced back and buried under a heap of high-sounding phrases.

I have before me as I write a new French book, in which the writers whom I mentioned at the outset have found the beautiful ideas to which I have referred, a book called *La Gerbe*.[1] It was issued last year by the publisher of the Archives Israélites, to commemorate the fiftieth anniversary of that publication. Had such a jubilee volume been published twenty years ago, it would undoubtedly have recounted with pæans of triumph all the victories of the " Frenchmen of the Jewish persuasion " during these fifty years. It would have described exultantly their success, their advance in every sphere of life, their present happiness and honored estate, their bright hopes for the future. But in fact it appears now, and not twenty years ago; and what is it that we hear? Without offence to its authors and admirers be it spoken: we hear cries of defeat, not pæans of triumph. It is in vain that we look for any sign of genuine rejoicing, of such " exaltation of spirit " as would be proper to this jubilee festival. Through the whole book, from be-

[1] La Gerbe: études, souvenirs, etc., Paris, 1890.

ginning to end, there runs an undercurrent of grief, a dark thread of lamentation.

First of all let us hear the editor himself, the central figure of the celebration, give his account of the achievements of his publication. " In the year 1840," he tells us, " fifty years after the promulgation of the principles of 1789, the Jews possessed rights on paper; but in practice their rights were non-existent. " And then he asks in a parenthesis, " Do they exist fully even in 1890? " After this question, which calls for no answer, he goes on to recount his battles against prejudice, and tells how he has tried unceasingly to spread the great principle of " social assimilation (*la fusion sociale*) with all its corollaries." What he says amounts to this, that even the second jubilee after the principles of '89 has not brought the desired happiness; that hatred of the Jews has revived even in France, despite the principles of '89, and despite all the battles against prejudice and all efforts to promote assimilation. And so—our respected editor promises to continue to fight and strive.

There follow a large number of articles, almost all written by distinguished men, and almost all, whatever their subject, working round as it were automatically to the question of anti-Semitism. Is not this a sure indication that this accursed question fills their whole horizon, so that they cannot turn their attention from it even for a moment, but it must needs force itself to the front, of whatever subject they may treat?

The writers in *La Gerbe* are certainly men of parts and distinction, and it is not for such men as these to turn back in fright at the sight of the enemy—still less to let others see that they are afraid. They know how to control themselves and make a show of looking at all these things from above; they know how to comfort themselves and their readers with pleasant hopes and fair promises, which read sometimes like little prophecies. One of the writers promises us on his word that this is the last battle between the Jews and their enemies, and it will end in complete victory for us, to be followed by real peace for all time. The great Revolution of '89 is always on their tongues. They refer again and again to the " rights of man " (*les droits de l'homme*), or, as some put it, " the new Ten Commandments " which that Revolution promulgated; and each time they express the hope—a hope which is also a sort of prayer—that the French people will not forever forget those great days, that the French people will not, *cannot* turn back, that the French people is still, as of old, the great, the enlightened, the glorious, the mighty people, and so forth, and so forth.

Whether these prophecies will be fulfilled or not is a question with which we are not here concerned. But in the meantime it requires no very penetrating vision to discern from them, and from the pages of *La Gerbe* generally, the true spiritual condition of the French Jews at the present time. There is here none of that " exaltation " which some would fain discover, but the exact opposite. Their condition may be justly defined as *spiritual slavery under the veil of outward freedom.* In reality they accepted this slavery a hundred years ago, together with their " rights "; but it is only in these evil days that it stands revealed in all its glory.

The writers of *La Gerbe* try, for instance, to prove to us and to our enemies that the fortunes of the Jews in every country are inextricably bound up with those of its other inhabitants, or even with those of humanity as a whole; that the troubles of the Jews in any particular country are not, therefore, peculiar to them, but are shared by all the other inhabitants, or even by humanity as a whole; and that for this reason . . . . but the conclusion is self-evident. One writer, wishing to reassure the *rich* Jews of France, whose apprehensions have been aroused by the anti-Semitic movement, tells them this very pleasing story. In 1840, during the February Revolution, a rumor got abroad in a certain Alsatian city that the revolutionaries intended to attack and loot the houses of the rich Jews. The Jews were very much perturbed, and hastened to seek the protection of the commander of the garrison which was permanently quartered in the city. He, however, refused to protect them, unless the National Guard would assist him. To the commander of the National Guard, therefore, they addressed themselves, only to be met with contemptuous jeers from men who did not see any harm in the looting of a few Jewish houses. So the Jews returned home in fear and trembling. But on the following day it became known that the revolutionaries had designs on all men of property, without distinction of creed, and were going to include the houses of rich Christians in their round of visits. At once both the permanent garrison and the National Guard appeared in the streets, and " the Jewish question was settled " —so our narrator concludes, with a smile of satisfaction: adding that he thinks it unnecessary " to expatiate on the *lofty moral* of this story." In truth, *we* can find a lofty moral in this story, from our own point of view. But shall we really find the " moral " which our narrator wishes to draw? At any rate, his moral is not exactly " lofty."

This trick of exciting sympathy with the Jews on the ground that it will benefit other people is very familiar to us here also. Our Russian Jewish writers, from the time of Orshansky to the present day, are never weary of seeking arguments to prove that the Jews are a milch cow, which must be treated gently for the sake of its milk. Naturally, our French *savants* do not condescend to use this ugly metaphor. They wrap up the idea in a nice " ideal " form. But when all is said, the idea is the same there as here; and a terrible idea it is, sufficient in itself to show how far even Western Jews are from being free men at heart. Picture the situation to yourself. Surrounded by armed bandits, I cry out " Help! Help! Danger! " Is not every man bound to hasten to my help? Is it not a fearful, an indelible disgrace, that I am forced to prove first of all that my danger affects other people, affects the whole human race? As though my blood were not good enough, unless it be mingled with the blood of others! As though the human race were something apart, in which I have no share, and not simply a collective name for its individual members, of whom I am one!

This slavery becomes more and more apparent, when the writers in *La Gerbe* come to deal with the internal affairs of Judaism. Valiantly they champion the cause of our religion against its rivals, knowing as they do that this is permitted in France, where neither the Government nor the people cares very much about such discussions. But when they have to disclose the *national* connection between the Jews of France and other Jews, or between them and their ancestral land, a connection in which it is possible to find something inconsistent to a certain extent with the extreme and zealot patriotism which is in vogue in France, then we discover once more their moral slavery—a spiritual yoke which throttles them, and reduces them to a condition of undisguised embarrassment.

One of the contributors, the distinguished philosopher Adolphe Franck, expresses the opinion that every Jew, *without distinction of nationality,* who enjoys the fruits of emancipation in any country, is bound to be grateful, first and foremost, to the Frenchmen of the Revolution, and must therefore regard France as his *first* fatherland, the *second* being his actual birthplace.

And here our philosopher finds it his duty suddenly
to add: "Jerusalem is [for the Jew] nothing more
than the birthplace of his memories and his faith. He
may give it a place in his religious service; but he himself belongs to the land of his birth." This way of
regarding Jerusalem is a very trite commonplace,
which our Western thinkers grind out again and again
in various forms. Not long ago another philosopher,
a German Jew, published a new volume, which contains
a *scientific* article on the Book of Lamentations. Now,
a scientific article has no concern with questions of
practical conduct; and yet the author finds it necessary to touch in conclusion on the practical question,
whether at the present day we have a right to read
this book in our synagogues. He answers in the
affirmative, on the ground that the Christians too read
it in their churches three days before Easter. "If
we are asked, 'What is Zion to you, and what are you
to Zion?' we reply calmly, 'Zion is the innermost
kernel of the inner consciousness of modern
nations.'" [1] This answer is not perhaps so clear as
it might be, even in the original; but the writer's object is perfectly clear. We have, therefore, no right
to be angry if our French philosopher also adopts this
view. But when we read the whole article in *La
Gerbe*, and find the author concluding that the Jews
have a special "mission," which they received *in
Jerusalem,* which they have not yet completely ful-

[1] Steinthal, Zu Bibel und Religionsphilosophie (Berlin, 1890),
p. 33.

filled, and for the sake of which they live, and *must live* till they do fulfil it completely, then we shall have a serious question to put. The duty of gratitude, we argue, is so important in our author's view, that he would have every Jew put France before the country of his birth—France, which was nothing more than the cause of our obtaining external rights, which we might have obtained without her, if only we had deserted our "mission." That being so, does it not follow *a fortiori* that Jerusalem, which gave us this very "mission," the cause and object of our life, has a claim on our gratitude prior even to that of France? Even so great a philosopher as our author could not, I think, find a logical flaw in this argument: and yet he could write as he has done. Is not this moral slavery?

Another thinker—a man who bears all the troubles of French Jewry on his shoulders, and is withal an active participator in work for the good of the Jews as a whole—recounts the good services rendered by the journal which is celebrating its jubilee; and one of them is this, that it has helped to strengthen the bond between the Jews in France and those in other countries. But as he wrote these words, the recollection of "beautiful France," and of the anti-Semitism which prevails there, must have crossed his mind; for he pauses to justify the slip of the pen by which he, a Frenchman, could welcome a strengthening of the bond between the Jewish community in France and Jewish communities elsewhere. He tries to show that

though the French Jews are well known for the
thoroughness of their patriotism and their devotion
to their country, yet it is no breach of duty on their
part to sympathize with their brother Jews, who are
still subject to disabilities in other countries, or to
rejoice with those of them whose position improves.
For my part, I have sufficient confidence in this distinguished man, and in his whole-hearted devotion to
his people, the Jews, to believe that, even if it were
proved to him beyond all doubt that French patriotism
is inconsistent with affection for his flesh and blood
in other countries, he would still feel that affection
for them secretly, in the depths of his being; that even
if all the Jews were blessed with full emancipation,
and there were no longer any room for " sympathy "
with these and " rejoicing " with those, he would still
desire to maintain permanently his connection with
the whole body, and to take part in all their interests.
But if this be so, what are all these excuses, what is
this constraint which he pleads, if not moral slavery?

But this *moral* slavery is only half the price which
Western Jews have paid for their emancipation.
Beneath the cloak of their political freedom there lies
another, perhaps a harder, form of slavery—*intellectual*
slavery; and this, too, has left its mark on the book
which we are considering.

Having agreed, for the sake of emancipation, to
deny the existence of the Jews as a people, and regard
Judaism simply and solely as a religion, Western Jews
have thereby pledged themselves and their posterity

to guard with the utmost care the religious unity of Israel. But emancipation demanded certain practical changes in religious matters; and not everybody could make this sacrifice. Hence people "of the Jewish persuasion" have split into various sects; the unity of the religion, on its practical side, has vanished. There remains, then, no other bond than that of religion on its theoretical side—that is to say, certain abstract beliefs which are held by all Jews. This bond, apart from the inherent weakness which it has in common with every spiritual conception that is not crystallized into practice, has grown still weaker of recent years, and is becoming more and more feeble every day. Scientific development has shaken the foundations of every faith, and the Jewish faith has not escaped: so much so that even the editor of *La Gerbe* confesses, with a sigh, that "the scientific heresy which bears the name of Darwin" is gaining ground, and it is only from a feeling of *noblesse oblige* that he still continues to combat it. What, then, are those Jews to do who have nothing left but this theoretical religion, which is itself losing its hold on them? Are they to give up Judaism altogether, and become completely assimilated to their surroundings? A few of them have done this: but why should they not all adopt the same course? Why do most of them feel that they cannot? Where is the chain to which they can point as that which holds them fast to Judaism, and does not allow them to be free? Is it the instinctive national feeling which they have inherited, which is independent of religious beliefs or practices? Away with the suggestion! Did they not give up this feeling a hundred years ago, in exchange for emancipation? Yet the fact remains that it is not in their power to uproot this feeling. Try as they will to conceal it, seek as they will for subterfuges to deceive the world and themselves, it lives none the less; resent it as they will, it is a force at the centre of their being. But this answer, though it satisfies us, does not satisfy them. They have publicly renounced their Jewish nationality, and they cannot go back on their words; they cannot confess that they have sold that which was not theirs to sell. But this being so, how can they justify their obstinate clinging to the name of Jew—a name which brings them neither honor nor profit—for the sake of certain theoretical beliefs which they no longer hold, or which, if they do really and sincerely maintain them, they might equally hold without this special name, as every non-Jewish Deist has done?

For a long time this question has been constantly troubling the Jewish thinkers of Western Europe; and it is this question which drove them, in the last generation, to propound that new, strange gospel to which they cling so tenaciously to this very day—I mean that famous gospel of " the mission of Israel among the nations." This theory is based on an antiquated idea, which is at variance with all the principles of modern science: as though every nation had been created from the first for some particular purpose, and so had a

" mission " which it must fulfil, living on against its
will until its Heaven-sent task is done. Thus, for example, the Greeks were created to polish and perfect
external beauty; the Romans to exalt and extol physical
force.[1] On this hypothesis, it is not difficult to find an
answer to our own question—an answer not inconsistent, on the one hand, with emancipation, and, on
the other hand, with the unity of Judaism. The
answer is this: Israel as a *people* is dead; but the
Jewish Church still lives, and must live, because the
mission of Israel is not completely fulfilled, so long as
absolute monotheism, with all its consequences, has
not conquered the whole world. Till that victory is
achieved, Israel must live in spite of itself, must bear
and suffer and fight: to this end it was created—" to
know God and to bring others to that knowledge."[2]
If, then, we wish really to fulfil our function, is it not
our duty to be God's apostles, to consecrate all our
strength to the diffusion of that knowledge for the
sake of which we live?

" Heaven forbid! " answer our " missionists "—and
their attitude needs no explanation—" it is not for us
to hasten on the end. God has entrusted the truth to
our keeping; but he has not imposed on us the task
of spreading the truth."[3]

How, then, shall we arrive ultimately at the fulfilment of our mission?

[1] Munk, Palestine (Paris, 1845), p. 99.
[2] Munk, ibid. ; La Gerbe, p. 7.
[3] La Gerbe, p. 12.

Munk answers thus: " Our mission advances cease-lessly towards its fulfilment *through the progress of religious ideas."* [1] And since our Scriptures are, according to the " missionists," the foundation and cause of this progress, they give us the credit of it, as though we ourselves were doing our duty on behalf of religious progress. It is for this reason, and for this reason alone, that we must remain loyal to our standard until the very end.

In itself, therefore, our mission is an easy and a com-fortable one. At least there is nothing disgraceful in being the teachers of the whole world, in regarding the whole human race, to the end of time, as pupils who slake their thirst at the fountain of our inspira-tion: more especially when this honorable task of ours involves no labor or worry on our part. We are like the Israelites at the Red Sea: the progress which emanates from the Scriptures is to fight for our mission, while we look on and rejoice. Now, this would be very well indeed, if the pupils on their side were amenable and docile, and paid the proper respect to their teacher. But in fact they are impertinent fellows, these pupils. They kick their teacher: they heap curses on him: they are forever besmirching his name, until his life becomes a positive burden to him. And so we are left face to face with the same question. We are no longer doing anything useful towards the fulfilment of our mission: the Scriptures, and consequently religious progress, are independent of us, and will do their

[1] Ibid. p. 7.

work without us: we are nothing but a monument on the path of religious progress, which marches on to its consummation without our assistance. Why, then, this life of trouble? The Greeks, who were created, according to this theory, for the sake of beauty, produced all those beautiful works of art, wrote all those beautiful books; and then, when there was nothing more for them to do, although their mission was not completely fulfilled, and although during all the centuries which separated them from the Renaissance their beauty lay hidden from the world—then history removed them from the stage, and left the rest to that progress which proceeded automatically from the Greek legacy of works of art and books. Why, then, should not history allow *us* to make our exit? We have done all that we could for our mission: we have produced the Scriptures. Further there is nothing for us to do: why, then, must we live?

One of our "missionist" thinkers, a learned preacher, deals with this question in an article entitled, "Why Do We Remain Jews?", and tries to answer the question from another side. We remain faithful to Judaism, he thinks, because there is no other religion for which we could change it. Every other religion contains something which we cannot accept. "Natural religion" would, indeed, be sufficient for us. But if we think of accepting natural religion, we must first know what are its principles. Let us, then, look for them in books which set out to expound them, for instance, in Simon's *Natural*

Religion. We find that this religion has three fundamental principles: creation, revelation, and reward
and punishment. At once we remember that as much
as five hundred years ago Rabbi Joseph Albo, author of
the *Principles,* based Judaism on three dogmas very
much like these. Judaism, therefoie, *is* natural religion,
and there is no need to change.

Now I might ask this preacher how he would answer
those Jews (and there are many of them nowadays)
for whom the religion of Simon and his school is an
antiquated philosophy, very far from being "natural,"
and who still desire to remain Jews, without knowing
why they so desire. But I will not ask him this question: for as a preacher he is only concerned with
philosophers who are also believers. And there is
another question which I might put to him. Does he
really and honestly believe that there is no difference
between Simon's "Revelation of the Godhead" and
Albo's "Law from Heaven"? But this also I will not
ask, because I know that it has always been the habit
of religious philosophy—a habit long since recognized
and sanctioned—to twist texts for the purpose of reconciling contradictions. The criticism that I do offer—
and it is one which deserves our preacher's attention—
I will put in the form of the following dilemma. If
Judaism includes, in addition to those principles mentioned above, certain things which have no parallel in
natural religion, then the question confronts us again:
Why should we not change the one for the other? But
if there is no real difference except that of name, then,

indeed, the question becomes more insistent: Why not accept a change of name, if by means of this purely external change we can win freedom from all our sufferings? It is not the name that is of importance to our mission, but the power to fulfil it: that is, the power to spread the knowledge of the Godhead in the Jewish sense: and our power to do this will surely increase out of all proportion if we substitute the name of " natural religion " for that of " Jewish religion." But in that case it is not merely permissible, it is *obligatory* on us to take this step, for the sake of that mission for which we were created.

It is perhaps superfluous to deal at length with this theory, which, indeed, it is difficult, in our day, to treat seriously. We are forced, despite ourselves, into a smile, a smile of bitter irony, when we see distinguished men, who might have shown their sorely tried people real light on its hard and thorny path, wasting their time with such pleasant sophistries as these; trying to believe, and to persuade others, that a whole people can have maintained its existence, and borne a heavy burden of religious observance and an iron yoke of persecutions, torments, and curses for thousands of years, all for the purpose of teaching the world a certain philosophy, which is already expounded in whole libraries of books, in every conceivable language and every conceivable style, from which who will may learn without any assistance from us: and especially at the present time, when the number of those who wish to learn grows less every day, nay, when we ourselves are every day forgetting our own teaching.

It is, indeed, surprising that such a thinker as Munk, and even the older thinkers of our own day, could and still can believe in the mission of Israel in the sense explained above. But we shall be less surprised if we remember that Munk wrote in the " forties," and that the older contributors to *La Gerbe* are for the most part children of that earlier generation which educated them—children of an age in which the idea of a " final cause " was intelligible and current as a scientific theory. It is, however, a stranger phenomenon, and more difficult to explain, that the same position should be adopted by thinkers and writers of the present generation. These men, who know and admit that " the scientific heresy which bears the name of Darwin " is gaining ground, that is to say, that the world is accepting gradually a scientific theory which does not admit the existence of purpose or end even where it seems most obvious—how can these men still cling to a doctrine which demands belief in the missions of nations generally, in the mission of Israel in particular, and, above all, in such a wonderful mission as this? There can be but one answer. They are *compelled* to do so, because they can find no other way of reconciling Judaism with emancipation. In the first place, Israel has no right to be anything but a Church consecrated to Heaven; in the second place, this heavenly bond has become too weak; and in the third place—and this is the important thing—they *feel,* in spite of it all, that Jews they are, and Jews they want to be. And so, in order to conceal the contradiction between these "truths," they are forced to take refuge in this antiquated theory. On all other questions of conduct or of scholarship they belong to their own generation; but on the Jewish question they cannot move from the position which their fathers took up fifty years ago. As though these fifty years had brought no change of idea and outlook into the world!

Thus this intellectual slavery also is a result of political freedom. If not for this freedom, emancipated Jews would not deny the existence of the Jewish nation; they would not have to climb up to Heaven, on an old and rickety ladder, to seek there what they might have found on earth. It might be maintained, indeed, that even then there would have been thinkers who inclined to look for some "mission" for their people, or, to speak more accurately, for some spiritual *aim* suited to its spiritual characteristics. But then they might have found a different aim—not, perhaps, a finer one, but still one that would have gained acceptance more readily, one more in accordance with the ideas of modern times and with the truths of logic and of history. For instance, they might have argued thus: Here has our people been wandering over the face of the earth for some two thousand years, in the course of which we do not find that it has ever consciously invented any new thing of importance, has ever beaten out any new highway on the tract of life. Its part has been always that of the huckster; it has peddled about all kinds of goods, material and spiritual,

of other people's making. All the good work which
the Jews did for the world's culture in the Middle
Ages was at bottom nothing but huckstering and ped-
dling: they picked up learning in the East, and gave
it to the West. "Yes" replies Munk, in extenuation,
"because the mission of Israel does not lie in making
new discoveries." [1] Well, so let it be! But now that
we see that Israel was fitted to be, and in fact has
been, a huckster of culture, surely common sense will
tell us that this is the occupation for Israel to follow
now, if some spiritual aim is wanted. Now, therefore,
that we have acquired culture in the West, let us
return and carry it to the East. And, if we are so
very fond of teaching, it is surely better for us to go
where there is a more evident lack of teachers, and
where it is easier to find attentive pupils.

But the truth is that if Western Jews were not slaves
to their emancipation, it would never have entered
their heads to consecrate their people to spiritual missions or aims before it had fulfilled that physical,
natural "mission" which belongs to every organism—
before it had created for itself conditions suitable to
its character, in which it could develop its latent
powers and aptitudes, its own particular form of life,
in a normal manner, and in obedience to the demands
of its nature. Then, and only then, after all this had
been achieved—then and only then, we may well believe, its development might lead it in course of time
to some field of work in which it would be specially

[1] Dictionnaire des sciences philosophiques, iii, article "Juifs."

fitted to act as teacher, and thus contribute once again to the general good of humanity, in a way suited to the spirit of the modern world. And if *then* philosophers tell us that in this field of work lies the " mission " of our people, for which it was created, I shall not, indeed, be able to subscribe to their view; but I shall not quarrel with them on a mere question of terminology.

But alas! I shall doubtless be dead and buried before then. To-day, while I am still alive, I try mayhap to give my weary eyes a rest from the scene of ignorance, of degradation, of unutterable poverty that confronts me here in Russia, and find comfort by looking yonder across the border, where there are Jewish professors, Jewish members of Academies, Jewish officers in the army, Jewish civil servants; and when I see there, behind the glory and the grandeur of it all, a twofold spiritual slavery—moral slavery and intellectual slavery—and ask myself: Do I envy these fellow-Jews of mine their emancipation?—I answer, in all truth and sincerity: No! a thousand times No! The privileges are not worth the price! I may not be emancipated; but at least I have not sold my soul for emancipation. I at least can proclaim from the housetops that my kith and kin are dear to me wherever they are, without being constrained to find forced and unsatisfactory excuses. I at least can remember Jerusalem at other times than those of " divine service ": I can mourn for its loss, in public or in private, without being asked what Zion is to me, or I to Zion. I at least have no need to exalt my people to Heaven, to trumpet its superiority above all other nations, in order to find a justification for its existence. I at least know " why I remain a Jew "—or, rather, I can find no meaning in such a question, any more than if I were asked why I remain my father's son. I at least can speak my mind concerning the beliefs and the opinions which I have inherited from my ancestors, without fearing to snap the bond that unites me to my people. I can even adopt that " scientific heresy which bears the name of Darwin," without any danger to my Judaism. In a word, I am my own, and my opinions and feelings are my own. I have no reason for concealing or denying them, for deceiving others or myself. And this spiritual freedom—scoff who will!—I would not exchange or barter for all the emancipation in the world.

SOME CONSOLATION
(1892)

In all this fresh outbreak of calamities that has
come upon us of late, there is nothing so distressing to
every Jew as the recrudescence of the " blood-accusation." This abominable charge, old though it is, strikes
us, and will always strike us, as something new; and
since the Middle Ages it has always profoundly agitated
the *spirit* of the Jewish people, not only in the actual
place where the cry has been raised, but even in distant
countries where the incident has been merely reported.

If I say that this blood-accusation has profoundly
agitated the *spirit* of the Jewish people, it is because
the roots of this phenomenon lie, to my mind, not in
any external cause, but in the innermost spirit of the
Jew. If in medieval instances of the blood-accusation we find that the whole people used to regard itself
as standing at the judgment bar together with the
wretches whom fortune made the immediate victims
of the scourge, we may explain this fact as a result
of the physical danger to the whole people, which was
involved in every local incident of this kind. Again,
if, fifty years ago, the Damascus blood-accusation so
cruelly disturbed the halcyon calm of European Jewry,
one might attribute this to just the opposite cause, to
the extreme jealousy of the emancipated Jews for

their newly-won dignity and privileges. But at the present day neither explanation is open. On the one hand, the physical danger is no longer serious, especially in the case of distant communities; on the other hand, we have grown used to listening with equanimity to those who revile us, and we are no longer consumed with a jealous regard for our dignity. Yet even to-day the blood-accusation comes as a rude and violent shock, which rouses the whole of Jewry to a passionate repudiation of this outrageous charge. Clearly, then, it is not a question of mere regard for personal safety or dignity: the *spirit* of the people is stung to consciousness and activity by the sense of its shame. In all else it might be said of us, in the words of the wise prince of old time, that "the dead flesh feels not the knife"; but here the knife cuts not only the flesh—it touches the soul.

Yet "there is no evil without good," that is, without a good moral. The great evil with which we are concerned here is not without its useful lesson, which it were well that we should learn. We are not masters of our fate: good and evil we accept from without, as perforce we must; so that it is fitting that we should always look for the useful lesson hidden in the evil that comes upon us, and find thus at least some consolation.

Convention is one of the most important factors in social life. There was a time when even philosophers thought that the universal acceptance of an idea was a certain proof of its truth, and used this as an argument in their demonstration of the existence of God. That is no longer so. Philosophers know now that there is no lie, no piece of folly, which cannot gain universal acceptance under suitable conditions. But this knowledge is confined to philosophers; for the mass of men there is still no greater authority than this conventional acceptance. If " everybody " believes that this or that is so, of course it *is* so; if I do not understand it, others do; if I see what appears to contradict it, why, " everybody " sees the same thing, and yet believes, and am I wiser than the whole world? Such is roughly the reasoning, conscious or vaguely conscious, of the plain man; and, having reasoned thus, he too accepts the idea, and helps to make it an accepted convention.

It is a powerful force, this of convention, so powerful, that, generally speaking, a man cannot escape its influence even when he is himself its object. If " everybody " says of such an one that he is a profound thinker or a sincere believer, that he has this or that good or bad quality, he ends by accepting this idea himself, even though at first he may not have discovered in himself that superiority or defect which others ascribe to him. Nay, more: this acceptance of an idea by its object moulds him little by little, until he approximates, or at least tends to approximate, to the state of mind in which " everybody " assumes him to be. For this reason educationalists rightly warn us against directing the attention of children, at the beginning of their development, to their moral shortcomings, and still more against attributing to them imaginary shortcomings: because by such means we may accentuate the real faults, and create a tendency towards the imaginary ones.

But of course "everybody" means something different for each man. For each of us "the world" is that society of which he considers himself a member, and with the other members of which he finds a certain point of contact. No man is affected by the conventional beliefs of groups which are entirely strange to him in spirit, with which he feels no connection in thought. Take for instance the "orthodox" and the "enlightened" Jews. Each school has its own conventional ideas; neither pays any attention to those of the other, even in matters which do not affect religion; and their mutual scorn and ridicule have not the least effect, because each regards the other as non-existent. But when conditions arise which force the members of the two schools into constant intercourse, and they get used to meeting on a broad basis of common humanity, then "the world" becomes a bigger world, and the views of all are affected in many ways by the conventional beliefs of "the world" in its new and wider sense.

This will explain why in the old days, when our ancestors believed in a literal sense that they were "the chosen people," the purity of their souls was not sullied by the shame which the world imputed to them. Conscious of their own worth, they were not in the least affected by the conventional ideas of the outside world, which was to them a society of alien beings, fundamentally different from and unrelated to themselves. In those days the Jew could listen unmoved to the tale of moral defects and sins of conduct which the world told and believed of him, without feeling any inner sense of shame or humiliation. What mattered the ideas of these aliens about him and his worth? All that he asked of them was to let him live in peace. But in modern times it is different. Our " world " has expanded: what Europe believes, affects every side of our lives in the most vital way. And since we no longer treat the outside world as a thing apart, we are influenced, despite ourselves, by the fact that the outside world treats *us* as a thing apart. It was recently asked by a Russian writer, in all simplicity: Since everybody hates the Jews, can we think that everybody is wrong, and the Jews are right? There are many among us Jews on whom a similar question half-unconsciously forces itself. Can we think, they ask, that all the vicious characteristics and evil practices which the whole world ascribes to the Jews are sheer imagination?

This doubt, once aroused, is easily strengthened by those false inferences from particular to universal which are so common among ordinary men. There is a well-known story about a traveller who, happening on an inn where the hostler stammered, wrote in his diary, " The hostlers in X. are stammerers." This story is a comic illustration of the kind of logic on which most of the plain man's general propositions are based. He generalizes from the particular instance to the whole class with the name of which that instance is normally labelled. He does not see that one particular may belong to several classes, that is, may have affinities with one class of things by virtue of one of its qualities, and with another class by virtue of a second, whereas its name only indicates its connection with one of these classes through a single aspect, not through all its aspects. It is in propositions of this kind that the universally accepted ideas about the Jews can and do find their support. " A and B are Jews by name and dishonest by character: *ergo,* the Jews are dishonest." True logic will reply, of course, that even if all the Jews of modern times were really dishonest, that would still not prove the general proposition, that " the Jews are dishonest," that is, that the quality of dishonesty, which belongs to every Jew, belongs to him by virtue of his inclusion in the class of Jews, and not by virtue of his inclusion in some other class—for instance, that of tradesmen—which embraces the individual Jew together with other individuals who have no connection with the class of Jews. In order to decide this question, we must first of all examine the other individuals who are included, together with the Jews, in other classes. If this examination shows that the quality of dishonesty does not belong to any class which embraces both Jews and non-Jews, then, but not till then, have we the right to lay down the judgment that Judaism is the source of dishonesty. But, as I have said, men are not usually very logical, and we cannot demand strict logic even of the ordinary run of Jews. They hear the universally accepted judgment; they see that it is actually true of a good many Jews; and this is sufficient to make them begin to subscribe to the judgment themselves. Thus " Jewish characteristics " pass from hand to hand like an honest coin, which, having become current in the outside world, gains currency also among the Jews. But there is this difference. The outside world recounts our bad qualities one by one, with a mocking and triumphant exultation; while we repeat the lesson after them word for word, in the still small voice of puling self-extenuation. For them (to borrow a simile from Talmudic law) we are the earthenware vessel which cannot be cleansed, but must be broken; for ourselves we are the vessel of metal, which may be cleansed by water and fire.

But this state of things, if it continues, may do us a great moral harm. There is nothing more dangerous for a nation or for an individual than to plead guilty to imaginary sins. Where the sin is real, there is opportunity for repentance; by honest endeavor the sinner may purify himself. But when a man has been persuaded to suspect himself unjustly, how can he get rid of his consciousness of guilt? " Remove the beam from your eye," they tell him; and he would fain obey, but cannot, because the beam is not really there. He is in the position of the monomaniac who, for some reason, has come to believe that a heavy weight is hanging from his nose and cannot be removed. But the evil goes further than this. Sometimes the conviction of sin actually produces in the individual that failing with which he believes the whole people to be infected, although, as an individual, he is entirely free from any predisposition towards it. For instance: a people which has produced men like Maimonides must number in its ranks even to-day systematic, orderly, and methodical persons, who might be able to permeate the work of the community in which they take part with their own habits, and to influence their fellow-workers in the same direction. But it is an accepted idea that objection to order and method is a Jewish quality; and we ourselves have accepted this idea, though it is by no means clear whether this characteristic, which is, in fact, common among a large section of Jews, belongs to the Jews as such, or is due, as appears more probable, to the Heder training. Hence those of us who have a love of order come to believe that there is no going against the national character, and are therefore powerless to reform. Indeed, if they are patriotic, they actually set about to conquer their own " anti-Jewish " love of order, and teach themselves to behave in true " Jewish " fashion.

What we need, then, is some means of emancipating ourselves from the influence of conventional prejudices as to the characteristics and the moral worth of the Jews. We must get rid of this self-contempt, this idea that we are really worse than all the world. Otherwise we may in course of time become in reality what we now imagine ourselves to be.

This necessary means of escape the world itself, with its accepted beliefs, affords us—through the blood-accusation. This accusation is the solitary case in which the general acceptance of an idea about ourselves does not make us doubt whether all the world can be wrong, and we right, because it is based on an absolute lie, and is not even supported by any false inference from particular to universal. Every Jew who has been brought up among Jews knows as an indisputable fact that throughout the length and breadth of Jewry there is not a single individual who drinks human blood for religious purposes. We ought, therefore, always to remember that in this instance the general belief, which is brought to our notice ever and anon by the revival of the blood-accusation, is absolutely wrong; because this will make it easier for us to get rid of the tendency to bow to the authority of " everybody " in other matters. Let the world say what it will about our moral inferiority: we know that its ideas rest on popular logic, and have no real scientific basis. Who has ever penetrated into the very heart of the Jew, and discovered his essential nature? Who has ever weighed the Jew against the non-Jew of the same class—Jewish tradesman against non-Jewish tradesman, persecuted Jew against persecuted non-Jew, starved Jew against starved non-Jew, and so on—who has carried out this test, scientifically and impartially, and found the balance incline to this side or to that?

" But "—you ask—" is it possible that **everybody can be wrong, and the Jews right?** "

Yes, it is possible: the blood-accusation proves it possible. Here, you see, the Jews are right and perfectly innocent. A Jew and blood—could there be a more complete contradiction? And yet . . . .

ANCESTOR WORSHIP
(1897)

Since the very beginning of the intellectual development of mankind various philosophers and men of
letters have been ceaselessly waging war on those
superstitions, those barbarous laws and customs, which
each generation inherits from its predecessors; but
never has this heirloom of the human race fallen on
such evil days as these. At first sight, indeed, it
appears as though its more aggressive opponents had
diminished in number; as though it were no longer a
target for so many keen arrows. But in reality the
battle has not ceased: only the weapons are different.

Formerly the philosophers and men of letters drew
their weapons from the armory of logic. They tried
to prove that a certain belief could not hold its ground
in the face of logical deduction or scientific evidence;
that this or that custom or law was opposed to
moral ideas, or was detrimental to the individual or to
society. Proofs of this nature were set forth in an
attractive literary form, expounded and emphasized in
a smooth and easy style, pointed by striking phrases
and epigrams. And yet they influenced but a handful
of individuals. The mass of men, and even the mass
of educated men, remained faithful to their inherited

opinions and traditional way of life, and paid little heed to the criticisms of logic and science. Nay, the effect of these criticisms on the world at large was actually in inverse proportion to their simplicity and clearness: whence arose that great generalization anent the progress of intellectual development, that the simplest and clearest truth is the least readily accepted by the majority of men. Thus in every generation we find these pugnacious critics complaining bitterly of the pig-headedness and inveterate stupidity of mankind. They do not stop to consider what is the root of this " stupidity "; it does not occur to them that they themselves, with their methods of warfare, supply their enemy with the strength to resist them. Yet such is in fact the case. For they provoke the antagonism of a powerful human feeling, that of respect for the past. This feeling has been a power in the human mind from the most distant ages; and there is much probability in the view held by many scholars, that in the childhood of mankind men went so far as to regard their ancestors as gods. Hence, every idea which seems to derogate from the respect due to our ancestors and mar the brightness of that vivid picture of them which is treasured by their descendants, inevitably rouses this feeling to determined opposition. It finds in this feeling an effective bar to its acceptance. " This belief, or law, or custom, which we have inherited from our ancestors is absurd "—why, it is as though one should say, " Our ancestors, who left us such absurdities, were fools." And the more obvious and indis-

putable the falsehood or the barbarism, the greater
the insult to the ancestors who clung to it, and the
greater, therefore, the obstinacy with which men resist
the idea that their ancestors were unable to see through
so crude a piece of error or folly. How could *they*
have helped noticing it?—this is the first question that
occurs to the plain man, whether he formulates it dis-
tinctly or not, when he hears any criticism of opinions
and customs which have the sanction of long acceptance. If the only answer vouchsafed to him is that
his ancestors were deficient in insight, or were the prey
of impostors—and this was the old method of account-
ing for the facts of history—then he is bound to come
to an exactly opposite conclusion. Our ancestors, he
decides, were certainly guided by wisdom in all that
they said and did, and their words and actions are
eternally right; but we are unable to understand them,
because they were giants, or we are pigmies.

But since the conceptions associated with the term
"evolution" arose in the domain of natural science,
and made their way subsequently into philosophy and
history, the situation has changed completely. In place
of invective and moral condemnation, tirade and
sarcasm, we now have *analysis*. The modern critic
analyzes human opinions and actions. He does not rest
content with a pronouncement that this belief is false,
or that custom absurd. He regards all human actions
and thoughts as natural phenomena, the inevitable
result of certain causes, fruits, as it were, of the human
tree, which came to birth and went through the slow

process of ripening according to definite laws, like
those which determine the growth of all things in the
vegetable and animal worlds. And just as the natural
scientist is not concerned to pronounce judgment on the
objects which he examines, to say, " this is good, that
bad; this is sweet, that bitter; this is beautiful, that
ugly "; just as he knows no distinction between the
most exquisite bird and the most repulsive insect, but
examines all alike with the minutest attention, doing
his best to penetrate into the mystery of their lives and
the process of their evolution: so, too, the student of
the spiritual life of mankind has no concern with good
and evil, wisdom or folly. For him it is all the fruit
of the human tree. All the phenomena alike attract
him and stimulate him to a thorough investigation, in
order that he may understand how such things come
into being, what internal and external conditions are
necessary for their life and development, why and how
they change from age to age, and so forth. For investigation of this kind there is no difference between
earlier and later generations of men. There are no
giants and no pigmies. All alike are men, all are
subject to eternal laws, and all in every age produce
such fruit as is determined by their condition and their
environment. Examination of this kind, in its analysis
and exposition of ancient beliefs and actions, does not
look down contemptuously on the ancients. It treats
with quiet courtesy and respect even the things that
we consider most barbarous or most wicked, those on
which the logical critics pour out torrents of abuse and

mockery, insult and vituperation. It recognizes—and
it alone recognizes—that our outlook differs from that
of our ancestors, not because we are essentially better
than they were, but simply because our mental condition has changed, and our environment is different;
that there is nothing so barbarous, so evil, that the
human mind cannot accept it and foster it, given suitable conditions; and that consequently many of the
sacred truths of every generation must become false-
hoods and absurdities in the next, and they who judge
to-day will not escape scot free from the tribunal of
to-morrow.

Hence the multiplication and diffusion of works
written in this spirit of historical criticism have done
much more to free the human mind from its subservience to the past than all the incisive reasoning of the
heretics of past generations. Every thinking man who
examines the past in this spirit becomes, as it were,
a reincarnation of the souls of all the ages. Understanding the mental life of past generations, and enter-
ing sympathetically into their ideals, he does not regard
it as a defect in them that their opinions and customs
do not in every respect come up to the standard of
our ideas and demands at the present day. Consequently, the feeling of respect for the men of the past
does not compel him to follow them in practice; he
recognizes that every generation has its ideals, every
generation its truths. And so the ancients do not
lose the respect due to them: their thoughts and their
actions were such as suited the conditions of their own

time, just as our thoughts and our actions correspond to the conditions in which we are placed to-day.

What I have said is true of the world in general; but in Jewish life the traces of this change of attitude are not yet visible. We are, indeed, always behindhand in these matters; "new" ideas dawn on us at a time when they have reached their twilight for the rest of the world. So with us the old struggle between respect for tradition and modern criticism is still fought on the old lines. Criticism of tradition involves contempt and depreciation of those from whom it has been inherited; and so, out of respect for them, we are bound to observe their tradition to the very letter. It is true that of late the noise of battle has subsided even among us, and for many years we have scarcely heard any dispute about the authoritative beliefs and laws of our people. But this is not because loud criticism has given place to quiet investigation: it is because the idea of nationalism has captured the best elements in our literature, and many adherents of this creed, which is based on a feeling of respect and affection for the national spirit, think it their duty to say Amen, though it be but with the lips, to all the hallowed traditions of the past. They too have fallen a prey to the mistaken notion that it is impossible to look at the past impartially, and to recognize how much of it seems strange from the point of view of modern conceptions, without at the same time pronouncing adversely on the intrinsic worth of the past—which of course would bring the nation into contempt, and would weaken the feeling of affection for the national spirit. Hence, in Western Europe, where most Jewish thinkers still regard Judaism solely as a religion, attempts are still made to reform the religious life of the Jews and purify their laws, by means of that logical criticism which can only judge the value of early institutions by our standards, and cannot examine their intrinsic qualities and their rise and development by the light of the ideas with which they were contemporary.

As a type of this kind of criticism take an article which I have before me, entitled " Research and Reform." [1]

Undoubtedly this article is right in the main. All the sections and paragraphs from the *Shulhan 'Aruk* which the author quotes are certainly quite foreign to our spirit at the present day; certainly " there is not a single Jew of modern education who can believe in them." But the inference which he draws, that " we must proclaim aloud, in season and out of season, that this is not our Law," is wrong, and has no more foundation than his hope that such proclamation will avail " to remove every stumbling-block from the path of the blind." The *Shulhan 'Aruk* is not (as he says)

---

[1] This article, written by an Italian Rabbi, A. Lolli, appeared in Ha-Shiloah, vol. ii, no. 4. It attacks the Shulhan 'Aruk, which contains so many laws that are distasteful to us, and demands that such laws should be abolished, and that we should "proclaim aloud, in season and out of season, that this is not our Law." [The Shulhan 'Aruk is a code of Jewish law, which is the final authority for orthodox Jews.]

" the book that we have *chosen* for our guide," but the book that has been *made* our guide, whether we would or not, by force of historical development: because this book, just as it is, in its present form, with all its most uncouth sections, was the book that best suited the spirit of our people, their condition and their needs, in those generations in which they accepted it as binding on themselves and their descendants. If we proclaim that " this is not our Law," we shall be proclaiming a falsehood. This *is* our Law, couched in the only form which was possible in the Middle Ages: just as the Talmud is our Law in the form which it took in the last days of the ancient world, and just as the Bible is our Law in the form which it took while the Jews still lived as a nation on their own land. The three books are but three milestones on the road of a single development, that of the spirit of the Jewish nation. Each corresponds to the nation's condition and needs in a different period.

In the Middle Ages exile and persecution left our people but one mainstay—the Torah; and since Torah was everything, everything was Torah, and no Jew moved a finger without first finding authority in the Torah. Religious precepts were regarded as laws of nature, which it was men's duty to know and live by, if they wished for life, without reasoning about them or distinguishing between the pleasant and the unpleasant. And just as medical science is not ashamed to treat of the hidden organs of the human body, so the Torah could not leave untouched any jot or tittle of

the minutiæ of life, be they never so repulsive. There
is a delightful story in the Talmud which illustrates excellently the mental outlook of our ancestors, and the
attitude to the Torah which had begun even then to
develop. King David, they say, went into his bath-
room naked, and was grieved to think that at that
moment there was no link between himself and the
Torah, until he remembered " the sign in his flesh,"
and was comforted! The Jew of those days felt his
life and his individuality only so long as he was surrounded by an atmosphere of Torah. Let him leave
that atmosphere for a moment, and it was as though
he had suddenly entered a strange world. All the
bitterness of his life in a foreign land, all the horror
of his position in this world, was borne in upon him
with overwhelming force, and threw him into a frenzy
of dark foreboding; till he turned and fled back into
his own retreat, where he could breathe the air that
was so dear to him. So completely was the soul of
the Jew in those days identified with the Torah, so
utterly unable to bear anything profane, that even so
simple and necessary a process as the morning rinsing
of the mouth had to be made a religious custom, and
provided with a " reason." Its object was—to cleanse
the mouth *for prayer!* [1]

Our reverend critic quotes the dictum of Samuel
David Luzzatto, that " the Mishnah and the Talmud
are not books which were originally intended to be a

[1] See Orah Hayyim, iv, 17, and the commentary of the
Wilna Gaon.

code of laws and ritual ordinances." After what we
have seen, it is not surprising that this view, correct
though it is, could never be accepted by the people at
large. What they needed in those days was not a
collection of the utterances of learned men, each
occasioned by particular circumstances, or a body of
different opinions which might be accepted or rejected.
They needed neither more nor less than " laws and
ritual ordinances," fixed immutably and beyond question, possessed of an authority backed by force, and
capable of giving a definite religious form to the whole
content of life, down to the smallest detail. Out of
this imperative need arose inevitably the new way of
regarding the Talmud, the only source from which
such laws and ordinances could be derived, as having
throughout the force of a living and eternal law. Out
of this need arose also the *Yad ha-hazakah*[1] of
Maimonides (to use a late subtitle which goes to the
very root of the matter), the *dogmatic* presentment of
the religious prescriptions as deduced from the Talmud
according to certain general principles of interpretation, which are purely external, and make no distinction between different laws on the ground of their
intrinsic value, and no attempt to exclude those which
had worth only in their own time and place. Any
such distinction, any such attempt, would have been

[1][Yad ha-hazakah ("Strong Hand") is the subtitle of Maimonides' Mishneh Torah, a codification of the whole of Jewish
law. The author regards it here as a hint at the *enforced*
authority of the prescriptions of ceremonial Judaism.]

opposed to the idea of the Talmud as a book of laws and religious ordinances intended for all time; but it was only on the basis of that idea that the dogmatic structure could expand and develop till it reached its full dimensions, and became all-embracing, in the *Shulhan 'Aruk.*

Now it is quite obvious that this need for a detailed code of religious observances is not widely felt in our own time. Even those Jews who still carry out every detail of the *Shulhan 'Aruk* do so only because they are slaves to the past. If the *Shulhan 'Aruk* had not been there already, our generation would certainly not have produced it. And yet it is a great mistake to think that the wall of tradition can be overthrown to-day by a blast of the trumpet. We have to take into account the powerful feeling of respect for antiquity, which guards the wall like an armed battalion, and is but roused by the trumpet sound to a more strenuous defence. In the day when there has been born and developed in us a new kind of need, a need to *understand* the rise and growth of traditional practices as a natural process; when we have a new Maimonides, gifted with the historical sense, to rearrange the whole Law, not in an artificial, logical order, but according to the historical evolution of each prescription; when in place of critics of the *Shulhan 'Aruk,* proclaiming that " this is not our Law," we have commentators of a new kind, who shall try to discover the source of its ordinances in the mental life of the people, to show why and how they grew up from within, or were imported and naturalized through stress or favor of circumstances: in that day, but not before, will there be a severance of the link between the feeling of respect for antiquity and practical life; and we shall be able to love and respect the spirit of our people perhaps even more than we do now, and to feel in every nerve the intense tragedy that lurks beneath even the most barbarous relics of our past, without being compelled to regard our tradition, in all its details, as a body of laws and ordinances superior to time and place.

THE TRANSVALUATION OF VALUES
(1898)

Amid the confused Babel of voices that are heard in the prevailing chaos of modern Jewry, there is one angry, strident, revolutionary voice which gains the public ear occasionally, and leaves a most extraordinary impression. To most men it is quite unintelligible: they stand amazed for one moment—and go their way. A few there are who understand at least where the voice comes from, and these, because they understand so much, sorrowfully shake their heads, and likewise go their way. But the younger men, ever on the alert, ever receptive of new ideas, drink in the new gospel which this voice proclaims; they are thrilled by it, attracted by it, without inquiring very deeply what is its ultimate worth, or whether the idea which it contains is really a new truth, worthy all this enthusiasm.

The new gospel is that of "the transvaluation of values"; and as for the idea which it contains, it is, indeed, no easy task to penetrate the darkness which envelops it, and to state it in clear and definite form; but if we examine the utterances of its votaries, and piece together the shreds and scraps of intelligible speech which sometimes float on the stream of incomprehensibility, we may perhaps describe it thus:

The whole life of the Jews from the time of the

Prophets to the present day has been, in the opinion of those who propound this new gospel, one long mistake; and it demands immediate rectification. During all these centuries Judaism has exalted the abstract, spiritual ideal above real, physical force: it has exalted the " book " over the " sword." By this means it has destroyed in the Jews the striving after individual mastery; it has subordinated the reality of life to its shadow; it has made the Jew a sort of appendage to an abstract moral law. In this condition it is impossible for the Jews to live on among the nations; still more impossible for them to restore their national life in their own country. Now, therefore, that the desire for a national rebirth has been aroused in us, it behooves us first of all to trans-valuate the moral values which are accepted among us at present; to overthrow, mercilessly and at a single blow, the historic edifice which our ancestors have left us, seeing that it is built up on this dangerously mistaken idea of the superiority of spirit to matter, and of the subordination of the individual life to abstract moral laws. We must, then, start again from the beginning, and build up a new structure on a foundation of new values. We must put the body above the spirit; we must unfetter the soul, which craves for life, and awaken in it a passion for power and mastery, so that it may satisfy all its desires by force, in unlimited freedom.

Like all the other new gospels which run riot in our literature, this gospel of the " transvaluation of values " is not a home product, nor did it spring into being in response to the demands of our own life. Our literary men found it ready-grown in a strange soil, and thought to give us the benefit of this precious plant, without considering how far, if at all, our own soil was suitable for its reception.

There arose in Germany, in this generation of ours, a philosopher-poet, thinker and seer in one, named Friedrich Nietzsche, who roused a large section of the youth of Europe to enthusiasm by a new ethical doctrine, based on the " transvaluation of all values " (*Umwertung aller Werte*). According to him, the function of the human being, like that of all other beings, is to develop and expand unceasingly the powers which Nature has given him, in order that the specific type may attain to the highest of which it is capable. Now, since the perfection of the specific type is only possible through the " struggle for existence " between the individual members of the species, in which the stronger advances ever higher and higher, recking nothing if his upward progress involves crushing and trampling on the weaker, it follows that the moral law is founded on an absolute mistake. It is wrong to regard that as good which brings welfare to the human race in general, and lessens the amount of suffering, and to call that evil which has the reverse effect. The moral law, working on this basis, has turned the world upside down; it has degraded the high, and exalted the low. The few strong men, whose superior endowments of body and mind fit them to rise to the top, and thus carry the specific type nearer to its perfection, are made subordinate to the many weaklings. Not alone are they unable to remove from their path this obstacle to their development: they are actually commanded by morality to *serve* the weak, to treat them with sympathy, to help them, to do them charity—in a word, to forgo the expansion of their own powers and their own individual growth, and to consecrate themselves wholly to the service of others, of the despicable and worthless multitude. The inevitable result is that the human type, instead of striving upwards, instead of producing in each successive generation stronger and nobler examples, and thus approaching nearer and nearer to its perfection, does in fact progress downwards, dragging down even the chosen few of every generation to the low level of the multitude, and thus ever widening the gulf that separates it from its true function. In order, then, to restore the power of self-perfection to the human type, we need a complete change of moral values. We must give back to the idea of good the meaning which it had of old, before " Jewish morality " overthrew Greek and Roman culture. " Good " is to be applied to the strong man, who has both the power to expand and complete his life, and the will to be master of his world (*der Wille zur Macht*), without considering at all how much the great mob of inferior beings may lose in the process. For only he, only the " Superman " (*Übermensch*), is the fine flower and the goal of the human race; the rest were created only to subserve his end, to be the ladder on which he can climb up to

his proper level. But we are not to regard the Superman as a sort of darling child of Nature, to whom
she has given the right to satisfy his desires and enjoy
all the good things of the world merely for his own
pleasure. No: what is honored in him is the human
type, which in him progresses and approaches nearer
to its perfection. For this reason the development of
his powers and the mastery of the world are not only
a privilege for the Superman; they are also a high and
arduous duty, to which he must sacrifice his personal
happiness as he sacrifices the happiness of others; for
the sake of which he must be as unsparing of himself
as of others. " Deem ye that I take thought for my
happiness? " says the Superman (*Zarathustra*) ; " it is
for my work that I take thought."   This work, the
advancement of the human type in each succeeding
generation, though it be but in a few examples, to a
higher level than that of the mass of men: this work
is in itself a desirable goal, quite independently of its
results from the point of view of the happiness or
misery, the advantage or disadvantage, of the multitude.   And so the moral and cultural value of any
period of history does not depend, as is generally supposed, on the level of happiness and culture reached
by the generality of men in that period, but precisely
on the extent to which the specific type, as manifested
in one or more individuals, is raised above the general
level.

   This is the fundamental idea of the doctrine of the
" transvaluation of values " in its original German

form.[1]   It desires not merely to change morality in certain details—to pronounce some things evil which were regarded as good, and the reverse—but to alter the very foundation of morality, the actual standard by reference to which things are pronounced good or evil.   Hitherto the standard has been the lessening of pain and increasing of happiness among the mass of human beings.   Everything that was calculated to assist in a greater or lesser degree towards the attainment of that object, whether directly or indirectly, whether at once or in the near or distant future, has been good; everything that was calculated from any point of view to produce the reverse effect has been evil.   Now we are told that moral qualities and actions are not to be estimated at all by reference to their effects in relation to the mass of men; that there is one thing which is essentially good, which is an end in itself, and needs no testing by any external standard—and that is the free development of individuality in the elect of the human race, and the ascent of the specific type in them to a level higher than that of the generality of men.   Thus—as Simmel rightly points out—Nietzsche rendered himself immune from any

[1] In Nietzsche's own works his teaching is enveloped in a cloud of extravagances and poetic exubeiances.   They are also full of contradictions in points of detail, so that it is very difficult to extract from them a single coherent system.   So far as this is possible, it has been done excellently by that acute philosopher Georg Simmel in his essay "Friedrich Nietzsche," printed in the Zeitschrift für Philosophie und philosophische Kritik, vol. 107, part 2.

criticism based on logic or experience.   All criticism of that kind must of necessity rest on the old standard which he will not accept.   It can only point to the injury which such a theory will inflict on human life in general, to its evil effects on the diffusion of culture, and so forth.   But according to the theory in question the whole life and the whole culture of the mass of men cannot weigh against a single Superman.

We see now whence our own literary men got the idea of the " transvaluation of values," and what they have done with it.   They found a new doctrine, universal in its scope, and certainly calculated to appeal to men of imagination; and its attraction for them produced a desire to propound a similar new doctrine, of special application to the Jews.   So far I have no fault to find with them.   The same thing has often been done before, from the Alexandrian period to our own day; and Judaism has more than once been made richer in new conceptions and stimulating ideas.   But here, as in every process which demands artistic skill, the essential thing is that the artist should understand the possibilities of his material, and know how to subdue it to the form.   He must not be mastered by his material, and let it turn under his hands into a useless piece of ware.

More than a year ago I crossed swords with these young writers, who complain of a spiritual " cleft " in their inner life, and think that they can bridge over the gap by introducing " European " ideas into Hebrew literature; and I said to them at that time: "It is not sufficient for us simply to import the foreign material; we must first of all adapt and assimilate it to our national genius. We see, for example, that the ideas of Friedrich Nietzsche have captured many young Jews, and have come into conflict with their Judaism, and produced a cleft in their inner life. What are we to do? Let us analyze these ideas, and divide them into their constituent parts, in order to discover what it is in them that attracts, and what it is that is at variance with Judaism. This analysis may prove to us at last that there is no essential connection between these two parts—that the first is a human element, while the second is simply German or Aryan, and has become associated with the other only because they happened to fuse in the mind of a particular man who was also a German. Then we shall be able to give these ideas a new form; to free the human element from its subordination to the German form, and subordinate it instead to our own form. Thus we shall have the necessary assimilation, and we shall be importing into our literature ideas which are *new, but not foreign*." [1]

If our Nietzscheans had adopted that course, they would have found that their master's doctrine does, in fact, contain two separable elements—one human and universal, the other merely Aryan; and that the first of these, so far from being opposed to Judaism, actually strengthens Judaism.

[1] See the essay called " Good Advice " [not included in this translation].

The human element in the doctrine of the " transvaluation of values " is that change in the moral standard which I have described above. The end of moral good is not the uplifting of the human race in general, but the raising of the human type in its highest manifestations above the general level. This postulate is, as I have said, one of those fundamental principles which each man admits or denies according to his taste and inclination, and which cannot be met by arguments derived from other premises. But if this postulate cannot be tested by any standard external to itself, that very fact imposes a restriction on those who lay it down. It is impossible for them to define clearly and convincingly the nature of that superior type which they desiderate. Seeing that the goal is the mere existence of the Superman, and not his effect on the world, we have no criterion by which to distinguish those human qualities of which the development marks the progress of the type, from those which are signs of backwardness and retrogression. Here again, as in the case of the postulate itself, we are dependent on our esthetic taste and our moral bent. Nietzsche himself, it is true, exalts physical force and external beauty; he longs for " the fair beast " (*die blonde Bestie*)—the strong, beautiful beast which shall rule the world, and act in all things according to its will. But it is obvious that this conception of the Superman does not follow by logical necessity from his fundamental postulate. It is no longer the philosopher as such who speaks; it is the man of Aryan race, who, with his excessive regard for physical power and beauty, depicts his ideal according to his own taste. We are, therefore, at liberty to suppose that this same Nietzsche, if his taste had been Hebraic, might still have changed the moral standard, and made the Super-man an end in himself, but would in that case have attributed to his Superman quite different character-istics—the expansion of moral power, the subjuga-tion of the bestial instincts, the striving after truth and righteousness in thought and deed, the eternal warfare against falsehood and wickedness: in a word, that moral ideal which Judaism has impressed on us. And what is there to prove that the change in the moral standard necessarily involves changing the Hebraic outlook, and substituting the Aryan: that man be-comes Superman not through moral strength and the beauty of the soul, but only through the physical strength and the external beauty of the " fair beast "?

Those who are at all expert in this matter do not need to be told that there is no necessity now for the creation of a Jewish Nietzscheism of this kind, because it has existed for centuries. Nietzsche, as a German, may be pardoned for having failed to understand Judaism, and having confused it with another doctrine, which sprang out of it and went off on another track. But his Jewish disciples ought to know that Judaism has never based itself on mercy alone, and has never made its Superman subordinate to the mass of men, as though the whole aim and object of his existence were simply to increase the happiness of the multitude. We all know the importance of the Zaddik, the "righteous man," in our ethical literature, from the Talmud and the Midrashim to the literature of Hasidism: we know that, so far from his having been created for the sake of others, "the whole world was only created for his sake," and that he is an end for himself. Phrases like this, as is well known, are of frequent occurrence in our literature; and they did not remain mere expressions of individual opinion, mere philosophic tags, but obtained popular currency, and became generally accepted principles of morality.

More than this: if we search deeper, we shall find this idea, in a wider presentation, at the very basis of the Jewish *national* consciousness.

Nietzsche himself complained, in his last book, that hitherto there had been no attempt to educate men deliberately with the object of producing the Superman. If such a man happened occasionally to be produced, this was merely "a happy accident, not the result of conscious will"[1] Indeed, it is easy enough to depict the Superman in lofty poetic images that fire the imagination; but if he is to be a phenomenon of constant occurrence, and not merely an occasional accident, the surrounding conditions of life must be adapted to that end. You cannot get water from a rock, or fruit from the parched soil of the desert. When all is said, man is a social animal; and even the soul of the Superman is a product of society, and cannot wholly free itself

[1] Comp. A. Riehl, "Friedrich Nietzsche" (Stuttgart, 1897), p. 125.

from the moral atmosphere in which it has grown and developed. If we agree, then, that the Super*man* is the goal of all things, we must needs agree also that an essential condition of the attainment of this goal is the Super*nation*: that is to say, there must be a single nation better adapted than other nations, by virtue of its inherent characteristics, to moral development, and ordering its whole life in accordance with a moral law which stands higher than the common type. This nation will then serve as the soil essentially and supremely fitted to produce that fairest of all fruits— the Superman.

This idea opens up a wide prospect, in which Judaism appears in a new and splendid light. Many of the " shortcomings " of Judaism, by which strangers judge us, and which our own scholars try to deny or excuse, become, when viewed in the light of this idea, positive superiorities, which are a credit to Judaism, and need neither denial nor excuse.

It is almost universally admitted that the Jews have a genius for morality, and in this respect are superior to all other nations.[1] It matters not how this happened, or in what way this trait developed: we certainly find that in the very earliest times the Jewish people became conscious of its superiority in this respect over the surrounding nations. This consciousness found its expression, in accordance with the spirit of that age, in the religious dogma that God had chosen out Israel

[1] Nietzsche himself often admits this: see, for instance, Zur Geschichte-der Moral (Leipzig, 1894), p. 51.

"to make him high above all nations." But this election of Israel was not to be a domination based on force, for Israel is "the fewest of all peoples." It was for moral development that Israel was chosen by God, "to be a peculiar people unto Himself . . . . and to keep all His commandments"; that is, to give concrete expression in every generation to the highest type of morality, to submit always to the yoke of the most exacting moral obligations, and this without any regard to the gain or loss of the rest of mankind, but solely for the sake of the existence of this supreme type.[1] This consciousness of its moral election has been preserved by the Jewish people throughout its history, and has been its solace in all its sufferings. The Jews have never tried, save in exceptional circumstances, to increase their numbers by conversion; not, as their enemies aver, out of jealousy, nor yet, as their apologists plead in excuse, out of tolerance, but simply because it is a characteristic of the superior type "that it will not consent to lower the value of its own duties by making them the duties of all men; that it will not shuffle off or share with others its own responsibility."[2] Judaism does indeed present, in this respect, a unique phenomenon. It distinguishes the Jews from the rest of mankind only in that it imposes on them exacting and arduous obligations; whereas

[1] Nietzsche says somewhere, that under certain conditions it is possible for whole families, or even whole tribes, to rise to the level of the Superman (Riehl, ibid.).

[2] Nietzsche, Jenseits von Gut und Böse (Leipzig, 1894), p. 264.

for the non-Jews the yoke is lightened, and they are
allowed the reward of a future life for the mere fulfilment of the most elementary moral duties, the so-
called " seven commandments given to the sons of
Noah." It is only during the last century, since the
French Revolution raised the banner of equality and
fraternity among all men, and made the general well-
being the supreme moral ideal, that Jewish apologists
have begun to be ashamed of the idea of Israel's election in its old sense. Finding this idea opposed to
that of absolute equality and the pursuit of the general
well-being, they have tried to adapt Judaism to modern
requirements by inventing the famous theory of " the
mission of Israel among the nations." Thus they reconcile the idea of the national election with that of
human equality, by making the one a means to the
other. Israel is, indeed (so they argue), the chosen
people; but for what end was he chosen? To spread
good-will and well-being throughout the world, by
teaching mankind the way of life according to that
true Law which was entrusted to him for this very
purpose. Now there is no need to repeat here the
oft-repeated criticism of this compromise, that it has
no foundation in actuality, and rests entirely on a
metaphysical dogma. It is enough to point out that
the Jewish people as a whole has always interpreted
its " mission " simply as the performance of its own
duties, without regard to the external world, and has
regarded its election, from the earliest times to the
present day, as the end of all else, and not as a means

to the happiness of the rest of the world. The Prophets no doubt gave utterance to the hope that Judaism would exert an influence for good on the moral condition of the other nations; but their idea was that this result would follow naturally from the existence among the Jews of the highest type of morality, not that the Jews existed solely for the purpose of striving to exert this influence. It is the nations who are to say, "Come ye and let us go up to the mountain of the Lord, ... and He will teach us of His ways, and we will walk in His paths." We do not find that Israel is to say, "Come, let us go out to the nations and teach them the ways of the Lord, that they may walk in His paths."

This idea of Israel as the Supernation might be expanded and amplified into a complete system. For the profound tragedy of our spiritual life in the present day is perhaps only a result of our failure to justify in practice the potentialities of our election. On the one hand, there still lives within us, though it be only in the form of an instinctive feeling, a belief in that moral fitness for which we were chosen from all the nations, and in that national mission which consists in living the highest type of moral life, in being the moral Supernation. But, on the other hand, since the day when we left the Ghetto, and started to partake of the world's life and its civilization, we cannot help seeing that our superiority is potential merely. Actually we are not superior to other nations even in the sphere of morality. We have been unable to fulfil our mission in exile, because we could not make our lives a true expression of our own character, independent of the opinion or the will of others. And so it may even be that many of our latter-day Zionists, who base their Zionism on economic and political grounds, and scoff at the national " election " and the moral " mission "—it may even be that many of these have been driven to Zionism simply by force of this contrast between the possibilities and the actualities of Jewish history: being forced thereby, all unconsciously, to seek some firm resting-place for their people, in order that it may have the opportunity once more of developing its genius for morality, and fulfilling its " mission " as the Supernation.

But enough. I meant no more than to show that the doctrine of the " transvaluation of values " is really capable of being assimilated by Judaism, and of enriching Judaism without doing violence to its spirit, by introducing " ideas which are new, but not foreign," or, rather, by introducing ideas which are not even essentially new. For, more than eight hundred years ago there lived a Jewish philosopher–poet, Rabbi Jehudah Halevi, who recognized the inner meaning and value of the election of Israel, and made it the foundation of his system, very much on the lines of what I have said above, though in a different style.[1]

And now what have our young writers done with this doctrine?

They have neglected what is essentially original in

[1] See his Kuzari, bk. i.

it, and have seized only on the new phrase and the
Aryan element which its author introduced: and with
these they come to their own people, as with a medicine to cure the diseases of its old age. For them the
essential thing is not the emancipation of the superior
type from its subservience to the multitude; it is the
emancipation of physical life from its subservience to
the limiting power of the spirit. Such a point of view
as this can never ally itself with Judaism. No wonder,
then, that they feel a " cleft in their souls," and begin
to cry, " Transvaluation! New values! Let the Book
give place to the sword, and the Prophets to the fair
beast! " This cry has become especially prominent
during the last year; and we are told every day that
our whole world must be destroyed root and branch,
and rebuilt all over again. But we are never told how
you can destroy with one breath the national foundation of an ancient people, or how you can build up a
new life for a nation after destroying the very essence
of its being, and stifling its historic soul.

One can understand—and one can tolerate—the individual Jew who is captivated by the Superman in
Nietzsche's sense; who bows the knee to Zarathustra,
throws off his allegiance to the Prophets, and goes
about to regulate his own private life in accordance
with these new values. But it is difficult to understand, and still more difficult to tolerate, the extraordinary proceeding of these men, who offer such a new
law of life as this to the whole nation, and are simple
enough to think that it can be accepted by a people

which, almost from the moment of its first appearance in the world's history, has existed only to protest vehemently and unceasingly on behalf of the rights of the spirit against those of the strong arm and the sword; which, from time immemorial to the present day, has derived all its spiritual strength simply from its steadfast faith in its moral mission, in its obligation and its capacity to approach nearer than other nations to the ideal of moral perfection. This people, they fondly imagine, could suddenly, after thousands of years, change its values, forgo its national preeminence in the moral sphere, in order to become " the tail of the lions " in the sphere of the sword; could overthrow the mighty temple which it has built to the God of righteousness, in order to set up in its place a mean and lowly altar (it has no strength for more) to the idol of physical force.

There is a further point that requires mention. These writers go much further than their master in waging war against the Book and all that it contains—that is, against the laws which set a limit to the supremacy of the individual will—and in lavishing affection on the dissenters and the rebels of the wilderness, who refused to subordinate the " glory of life " to abstract laws, and to change the fleshpots of Egypt for the heavy yoke of moral obligations. Nietzsche himself, for all his worship of the strong arm and the glory of physical life, regards righteousness as the highest perfection attainable on earth: so much so, that he finds it hard to believe that it is within the power of man, even of the Superman, to conquer the feeling of hate and revenge, and to be guided by absolute justice in his relations with friends and foes alike. Hence he finds it a great advantage that righteousness should be embodied in fixed abstract laws, which enable a man to test the justice of his actions in relation to the objective rule, without being compelled to remember, in the moment of his self-examination, the living enemy, who arouses his passions, so that his judgment is obscured by his subjective inclinations.[1]

And here I am reminded that these writers of ours are in the habit of paying me an undeserved honor. They applaud me because in one of my essays[2] I, too, have protested against our being " the people of the Book." To be sure, they think that I am inconsistently denying my own " heresy " when I couple this protest with praise of our " national possessions " and their natural development, and do not demand, as they do, the complete destruction of the Book. But here again they have simply found a new phrase and seized on it, without examining its true inwardness. My regret was not for the existence of the Book in itself, but for its petrifaction. I lamented the fact that its development has been arrested, that it no longer corresponds to the inner moral feeling, as it used to do, in the earlier days of Jewish history, when " the voice of God in the heart of man " used to draw its inspiration direct from the phenomena of life and nature,

[1] Genealogie, pp. 82-84.
[2] "The Law in the Soul." [Not included in this translation.]

and the Book itself was compelled to change its contents little by little, imperceptibly, in order to conform to the moral consciousness of the people. And so I was not advocating the dominance of the sword over the Book; I was pleading for the dominance of that moral force which was implanted in our people centuries ago, which itself produced the Book, and renewed the spirit of the Book in each successive period, according to its own needs. It was only after a long spell of exile that much suffering quelled the spirit, and the moral feeling practically ceased to develop, so that there were no further changes made in the contents of the Book, and the people became absolutely enslaved to a series of lifeless letters. And it is in accordance with this view, and not in contradiction to it, that I maintained in the essay in question, as I always maintain, that there is no call for uprooting, or for proclaiming the change of values with the blare of trumpets; but only for the introduction of what I have called " a new current of life " into our spiritual world: this new current being " a living desire for the unity of the nation, for its rebirth, and its unfettered development along its own lines, as one of the social units of humanity." This new current would bring fresh life to our people, and would restore to it the faculty of moral self-development; and then, as a natural consequence, the Book, too, would develop once more, responding to the true needs and demands of the national spirit, and not to the shrieks of a few imaginative young men, who have eaten the sour grapes of a foreign philosophy, and want the whole nation's teeth to be set on edge.

On more general grounds, too, these writers of ours should have studied the laws of historical evolution a little more deeply before trying their hands at pulling down and building up. It is true that Nietzsche himself hated historians, and stigmatized Darwin and Spencer, the authors of the evolutionary theory, as mediocrities. But this did not prevent even him from inventing historical hypotheses in order to explain the progress of morality, or from taking the cornerstone of his new system from Darwin. These writers of ours seem to regard the moral code of each nation as something external, manufactured from beginning to end by certain individuals, who were fully conscious of what they were doing, and had a definite end in view. In order, therefore, that this moral code may be changed—or, rather, in order that it may be utterly destroyed, and another set up in its place—all that is needed is that certain other individuals should proclaim, loudly and savagely, that a change of values is imperative. An idea of this kind was all very well years ago, in the time of Rousseau and his school. But these modernest of modern writers, who consider themselves the writers of the *future,* ought to know that you cannot manufacture a new moral code for a nation, any more than you can manufacture it a new language. The laws of morality, like those of language, are an outcome of the national character; they are a fruit which ripens little by little through the ages, under the influence of innumerable causes, some permanent, some transient, not in accordance with a system laid down and defined at the outset. Hence it results that in both cases logical contradictions abound, the norm and the exception live side by side. No man has the power to pull them down and build them up according to his desire and taste: they change constantly of their own accord, reflecting the changes in the nation's circumstances, character, and needs. Now, despite all this, Volapük as a language has some value; it may serve as an artificial aid in time of need. But a moral Volapük is a piece of utter fatuity, as unprofitable as it is unnecessary; it serves no purpose but to waste time, and to confuse ardent young men who are athirst for exciting novelties. The inventor of Volapük, wishing his language to be accepted universally, found it necessary to expunge the letter *r* from his alphabet, because it cannot be pronounced by—the Chinese. But the authors of our moral Volapük do not trouble to inquire as to the capabilities of the nation for which they are building: they hold a pistol to your head, and offer you the blessing of a new law, against which every fibre of your being revolts, without first inquiring whether you can accept it.

" It is a thing of the highest importance to instil into the minds of the people . . . . that feeling of reverence which will teach them that there are certain things which they may not touch, certain sanctuaries which they may not approach without removing their shoes, which must be preserved from the hand of profanation. . . . And, on the other side, when we consider the so-called 'men of culture,' those who believe in 'modern ideas,' there is nothing that so disgusts us as their apparent lack of a sense of shame, and that easy effrontery of hand and eye with which they maul and finger everything."

That is a hard saying, but it is not one for which I need ask pardon of our Nietzscheans. The saying is not mine: it comes from their own Bible. It was Nietzsche who wrote these words; and they were directed against those who lay irreverent hands on the Hebrew Book—on the Scriptures. " Such books as this," he adds, " with their fathomless depth and their priceless worth, need an external authority, backed by force, to protect them, in order that they may remain in existence for all the thousands of years which are necessary before their wealth can be exhausted." [1]

These are the master's words. Hearing, after this, the words of his Jewish pupils, one cannot resist the thought that it is better for our children to wander abroad themselves, and draw the noxious water from the fountainhead, than to get it at second hand in this Hebrew " cleft " literature, which promises to reconcile the claims of Judaism with those of human life in general.

[A criticism of the foregoing essay appeared in Ha-Shiloah, to which Ahad Ha-'Am replied in the same journal. The fol-

[1] Jenseits, p. 254.

lowing paragraph from his reply puts very clearly the point at issue between the "young men" and himself.]

I have never yet discovered what phraseology or what style must be used to convince people of the truth that a belief in the fundamental morality of the Jewish spirit is not in the least opposed to the ideal of the national revival, but rather affords the true historical basis and logical substructure of that ideal. Times beyond number, in all shapes and forms, have I urged this view. Indeed, if I mistake not, I was one of the first to point out the absolute necessity of awakening our dormant genius for morality in order to overcome the petrifaction which has seized on our life, and to give us an immediate link with nature, without the intervention of " the Book." As regards the very point on which the author of this article attacks me, I have explained again and again that there is no inconsistency between the striving after a healthy national life and the cultivation of our moral strength. And yet the champions of our " young men " can still go on repeating that " we must pay attention also to our physical resources, and strive after a national life like all other nations." As though that were anything new! What they have discovered is not the *need* for a change, for a return to nature: that idea they found ready-made in books of the old-fashioned moral school. The real foundation of their theory is the antithesis between this need and the bent towards morality, which has been characteristic of the Jewish spirit since the Jews existed. Consequently, those who wish to defend them, and to reply to the criticisms of their opponents, are bound to demonstrate the reality of that antithesis, and the necessity for the destruction of this moral bent. To come and argue, on behalf of the " young men," simply that we stand in need of a healthy national life, like all other nations, is merely to bring coals to Newcastle; and to add naïvely that the existence of this need proves " the moral theory of Rabbi Jehudah Halevi " obsolete—this shows that the critic is unacquainted with what he is criticising. For the whole object of my arguments has been to show that there is no incompatibility between the need for a national revival and the " moral " theory of Judaism, and that this theory does not necessarily involve acceptance of the point of view indicated by such phrases as " the people of the Book," and " exceptions to all historical laws." It is, on the contrary, actually opposed to that point of view, because it attempts to apply universal historical laws to Jewish life, and for that very reason cannot stomach the ideas of our " young men," who ride roughshod over history and its universal laws.

A NEW SAVIOR

(1901)

The Annual Meeting of the Council of the Jewish
Colonization Association, held at Paris in October last,
at which the fate of the Jewish agricultural laborers
in Palestine was decided, is now a matter of history.
These unfortunate laborers sent a deputation to Paris,
to call on the members of the Council before the meeting, and explain the position to each one separately,
so that he might be able to consider the matter at
leisure, and need not say a hasty Amen to other people's
views at the meeting itself.   There were gentlemen
among the members of the Council who received the
deputation courteously, and listened to their suggestions with patience and sympathy, though they knew
beforehand that these suggestions had no chance of
being carried out.   But one member shut his door in
the face of the humble Palestinians, and gave them,
instead of spoken comfort, a written insult—a proced-
ure which was hardly becoming to a cultured aristocrat
of his type.   He thus laid himself open to the suspicion
of entertaining a hatred and contempt for Oriental
Jews so strong as to overcome the good breeding of
the Frenchman, and make him trample under heel
the rudiments of polite behavior.

But, in truth, we mortals judge by appearances. The end of the story puts a different color on the beginning, and shows that this gentleman, at the very time when he was outwardly so unkind to these unfortunate men, was secretly bubbling over with sympathy for all his unhappy brethren in the East. We find that while the laborers' deputation stood on his door-step and could not gain admittance, he was sitting in his study and seeking a remedy for an evil far greater than the hard case of some hundreds of workmen: to wit, the moral and material poverty of all the myriads of Jews in the East.

Nor did he seek in vain. Scarce had the ink dried on the pen with which he wrote his reply to the deputation and their " insane suggestions " (*propositions insensées*), when lo and behold! he writes and publishes in a French Jewish paper an article on " The Internal Emancipation of Judaism," in which he calls on the " enlightened " Jews of the West to unite in aid of their brethren in the East, so as to free them from that " inner slavery " in which they are sunk at present, and which is responsible for all their troubles. Another contributor to the same journal attacks his views, of course with much bowing and scraping and profuse expressions of gratitude, in the name of Judaism, for the fact that so great a man should patronize it, and condescend to take an interest in its problems; and our distinguished friend actually goes to the trouble of writing a second and even a third article, both breathing an intense pity for his poor benighted brethren, so sadly in need of the light which he is prepared, at some personal sacrifice, to shed on them—although (this may be read quite clearly between the lines) he is what he is and they are what they are![1]

Now what, think you, is this "inner slavery" with which we are infected? It is nothing more or less than the observance of the Sabbath and the dietary laws. The dietary laws make our meat dear, and prevent us from having the benefit of "healthy and cheap forms of food, such as swine's flesh"; and the Sabbath involves heavy loss to business men, and does not allow poor men to obtain work in factories. But this, in the opinion of our distinguished friend, is not the main point. To lose money is a bad thing; but much worse, much more bitter, is the moral loss in which these rites involve us. " Now, when the progress of science and the moral consciousness has done so much to draw the hearts of men nearer together, the Jews are cut off by their religious precepts, which surround them with a gulf deeper than that of hatred and prejudice, by encouraging the false idea that they are strangers among the nations." " This is the real yellow badge, which we must remove from our brethren "—such is the trumpet-call with which our distinguished friend concludes his last article.

Do you wish for proof that all these rites have lost their potency? Why, " almost all those Jews who, since the time of Spinoza have been to the outside

[1] S. Reinach, L'émancipation intérieure du judaïsme (L'Univers Israélite, nos. 6, 8, 12).

world the fine flower of Judaism, have emancipated themselves more or less completely from religious observances. The belief in one God, the belief in progress and the triumph of right, the bed-rock on which the Jewish outlook is based, have nothing to fear from the abolition of the Sabbath and the dietary laws." Of course, our distinguished friend is himself one of those Jews who are to the outside world the fine flower of Judaism, and so he is not ashamed to open his door to the world (that same door which was closed in the faces of the poor laborers), and let everybody see how things are conducted inside. " I do not ask for emancipation for myself: I have already achieved it, and need no external aid. But I do ask for an attempt to emancipate, by means of organized propaganda, the great mass of the members of my communion, the poor who believe."

The thought may spring to one's mind, If he was able to emancipate himself without external aid, is it not possible that the poor Eastern Jews also may attain the same result by their own efforts, without his assistance, when circumstances really make it necessary that they should do so? But our distinguished friend scouts any such idea. These poor people believe that religious ceremonies are holy, and must not be touched ; " and in order to show them their mistake, there is need of reasoned argument, explanation of the social basis of morality, historical expositions, and so forth, all of which must be brought to them *from without.*" The Jews of France were able to emancipate themselves from the burden of these observances, "because they lived in an atmosphere of enlightenment"; but the case of the Eastern Jews is different. "How can you hope," cries our author, "that all the millions of Jews in Russia and Roumania will be brought into an atmosphere of philosophy and science like ours in the West? It is heartless, then, to expect them to emancipate themselves. We must assist them."

Assist them—but how and wherewith?

The answer is very simple. The emancipated Western Jews are to put into our hands the weapon which we lack, rational criticism, and with this weapon we are to cut the stout cords that bind us; and then we are free! It is a very powerful weapon, this of rational criticism. By its means "it is possible to awaken doubts in simple, trusting minds; it is possible to make respectable inhabitants of every small Polish town ask the hitherto forbidden question, Why do we not follow the example of our Western fellow-Jews? Why should we not be content to be Jews of their type?"

And while he is waiting for others to come and help him in bringing us this weapon of rational criticism, our author does his own little best, and stretches out to us, for the time being, just the butt-end of the knife, in this wise: Do you imagine, he says, that from time immemorial the Sabbath has been a day of rest for the weary, and that it has therefore a moral value? You are mistaken! Even before the giving of the Law it was the practice to refrain from work on that day, because it was regarded as a day of evil omen, on which nothing could prosper [1]; and this is an idle superstition, which must be rooted out. Do you think, again, that from time immemorial your ancestors used to sacrifice their lives for the sanctity of the Sabbath, and would suffer heavy loss rather than profane it? You are mistaken! Mattathias, the father of the Hasmoneans, allowed his men to defend themselves against the enemy even on the Sabbath. This proves that self-preservation is the first of all laws; and therefore you, too, are in duty bound to go to your work on the Sabbath, in order not to suffer loss in your business; you, too, are in duty bound not to waste your money on kasher meat, when swine's flesh is so cheap.

So this weapon of rational criticism is not a very sharp one, nor a very new one. On its own merits, indeed, it is not worth a moment's notice, after a century of attempts at "religious reform," many of which have been much more able and intelligent. But the novelty of this attempt lies not in itself, but in its being made for the sake of other people, as a kind of charity; and for this reason I have thought it worth bringing to the notice of our own community. Throughout the nineteenth century we have been used to seeing the Reformers working each for the benefit of the Jews in his own country, and leaving the Jews in other countries to look after themselves and intro-

---

[1] This is a well-known theory, based on records of a Sabbath of this kind in the ancient history of Babylon. See for example Sayce, Religion of the Ancient Babylonians (1887), p. 76.

duce reforms suited to their own way of thinking and
the local conditions, of which they were the best
judges. But now we have a really *fin-de-siècle* idea
in Reform: to send a reforming weapon of foreign
manufacture to those poorer brethren who lived in
countries where it is not produced.

One is inclined to smile at the simplicity of this
learned scholar; but the smile vanishes as one remembers that it is men of this kind who stand at the head
of powerful organizations, whose yea or nay deter-
mines the fate of measures of the highest importance
in our national life. We are not concerned here with
the learned scholar, the member of the *Académie
française;* we have already grown accustomed to these
scholars who do not know their people, and hurl their
utterances down from the lofty heights of Olympus.
But here we have a man who has been appointed a
steward of the congregation, of the whole people, who
is one of the leading members of the Jewish Colonization Association and the *Alliance:* and *this* man is so
far removed from the general body of his people as to
suppose, in all sincerity and simplicity, that the myriads
of Eastern Jews have never heard this profound wisdom of his, and are incapable of grasping it, unless he
and his like hand them the " weapon of rational criticism." If you tell him that this same weapon has
been lying about our streets for years past, and has
actually become rusty, he will not believe you, or, what
is worse, will not understand you, even if he does believe. Men of this kind, themselves without any

vestige of true Jewish feeling, cannot by any means be brought to understand how there can be among us intelligent men, familiar with all the theories of the learned world about the origin of the Sabbath and the other religious observances, who know also what our author himself affects not to know, that even " the bed-rock on which the Jewish outlook is based " did not spring into being full-grown, but was gradually evolved, like the conception of the Sabbath, out of the crude beliefs and emotions of primitive man, and who can still find the Sabbath a delight, can respect and hold sacred the day which has been sanctified by the blood of our people, and has preserved it for thousands of years from spiritual degeneration, although they may not be scrupulously careful as regards all the details of the multifarious kinds of forbidden work. They cannot understand how such men, though they may not be very particular about what they eat away from home, can still observe Kashrut in their houses, because they do not wish their tables to be regarded as unclean by the Jewish public: not that they *fear* the public, as our author erroneously supposes in one of his essays, but that they value the national tie that unites them with it: and how even those who act otherwise would yet regard it as the height of impertinence for a Jew to boast publicly that he is no longer at one with the great mass of his people as regards his domestic life and his food. All this is quite unintelligible to Western communal leaders of the type of our author. And not only that: even the real significance of historical events, which are all that remains to them of Judaism, is now quite beyond their comprehension, because they have lost the national feeling. Remember Mattathias the Priest, that national hero who turned his back in scorn and loathing on the Syrian officer, with his promises of life and wealth and glory, and sacrificed himself and his family for the honor of his people and his religion. Remember that passionate cry of his, " Our holy things, our pride and our glory, have been laid waste; why then should we live?" *This* is the hero whom our French savior brings in evidence that it is our duty to abolish the Sabbath, because " a man must live "! Our Member of the Academy does not understand that if Mattathias allowed fighting on the Sabbath, he only did so in order to preserve the whole nation, in order that the Jews might be able to remain separate from other nations in their inner life, and develop in their own way as a distinct and individual people. That is to say, his purpose was exactly the reverse of that with which our distinguished friend now suggests the abolition of the Sabbath. If Mattathias had heard our friend putting him to this use, and then adding that " in our day the Jews are no longer a nation," I fear that he might have treated him as he treated the first Jew who went up to the Syrian altar.

One is reminded of the Polish nobles of a former generation, and the way in which they treated " their " Jews. The poor Jew stands with bared head before his lord, as needs he must for his belly's sake; and the lord treats him with the utmost contempt, imagining the while, guileless creature that he is, that the Jew himself is conscious of his own worthlessness, and acknowledges the lofty superiority of his lord and feeder. He does not know that in his heart of hearts the Jew despises him and his like, and thinks nothing of all their glory and riches and wisdom, because he is fully aware that he himself, for all his material poverty, stands morally far above all these lords of his, who are slaves to this temporary life. So it is with us and our distinguished brethren of the West. They see the Jews of the East coming to beg material aid of them in time of trouble; and apparently they are crass enough to suppose that these Jews confess also to a spiritual inferiority, and are waiting for the West to emancipate them not only from their external poverty, but also from their inner slavery. Could these saviors of ours but know what *we* think of *them,* of that inner slavery to which *they* condemn themselves when they barter their national spirit for paper privileges; of that " slavery in freedom " of which the French Jews have taken so liberal a dose: could they but know this, they might perhaps understand how profound is the contempt which we, ingrates that we are, return them for their kindness when they come to emancipate us from our spiritual bondage.

Slaves that you are, emancipate *yourselves* first!

But you cannot! It is not in you to emancipate yourselves. " It is heartless to expect you to emancipate yourselves." That is a task beyond your moral

strength. It is not you, but we, " the poor who believe," in the East, who will emancipate you from that
inner slavery in which, all unconscious, you are sunk.

We will fill your spiritual emptiness with Jewish
feeling; we will bring you Judaism, not the fair-
sounding, meaningless lip-phrase which is your con-
fession of faith, but a living Judaism of the heart,
inspired with the will and the power to develop and to
renew its strength. And then you will change your
tune about slavery and emancipation.

If you have eyes to see what is going on around
you, use them! Here are these paupers coming
from the East, and beginning already to exercise an influence on your communities, while you disdain to take
notice of them. Even so the lordly Romans in their
day looked down with contempt on the " paupers
from the East," until these paupers came and over-
turned their world.

THE SPIRITUAL REVIVAL.[1]

(1902)

It is not a mere accident that the question of Jewish culture has come to the front with the rise of " political " Zionism. Zionism—unqualified by any epithet—existed before, but it knew nothing of any problem of culture. It knew only its own plain and simple aim: that of placing the Hebrew nationality in new conditions, which should give it the possibility of developing all the various sides of its individuality. This being the aim of the earlier Zionists, the first article in their programme was naturally the creation of a fixed, independent centre for our nationality in our ancestral land. But at the same time they kept a watchful eye on every side of the life of the Hebrew nationality as it exists at present, and used every suitable means of strengthening it and promoting its development. A society of Zionists in Warsaw, for instance, was engaged at one and the same time in founding a colony in Palestine, a school of the modern type in Warsaw, and an association for the diffusion

[1] [This essay was originally an address delivered before the general meeting of Russian Zionists at Minsk, in the summer of 1902. Only a part of it, that part which deals with the question of Jewish culture in its broader aspects, is here translated. The omitted portion is not of any considerable length.]

of Hebrew literature. That is to say, these men thought it their duty to combine " political " with " cultural " work; and all this in the name of Zionism (or Hibbat Zion, as it was then called). Nobody challenged this combination; nobody raised the question whether this " cultural " work was right or wrong, obligatory or permissible. It was understood on all sides that the conception of Zionism must include all that comes within the definition of Hebrew nationality. Any piece of work which would assist in strengthening and developing the nationality was Zionist work beyond all manner of doubt.

And now a new Zionism has arisen, and has adopted the term " political " as its descriptive epithet. What, we may inquire, is the precise point of this epithet? It adds nothing to the older Zionism, for Zionism has always been, in its hopes for the distant future, essentially " political." From its inception Zionism had at its very root the hope of attaining in Palestine, at some distant date, absolute independence in the conduct of the national life. That was a necessary condition of the unhindered and complete development of the national individuality. Now, even the newer Zionism cannot bring the Messiah " to-day or to-morrow "; hence it also is " political " only in its hopes for the future. Small wonder then that the epithet, which clearly added nothing, was often understood as taking something away. It was taken by political Zionists to mean something like this: The earlier Zionists included in Zionism everything germane to the development of the Hebrew national individuality; whereas for us it has only a political aim. Zionism for us means simply the foundation in Palestine, by means of diplomatic negotiations with Turkey and other powers, of a " safe refuge " for all oppressed and persecuted Jews, who cannot live under tolerable conditions in their native countries, and seek a means of escape from poverty and hunger. Even the Basle programme helped to fix this idea in people's minds, because in its first paragraph it defined the aim of Zionism thus: " To found in Palestine a safe refuge for the Jewish people," and made no mention of the *Jewish nationality*. The various speeches of Zionist leaders at Basle, in London, and elsewhere, which were a sort of commentary on this paragraph, stated emphatically and repeatedly that Zionism had come to solve once for all the economic and political problem of the Jews; that its aim was to gather all the oppressed of Israel into one place, into the Jewish State, where they could live in security, and be no longer foreigners and aliens, whose struggle for existence excites the jealousy and ill-will of the native population. This is not the place to examine this form of Zionism with a view to discovering how far its promises as to the solution of the Jewish problem were capable of fulfilment in the natural course of events. I have dealt with this point on several occasions elsewhere. Here I only wish to point out that these promises had the effect of attracting attention mainly to the political aspect of Zionism, until the Zionist conception became narrowed down, and lost half its meaning.

Thus the "problem of culture" was a child of political Zionism. For centuries our people have suffered torments for the sake of the preservation of the products of their national spirit, seeing in these products the be-all and end-all of their existence. And now that they have at last come to recognize that suffering alone is not enough, but that it is necessary to work actively for the national revival—now, forsooth, it has become a "question," whether the strengthening of the national spirit and the development of the nation's spiritual products are essential parts of the work of the revival. And this question is answered by many in the negative!

But it must be added that this negative attitude, if we may trust those who adopt it, does not involve any opposition to "cultural" work as such. "Far be it from us," they say, "to deny the usefulness of such work. Though we do not regard it as Zionist work, we do not say that Zionists should not take it up. On the contrary, we actually encourage them to take part in cultural work so far as they can. But we do not wish to make it obligatory on them, because that would be mixing up Zionism with matters which are not essential to it, and have no necessary connection with its principles." Certainly it cannot be denied that many of these Zionists, who regard "culture" as something foreign to the conception of Zionism, do in fact take part in cultural work, do in fact found schools and libraries, and in some cases even help in the diffusion of Hebrew literature and so forth. Nay, more: if you

examine Zionist societies in various places, you will
find that it is precisely such work that keeps them
alive. Wherever a Zionist society really lives, its life
is generally a result of cultural work, because such
work can obtain a hold on the members, and give them
the opportunity of devoted and persistent activity of
a concrete nature, which has a visible usefulness. And,
on the other hand, where a society is content to do no
more for Zionism than sell " shekolim " and shares and
hold " political " lectures, there you will generally
notice a feeling of emptiness and the absence of a
life-giving force; and in the end such a society pines
and wastes away for lack of food, for lack, that is, of
solid and constant work, which can rivet the attention,
occupy the mind, and rouse the emotions and the will
without intermission. All this is quite true. But to
what conclusion does it drive us? Those who oppose
" culture " conclude that there is no need to talk a
great deal about " cultural work," or to argue and
dispute about the purely theoretical question, whether
such work is essentially bound up with the conception
of Zionism, or not. This question, they say, is purely
one of theory; in actual practice most Zionists do perform their share of this work to the best of their ability.
But this conclusion is right only from the point of
view of the interests of culture; it is not right from that
of the interests of Zionism. It may be true that cultural work needs no express sanction from Zionism,
so long as Zionism, in its purely political form, cannot
provide its adherents with any other form of work

which has greater attractions and a stronger hold. So long as that is the case, political Zionism is bound to rely on the help of cultural work, which is better able to satisfy the mind and provide an outlet for the energies of those who detest waste of time and idle talk. But if this sanction is not necessary to culture, it is most emphatically necessary to Zionism. Every true lover of Zionism must realize the danger which it incurs through the diffusion of the idea that it has no concern with anything except diplomacy and financial transactions, and that all internal national work is a thing apart, which has no lot or portion in Zionism itself. If this idea gains general acceptance, it will end by bringing Zionism very low indeed. It will make Zionism an empty, meaningless phrase, a mere romance of diplomatic embassies, interviews with high personages, promises, *et hoc genus omne*. Such a romance appeals to the imagination; but it leaves no room for creative work, which alone can slake the thirst for activity.

When, therefore, we demand a clear and explicit statement that work for the revival of the national spirit and the development of its products is of the very essence of Zionism, and that Zionism is inconceivable without such work, we are not giving utterance to a mere empty formula, or fighting for a name. We are endeavoring to save the honor of Zionism, and to preserve it from that narrowness and decay which will be the inevitable, though undesired, result of the action of those leaders and champions of the movement who wish to confine it to the political aspect.

But before we attempt to make cultural work a part of the Zionist programme, we must distinguish between the two branches of that work. These two branches, though they differ in kind, have hitherto been confused, with the result that the question has become still further complicated.

The degree of culture to which a nation has attained may be estimated from two points of view: from that of the culture which it has produced, and from that of the state of its cultural life at any given time. In other words, " culture " has both an objective and a subjective meaning. Objectively, a nation's culture is something which has a reality of its own: it is the concrete expression of the best minds of the nation in every period of its existence. The nation expresses itself in certain definite forms, which remain for all time, and are no longer dependent on those who created them, any more than a fallen apple is dependent on the tree from which it fell. For instance, we still have the benefit of Greek culture: we drink in the wisdom of Greek philosophers, and enjoy the poetry and the art which that great nation has left us, though the nation itself, which created all this culture, has vanished from the face of the earth. But the " state of the cultural life " of any nation is purely subjective and temporary: it means the degree to which culture is diffused among the individual members of the nation, and the extent to which its influence is visible in their private and public life. The " state of the cultural life " is thus essentially dependent on the individuals of whom it is predicated, and with them it passes and changes from one period to another.

Culture in the objective sense and culture in the subjective sense do not necessarily reach the same degree of development at the same time. There are periods in the history of a nation in which all its spiritual strength is concentrated in a few exceptionally gifted minds; and these produce an original culture of high value, which the generality of their countrymen (such is their " state of culture " at that particular time) cannot even fully understand. The England of the seventeenth and eighteenth centuries affords an illustration. Shakespeare, Bacon, Locke, Hume, and the other great English writers of that period, a large body of men, relatively speaking, created new worlds in literature and philosophy, by the light of which men still walk at the present day. But the great mass of the English people was then in a low state of culture, which did not by any means correspond to the level reached by these giants. On the other hand, the intellectual forces of a nation in a particular period may find their expression in the general state of culture: education may be universal and the tone of life throughout enlightened and refined: while, at the same time, this culture may be barren, producing no master-minds able to express the spirit of the nation in original creative work, but dependent entirely on its own past, or on borrowings from other nations. This is the condition, for instance, of the Swiss at the present day. They are all educated in excellent schools, which satisfy the highest demands of European enlightenment; in many departments of the national life they show a high, and perhaps unequalled, level of culture. But from the point of view of *objective* culture Switzerland is unproductive: as yet there has arisen no great creative intellect, capable of embodying the Swiss spirit in an original national culture; and even the best teachers in the Swiss universities have to be imported from abroad.

In dealing, therefore, with the question of spreading culture among the Jewish people, we must remember that there are two terms involved: on the one hand, the culture (in the objective sense) which we wish to spread; on the other hand, the people in relation to that culture. Our task thus falls into two halves. We have in the first place to perfect the body of culture which the Jewish people has created in the past, and to stimulate its creative power to fresh expression; and in the second place to raise the cultural level of the people in general, and to make its objective culture the subjective possession of each of its individual members. And in order to discover what we ought to do, and what we can do, in each of these two directions, we must clearly understand the position and the needs both of the culture and of the people.

I propose to deal in turn with each of the two halves into which I have divided the main question.

The existence of an original Hebrew culture needs no proof. So long as the Bible is extant, the creative power of the Jewish mind will remain undeniable.

Even those who deny that the Jews are a people at the present day are compelled to admit that when they were a people they were a *creative* people, and the products of their creative power bear the indelible impress of their native genius. This being so, all those of us who believe, or rather *feel,* that the Jews are still a people, have the right to believe equally, without looking for any special proof, that the Jewish creative genius still lives, and is capable of expressing itself anew. But a different idea has gained currency of late, and especially among Zionists: to wit, that there is no true Hebrew culture outside the Scriptures, which the Jews produced while they lived and worked in a normal manner on their own land; that all the literature of the Diaspora does not express the true Hebrew genius, and has no connection with the earlier literature, because the heavy yoke of exile crushed the creative faculty and made it sterile. Those Zionists who hold this view apparently think that it strengthens the case for Zionism, because it belittles yet another side of the life of the exile. But as a matter of fact, if this view were correct, we should be compelled to doubt whether there were any hope for a revival of our creative power, even after the return to our own land. Every vital function which ceases to work becomes weaker and weaker, until at last it atrophies; and two thousand years of disuse would be sufficient to kill the strongest function imaginable. But, fortunately, this view has no foundation. The unfavorable conditions in which we have lived since the Dispersion have naturally left their mark on our literary work; but the Jewish genius has undergone no change in its essential characteristics, and has never ceased to produce. For instance, it is the fashion amongst non-Jewish scholars (and of course most Jewish scholars adopt the fashion, as usual) to emphasize the essential and fundamental difference between the teaching of the Prophets and the practical Judaism which grew up in the time of the second Temple, and received its final form after the destruction of that Temple. The teaching of the Prophets, they say, was exclusively moral, and was directed towards a lofty spiritual ideal; whereas the later practical Judaism concerned itself only with external regulations, and wasted its strength in the creation of innumerable trivial ordinances, with no moral value whatever. The difference is, in their view, so patent that it cannot possibly be denied. And yet, if we look more closely, we shall find that these two Judaisms, widely as they differ in content, are products of one and the same spirit, whose impress they bear in common. It is a fundamental characteristic of the Jews that they do not readily compromise, and have no love for half measures. When once they have recognized the truth of a particular conception, and made it a basis of action, they give themselves wholly to it, and strive to work out its every detail in practice; there is no regard for side issues, no concession to existing interests. It was this characteristic that produced first of all, in the days of our freedom, the teaching of the Prophets, with its extreme insistence on morality; it was this that produced afterwards, in the days when we were slaves, the teaching of the Talmud and the *Shulhan 'Aruk,* with its equally extreme insistence on practice. The nation was driven to emphasize the aspect of practical observance by the necessity of preserving itself in conditions of slavery and dispersion: hence the belief that " the Holy One, blessed be He, wished to bestow merit on Israel; wherefore he multiplied for them the Law and the commandments." Once entered on the path of the multiplication of commandments, we went on multiplying and multiplying without end. We did not discriminate between the important and the trivial; we could not give up the pettiest of petty details.

The national creative power, then, is not dead; it has not changed, nor has it ceased to bear fruit in its own way; only the changed conditions have given its fruit a different taste. The fruit produced by a tree in the place where it grows naturally and freely is unlike that which it bears when it is preserved by artificial means in a strange soil; and yet the tree is the same in its essential nature, and so long as it lives it produces fruit of its own specific kind. So it is with the Hebrew spirit: it bore fruit after its own kind, and created a literature in a mould original and peculiar to itself, not only while the Jews lived in their own country, but also in the lands of their exile, so long as the conditions were such as to leave the nation any possibility of devoting its whole spiritual energy to its own work.

It is only in the latest period, that of emancipation and assimilation, that Hebrew culture has really become sterile, and has borne practically no fresh fruit at all. This does not mean that our creative power has been suddenly destroyed, or that we are no longer capable of doing original work. It is the tendency to sink the national individuality, and merge it in that of other nations, that has produced two characteristic phenomena of this period: on the one hand, the conscious and deliberate neglect of our original spiritual qualities and the striving to be like other people in every possible way; on the other hand, the loss to ourselves of the most gifted men whom we have produced in the last few generations, and their abandonment of Jewish national work for a life devoted to the service of other nations.

Indeed, these very men, with their great gifts, are themselves a proof that we still have within us, as a people, a perennial spring of living creative power. For try as they will to conceal their Jewish characteristics, and to embody in their work the national spirit of the people whose livery they have adopted, the light of literary and artistic criticism reveals quite clearly their almost universal failure. Despite themselves, the spirit of Judaism comes to the surface in all that they attempt, and gives their work a special and distinctive character, which is not found in the work of non-Jewish laborers in the same field. It is beyond dispute, therefore, that, if all these scattered forces had been combined in working for our own national culture, as

in earlier times, that culture would be to-day one of
the richest and most original in the whole world. We
might attempt to find satisfaction in this thought. But,
unfortunately, it can only serve to increase our de-
spondency, when we see our people exporting without
importing, and scattering the sparks of its spiritual
fire in all directions, to augment the wealth and the
fame of its enemies and its persecutors, while for itself
it has no enjoyment of its own wealth, and its national
treasury is none the richer for all the work of its most
gifted sons. At the present day we are suffering
heavily from that " evil " which the writer of Ecclesiastes long ago noticed as " heavy upon men,"—
" a man to whom God giveth riches, wealth, and honor
. . . . yet God giveth him not power to eat thereof,
but a stranger eateth it."

But we have already gone so far in renouncing our
national individuality that we are no longer even conscious of the evil; and the dispersion of our intellectual
forces scarce claims a passing sigh of regret. Nay,
when we see a Jew earning fame by distinguished work
in any non-Jewish world of culture, our hearts swell
with pride and joy, and we hasten to proclaim from the
housetops that " so-and-so is one of our people,"
though " so-and-so " may be doing his utmost to forget and bury the relationship. Occasionally such
an incident as this may provoke some of us to lament
the sorry plight of a nation which can only till the
fields of other peoples, while its own lies neglected and
untended; but many of our " superior " and " broad-

minded " brothers treat us with a lofty contempt, and
regard our complaint as treason to " humanity."
" What do we care," you will hear them argue,
" whether a man works for his own people or for
another? Enough that his work benefits humanity at
large. The good of humanity—that is the one ideal
of the future; to set up any other is a sign of petty
tribalism and narrow-mindedness." This is certainly
a " broad " view: but it overlooks the fact that greatness is a matter not of breadth only, but of depth. In
reality, this view, for all its breadth, is utterly superficial. For consider the two sides of the antithesis.
In the one case a man works among his own people,
in the environment which gave him birth and endowed
him with his special aptitude, which encircled the first
slow growth of his faculties and implanted in him the
rudiments of his human consciousness, his fundamental
ideas and feelings, thus determining in his childhood
what should be the bent and character of his mind
throughout his life. In the other case he works among
an alien people, in a world that is not his own, and in
which he cannot become at home unless he artificially
change his nature and the current of his mind, thereby
inevitably tearing himself into two disparate halves,
and foredooming all his work to reveal, in its character
and its products, this want of harmony and wholeness.
Is there really no difference?

It follows, then, that humanity at large suffers to
some extent from the dispersion of our cultural forces;
and therefore our staunchest champions of humanity

have a perfect right to share unhesitatingly in our concern at this dispersion. But even if they think that the loss to humanity is not so great as to justify them in feeling concerned about it, we at least, we who are nationalists, need not be ashamed, I think, to publish abroad our distress at this enslavement of our capacities to alien races, and at the resulting loss to our internal national life. Even the most ardent " liberals," whose watchword is humanity, and whose lodestar is progress, even they certainly permit themselves and others to take suitable measures for attaining their own particular ends, so long as those measures do not involve any loss to humanity or progress; and if this is permitted to individuals in their private lives, why should it be forbidden to a whole nation in its national life? We need not, therefore, answer those who ask what humanity *loses* by our loss: it is rather for them to explain to us what humanity *gains* by our loss, and what humanity would lose if we, and not an alien people, were to derive a national advantage from the men of genius whom we produce; if we, and not an alien people, were to lay on the altar of humanity the offerings of our own sons, who owe to us their existence and their inspiration.

Recently, for instance, we buried and mourned for Antokolsky. While the tears yet flow for the premature death of this great artist, the time has not come to examine in detail, and without fear or favor, his relation on the one hand to his own people, which gave him inspiration and genius, and on the other hand to the alien nation from which he derived riches and honor. But there is one general truth which we cannot hide. The mourning which his death has caused throughout the whole world, and especially in his native land, must cause us a secret pang, when we see that others arrogate to themselves the glory of his name now that he is dead, just as they took the fruits of his genius while he was alive: and we, meanwhile, can only reflect sadly on what Antokolsky might have given, but did not give, to his people, and on the terrible poverty and degradation of our national position, but for which men like Antokolsky would not look abroad for an outlet for their genius.

And who will dare to say that this pang which we feel is a sin against humanity and progress? How would progress have suffered, what would humanity have lost, if Antokolsky had devoted his genius, or at least some considerable portion of it, to the service of his own people's culture; if the matter which he endowed with form and soul had been taken from our national life, which was undoubtedly much closer to him in spirit, much more intelligible to him, than the alien life in which he sought his subjects?

Of course, it is easy to solve the difficulty by a generalization. It is easy to say—and we do in fact hear it said very often—that Jewish life is very circumscribed, and does not afford sufficient material for a creative work of genius; that therefore great artists are compelled to rely on non-Jewish life as a medium for the expression of their ideas. But this solution vanishes like smoke as soon as we pass from the generalization to the individual instances. Thus, to take one example, Antokolsky wished to produce a statue of a violent and cruel tyrant, steeped in bloodshed, universally dreaded, and yet not wholly dead to the voice of conscience, but alternating always between crime and repentance. Could there be a more perfect type of such a tyrant than Herod, as history portrays his character and his actions? And if Antokolsky nevertheless chose as his model not Herod, but the Russian king, Ivan the Terrible, was it really because there was a richer and fuller interest, a more broadly human appeal, in the figure of this obscure tyrant, almost unknown outside his own country, and scarcely intelligible to any but his own countrymen, than in that of Herod, which was bound up by a thousand links with the general culture of his era, which exercised a certain influence on the history of the world, and which was certainly familiar to the artist himself before ever he heard even the name of Ivan the Terrible? And here is yet another instance. When Antokolsky wished to create a type of a lonely recluse, writing his books in the isolation of his own chamber, he went back to the eleventh century, to a monastery in Kieff, to find the well-known Russian monkish chronicler Nestor; whereas he had seen in his own birthplace, Wilna, a recluse type of a much broader human appeal, and much closer to himself in spirit— the type, I mean, of the " perpetual student " whom a

Hebrew poet has so brilliantly depicted,[1] the recluse who does not shut himself out of the world in a monastery, but lives in society, and is yet as far as any monk from the bustle and turmoil of life, knowing no world but that of the books which he reads, or, if he is a great man, the books which he writes. When Antokolsky was a small boy he must certainly have listened with reverence to the stories told by the old men of his town about the great recluse who lived there a hundred years before, whose whole life was one long day of study and writing, without pause or rest. But Antokolsky, the great artist, did not remember the Gaon of Wilna, who fired the boy's imagination: he wandered far afield to a medieval Russian monastery, outside the ken of himself and his ancestors, in order to find there what he could have found among his own people, and in his own town.

Was this really so necessary, so essential to the welfare of art and the good of humanity, that we have no right to lament our loss, and to lament it aloud?

Yet there were some among us who thought it their duty to hide this national grief under the veil of love for humanity; and some of these even allowed themselves, according to reports in the press, to bear false witness against their people over the coffin, actually *congratulating* the house of Israel on the fact that

[1] [Ch. N. Bialik, the greatest poet produced by the modern Hebrew revival, has drawn in his "Ha-Matmid" a masterly picture of the "perpetual student," who allows himself scarcely five hours' rest in the twenty-four from the study of the Talmud.]

Antokolsky's genius and his creations had passed into other ownership![1]   And the endeavor to show the world how far we are always prepared to shrink and double ourselves up in order to make room for others, has gone to such lengths that Jewish writers have not stopped short of disclaiming, with gratuitous generosity, the characteristics of their own people, and ascribing them to others, in order that they might be able to point out that Antokolsky was a Russian to the very core. " The characteristics of Antokolsky's work," so writes a Jew in a Jewish paper, " are essentially characteristic of Russian art in general: idealism in conception and realism in execution. . . . . You cannot find among Antokolsky's productions even one dedicated exclusively to beauty of form, say of the human body. He always looks for the soul abiding in that body." [2]   So these characteristics, which have notoriously distinguished the spirit of Israel from time immemorial, came to Antokolsky not from his own people, but, if you please, because he acquired " the essential characteristics of Russian art "!

But Antokolsky is not the only Jew who has consecrated the force of his genius to the service of an alien people. All our greatest artists, thinkers, and writers do the like. They leave our humble cottage as soon as they feel that their exceptional abilities will open the doors of splendid palaces. And when they achieve greatness and renown, we gaze at their elevation from

[1] See the Voschod, July 11, 1902 (no. 28).
[2] The Jewish Chronicle, July 25, 1902.

afar, and share in the pride and the joy which they feel at having had the good fortune to escape from our darkness into the foreign light. But even this pitiable pride of ours is regarded by our enemies as the height of impudence: as though a slave should dare to remind you that he also has a share and a stake in his master's property. They grow rich by our poverty, prosperous by our decay; and then they cry out on this despicable nation, which has not a single corner of its own in the temple of modern culture! Such, it seems, has ever been our fate. Several nations have even annexed our God, and now scornfully ask us, " Where is *your* God? "

But there is another side to the picture. Our best and most original minds—those whose Hebrew originality reveals itself, in their own despite, even when they work in alien fields—stand, as we have seen, outside our own body politic. What then remains inside? For the most part, only the smaller minds and those of poorer grain; and these are carried away, root and branch, by the current of the alien culture in the midst of which they live. Thus all their work in the sphere of Jewish culture is in the main nothing but an imitation of the foreigner, an imitation without any quality of originality, restraint, insight, or proportion.

There is one department of learning that belongs wholly to us, both in name and in substance—I mean the so-called " Jewish Science." [1] Here certainly was an outlet for our intellectual energies, an opportunity

---

[1] [See note on p. 65.]

for us to reveal our latent originality. But what happens in practice? The most eager and most original workers in this field are non-Jewish scholars; and these are slavishly followed and imitated by the Jewish scholars, who never turn a hair's breadth from the general principles and lines of research laid down by their masters, even where they are by no means above criticism. Until quite recently there was no sign of any attempt on the part of Jewish scholars to controvert even this axiom of Christian investigators, that the historical evidence of Greek and Roman literature is always to be accepted as against that of the Talmud and the Midrashim, where the two are in conflict. It is only this year that a Jewish scholar [1] has examined this general principle in connection with a particular question, and has found that it has no foundation, but that, on the contrary, the Talmudical references are more in accordance with historical truth. The logical method of the Talmud, again, has not yet been thoroughly investigated by Jewish scholars; and the idea which the outside world has formed of the Talmudic style of argument, that it is opposed to true logic and sound sense, has become current among us also to such an extent that the phrase " Talmudic sophism " has become with us a nickname for every crooked and far-fetched piece of quibbling. But last year a Jewish scholar [2] showed that the Talmudic

[1] [Dr. Büchler, then in Vienna, now principal of Jews' College London.]

[2] [Dr. Schwarz, of Vienna.]

method rests on sound foundations, and will repay study; and that, in fact, the difference between that method and Greek logic is not accidental, and does not convict the Jewish Rabbis of ignorance, but has its roots in a deep-seated and fundamental difference of spirit between the Jews and the Greeks.

But such instances of independent investigation, real *free*-thinking we may call it, are very rare in the history of " Jewish Science," and have only begun to appear recently; and it may be that they are one of the results of the modern revival of the spirit of nationalism among the Jews. However that may be, " Jewish Science " as a whole is still a bondslave to the alien; the genuine Hebrew spirit has not found full and original expression in this movement, as we might legitimately have hoped.

But in truth such a hope was *not* legitimate, not if we remember in what manner the birth and growth of the " Jewish Science " movement came about, and to what end they were directed. When Jewish scholars turned their eyes to the past, they were not impelled to do so by something within them that demanded that the national spirit should continue to develop in the future; they were not looking for a spiritual thread to bind together all the successive phases of our national life; they were not seeking to strengthen this thread by the aid of a clear historic consciousness. " Jewish Science " owes its being not to any nationalist impulse of this kind, but to other impulses of a temporary and accidental character, which were calculated for the most part to sever the national bond not merely as between past and present, but even as between the scattered groups into which the nation is divided to-day. Zunz, who led the founders of the movement, regarded it as a means of converting the world to more friendly feelings towards the Jews, and of obtaining the supreme ideal of those days—equality of rights. Geiger threw himself heart and soul into "Jewish Science," in order to find support for *his* great ideal—religious reform—which was itself essentially a means to the acquisition of equal rights. Even Zechariah Frankel, who was closer than they were to the Hebrew spirit, did not hesitate to publish in the "sixties," at the beginning of one of the numbers of the Monatsschrift which he founded for "Jewish Science," the opinion that the national life of the Jews of Prussia had ended with the removal of the last of their civil disabilities in that country, and that thenceforth it was their duty to give themselves whole-heartedly to the life of the nation in which they lived. Since, therefore, he went on, the Jews have no longer a separate history, historical investigation of their past will in future have no connection with their life in the present and the future, but will be a purely theoretical science.[1] Such ideas, of course, could not restore to the Jewish spirit its independence and its capacity for original expression; and so "Jewish Science" became nothing more than a memorial tablet to our dead spiritual activity.

[1] The number of the Monatsschrift is not before me as I write, and I give the substance of Frankel's remarks from memory.

And we find another memorial tablet in that branch of literary work in which the national spirit of every people finds its chief expression,—I mean, in our *national* literature.

Our " national literature " is often taken in a wide sense, to include everything that has been or is written by men of Jewish race in any language. If we accept that definition, we cannot complain of the poverty of this literature. Heine's love-poems, Börne's crusade against the political reaction in Germany, Brandes' critical essays on all the literatures in the world except the Hebrew—all these are ours, are parts of our national literature. But this conception is fundamentally wrong. The national literature of any nation is only that which is written in its own national language. When an individual member of that nation writes in a foreign language, what he writes may, indeed, reveal traces of his own national spirit, even if his subject has no connection with his nation (and this is, in fact, the case with the great Jewish writers whom I have mentioned, and others whom I have not mentioned) ; it may even influence the history of his nation, if it deals with questions affecting their life. But *national* literature it is not: it belongs wholly to the general body of literature of that nation in whose language it is written. North America has many able writers; a flood of new books, some of them of great merit, pours forth there every year, to say nothing of innumerable periodicals: and in spite of this the Americans have as yet no real national literature, because they have no separate national language, and there is no clearly defined and recognized border line between American literature and its stronger and richer sister, English literature, which annexes all that is written in the English language. So with the Swiss: their literary productions go to swell the literature of the three great nations in whose languages they write, and they themselves have no national literature of their own, if we exclude what little has been written in the prevailing dialect of German Switzerland.

Our national literature, then, is that alone which is written in our national language; it does not include what Jews write in other languages. If they write on subjects which concern other nations as well, or other nations only, their books belong to the literature of the nation in whose language they are written; and the best of them find a place in the history of that literature, though not always a place commensurate with their value, side by side with the native writers. If they write exclusively on matters concerning the Jewish people and its national life, they are building themselves a Ghetto in a foreign literature: and this Ghetto, like any other, is regarded by the native population as of no account, and by the Hebrew community as a merely temporary product, which is not destined to endure as part of its national life, which it may and does enjoy at that time and in that place, but which cannot call forth, as a national literature does, a living and imperishable sentiment. Thus, for example, our community has already almost forgotten the name of

Levanda : his sketches of Jewish life in Russia, which twenty years ago were still among the most popular in Russian Jewish circles, have now very few readers indeed. But Smolenskin's stories, very similar to those of Levanda in subject, and much inferior to them in ability and taste, are still as widely read and as popular as though they had been written yesterday. The only reason that I can find for this difference is that Smolenskin wrote his stories in Hebrew, and Levanda in Russian. This example, which is not unique, proves that the Jewish nation recognizes as its national literature only what is written in its own language. For this reason it retains its affection for Smolenskin's stories, which enriched its national literature, even now when they belong to a bygone age; while writers like Levanda, who use a foreign language, are popular only so long as their books are fresh, and are then forgotten, being indeed but a temporary phenomenon, which had its uses for a certain time, but did not permanently increase the national wealth.[1]

But I touch here on a fresh question, which has come to the front only in our own time: I mean the

[1] Even Abraham Geiger, far removed as he was, by the trend of his ideas, from recognizing the value of Hebrew at the present day *as the national language,* was forced to confess that Hebrew works of scholarship or general literature are much more highly valued by the people, and retain its affection and respect much longer than books on the Jews and Judaism written in other languages (A. Geiger, Nachgelassene Schriften, ii, pp. 286-288).

question of the " Jargon."   Our ancestors in every
generation, though they always spoke the languages
of the countries to which they were exiled, recognized beyond all shadow of doubt that we had but one
national language—Hebrew.   Even the Jewish-Ger-
man Jargon, which has been spoken by Jews in
Northern Europe for so many centuries, never had
for them any greater importance than the other languages of the Diaspora, and they used it, like other
languages, only under compulsion, for the sake of those
who were ignorant of Hebrew.

But now there is among us a party which would
raise this Jargon to the dignity of a national language.
Since, they argue, the majority of the Jews have in
course of time acquired a new language, which is
peculiar to them, and is not shared by any other
people, we must accept facts as they are, and acknowledge, whether we will or not, that this is our national
language to-day, and not Hebrew, which has not been
spoken for two thousand years, and in the present
generation is known to very few even as a literary
medium.   This theory as to the national language leads
logically to a new view of the national literature.   If
the Jargon is our national language, then, of course,
the Jargon literature is our national literature; and as
such it claims our affection and respect, and demands
that we should give our best energies to the task of
perfecting it and making it worthy of its honored
name.   We must no longer waste time on Hebrew
literature, which is a mere survival, galvanized for the
time being into an artificial life.

This is not the place to enter into a detailed discussion of this question. But it seems to me, speaking generally, that it is just the upholders of the view which I have mentioned, with their appeal to facts as they are, who really turn a blind eye to the actual facts, and wish to create an artificial state of things on an unstable foundation.

In the first place, the actual facts of history are against them. Never since the world began has it happened that a nation has accepted as its national language an alien tongue acquired in a strange land, after a long history during which it knew nothing of this tongue, but had another national language, always recognized as such, in which it produced a literature of wide range and glorious achievement, expressing every side of its national individuality. There is not a single nation, alive or dead, of which we can say that it existed before its national language—that whole periods of its recorded history passed away before its national language was known to it. No man can regard as his own natural speech any language which he has learned after arriving at manhood. His language is that in which his cradle-songs were sung, that which took root in his being before he knew himself, and grew up in him together with his self-consciousness. Similarly, a nation has no national language except that which was its own when it stood on the threshold of its history, before its national self-consciousness was fully developed—that language which has accompanied it through every period of its career, and is inextricably bound up with all its memories.

In the second place, the actual facts of the present are against them. This Jargon, though it is to-day the language of most Jews, is gradually being forgotten all over the world, and will have disappeared some generations hence. In America, where the Jargon and its literature are most flourishing (save the mark!), it is in reality only the language of the older generation, which brought it from Europe. The younger generation, born in America and educated in American schools, speaks English and does not understand the Jargon. If not for the yearly inrush of Jargon-speaking immigrants, there would not be a vestige of the language left in the New World. But the volume of immigration into America is bound in the nature of things to decrease in course of time; and with it the Jargon-speaking population will also decrease, until the Jargon is extinct. Even in its native countries— Russia, Galicia, and Roumania—the Jargon is being driven to the wall by the language of the country, just in so far as education is spreading among the Jews. Thus, even at the present day, there are in those countries thousands of families from which the Jargon is banished. There is therefore no doubt that before long Yiddish will cease to be a living and spoken language. The process of its decay is an inevitable outcome of the conditions of life; and all the efforts of its supporters to raise it in the popular estimation by the agency of an attractive literature will not avail to stem this process, any more than Hebrew literature, which certainly has always stood high in the popular estimation, availed to preserve Hebrew as a spoken language when the conditions of life demanded its abandonment in favor of other forms of speech. Their labors in the service of Yiddish can have only this result: that after two or three generations we shall have *two* dead literary languages, instead of one, as at present, and that our descendants will consequently be morally bound, in the name of nationalism, to learn both of them from books.

But I am confident that we shall not be brought into this absurd position. The Jargon, like all the other languages which the Jews have employed at different times, never has been and never will be regarded by the nation as anything but an external and temporary medium of intercourse; nor can its literature live any longer than the language itself. So soon as the Jargon ceases to be spoken, it will be forgotten, and its literature with it; and then nobody will claim for it, on the ground of national sentiment, what our best men have always claimed for Hebrew—that it should be an obligatory subject of study.

In cases of aphasia it often happens, so doctors tell us, that the patient forgets all the languages that he has ever learned from books, including even the one that he was in the habit of using before his malady began, but remembers his native language—his mother tongue—and can use it with ease, even though he may not have spoken it since his childhood. Such is the strength of the natural, organic link between a human being and his own language. There is the same link between a nation and its real national language. True, an evil fate has bereft us of our national language, and forced us to use others in its stead; but no other language has ever ousted it, or can ever oust it, from its place in the roots of our being. All of them, the Jargon not excluded, obtain a foothold as the result of temporary circumstances, and lapse into oblivion again when circumstances change, and we have no further need of them. But Hebrew has been our language ever since we came into existence; and Hebrew alone is linked to us inseparably and eternally as part of our being. We are therefore justified in concluding that Hebrew has been, is, and will always be, our national language; that our national literature, throughout all time, is the literature written in Hebrew. We are at liberty to use any other language that is generally understood among our people for the diffusion of ideas and knowledge; and such use undeniably serves a practical purpose for the time being. But it is a very long step from this temporary usefulness to the dignity of an undying national literature: so long a step that it is matter for wonder how sane men can confuse two such different ideas. Indeed, if I am not mistaken, the best of the Jargon writers are themselves conscious that the Jargon and its literature are doomed to oblivion, and that only Hebrew literature can survive among the Jews forever; and it is for this reason that they have their works translated into Hebrew, in

order to gain them admittance into our national literature, and to secure their survival.

I have dealt perhaps at undue length with this question, which is not an essential part of my subject. My
excuse must be that I could not pass over the confu-
sion of thought that has latterly prevailed among us
on the question of our national literature. But now to
return to our subject.

We have decided that Hebrew literature alone is
our true national literature. But how poor, how
meagre has this literature become of late years!

Some time ago I had occasion to discuss the present
position of our literature; [1] and for that reason I do not
propose now to enlarge on this subject, which in any
case calls for no long exposition. Any qualified judge
must admit that our literature has reached a high level
of perfection in one branch only—that of self-advertisement. If you took our literature at its own present
valuation, you might suppose that it was achieving
wonders and growing richer and richer every day.
But the sober truth is that this self-advertisement is
the sum total of its wealth: it is a case of *vox et
prætærea nihil.*

Before the Haskalah period [2] we had indeed an
original national literature. This literature is open to
adverse criticism from various points of view: it may
be censured alike for its content and for its form,
though most of its critics have exaggerated its de-

---

[1] In the essay entitled "After Ten Years" [not included in
this translation].
[2] [See note on p. 64].

fects; but at least it cannot be denied that this literature is *ours,* that it was a product of the Jewish spirit, that it was a faithful expression of the contemporary inner life of the nation, and that all our best intellects contributed to its making in each successive age. But in recent times, from the day when we left the Ghetto, and began to scatter our energies to the four winds of heaven, our literature has been smitten by the same curse that has fallen on every branch of our national culture. The really original intellects desert their own poverty-stricken people, and give their efforts to the enrichment of those who are already rich; while our literature remains a barren field for dullards and mediocrities to trample on, with that excessive unrestraint which a man may use in his own bedroom. Even what is good in our literature—the work of the few writers who deserve the name—is good only in that it resembles more or less the good products of other literatures. From the beginning of modern Hebrew literature to the present day we have produced scarce one really original book to which we could point as an individual expression of our national spirit. It is almost all translation or imitation, and for the most part badly done at that: the translation being too far from the original, and the imitation too near. And the translation and the imitation have this in common, that they are foreign in spirit. We cannot feel that our national life is linked with a literature like this, which is in its essence nothing but a purveyor of foreign goods, presenting the ideas and feelings of foreign writers in a vastly inferior form.

With shame we must confess it: if we wish to find even the shadow of an original literature in the modern period, we have to turn to the literature of Hasidism, which, with all its follies, has here and there a profound idea, stamped with the hall-mark of Hebrew originality. The Haskalah literature has not nearly so much to show.

Such, then, is the condition of our national culture in all its branches.

The whole world is reverberating just now with the cry of our wandering poor for bread. Help is offered from every side, in large measure or in small. In time they will find a resting-place, though it be only temporary, one here, one there, and the Jewish people will not be wiped off the face of the earth. But meanwhile the rot is spreading internally, and no cry is raised. Our national spirit is perishing, and not a word is said; our national heritage is coming to an end before our very eyes, and we are silent.

Deep indeed must be our degradation, if we have no understanding, no feeling left for anything but the physical suffering which touches our flesh and bone.

There are indeed a few individuals among the Zionists who recognize and acknowledge that the spiritual trouble of which I have spoken hitherto is fraught with danger to our people's future no less than the physical trouble; and that a "home of refuge" for the national *spirit* is therefore not less imperatively necessary than a home of refuge for our homeless wanderers. But they imagine that there is one method of solving both problems; that the very attempt to create a healthy and well-ordered settlement in Palestine involves the creation of that national basis which is necessary for the revival of the national spirit in that country—that basis without which we cannot hope to give firmness and stability to the national spiritual centre of our aspirations. It is, indeed, impossible to maintain that the material settlement has no bearing on our spiritual problem, or that this problem can be solved without the aid of such a settlement. On the contrary, the whole point of the material settlement consists, to my mind, in this—and it makes no difference whether those who are engaged in the work of settlement realize it or not—that it can be the foundation of that national spiritual centre which is destined to be created in our ancestral country in response to a real and insistent national demand. The material problem, on the other hand, will not disappear even after the creation of a home of refuge, because in the ordinary course of things immigration into the Jewish settlement cannot counterbalance the natural increase of the Jews in those countries where the majority of them live at present. I have endeavored to make this clear in other essays, which probably are familiar to most of my readers; [1] and it is not necessary to enlarge

[1] [The reference is to a number of controversial Essays in which the author criticised the Herzlian conception of Zionism. These Essays, which are familiar to most readers of Hebrew, are not included in the present translation.]

on the subject here. But it does not at all follow from this admission that we must pay no attention for the present to the spiritual revival, but must sit and wait with folded arms until it comes of itself, until, that is, the material settlement is sufficiently established and completed. It is impossible, in my opinion, to deny that only a very large settlement could be sufficient for that purpose. Not twenty agricultural colonies, not even a hundred, though they be never so well ordered, can automatically effect our spiritual salvation, in the sense of a reunion of our scattered forces and their concentration in the service of the national culture. That result may be achieved when we have an extensive and complete national centre, embracing every department of human life, and producing in each department new demands and new means to their fulfilment. But can we sit and wait for the realization of this great dream—a realization which, by universal admission, cannot be speedy—and meanwhile allow our spiritual strength to waste away before our very eyes?

It is for this reason that I maintain that work for the national revival cannot be confined to the material settlement alone. We must take hold of both ends of the stick. On the one side, we must work for the creation of an extensive and well-ordered settlement in our ancestral land; but on the other side we are not at liberty to neglect the effort to create there, at the same time, a fixed and independent centre for our national culture, for learning, art, and literature. Little by little, willing hands must be brought into our country, to repair its ruins and restore its pristine glories; but at the same time we must have hearts and minds, endowed with knowledge and sympathy and ability, to repair our spiritual ruins, and restore to our nation its glorious name and its rightful place in the comity of human culture. And so the foundation of a single great school of learning or art in Palestine, the establishment of a single university for the study of language and literature, would be, to my mind, a national work of the highest importance, and would do more to bring us near to our goal than a hundred agricultural colonies. For such colonies are, as I have said, nothing more than bricks for the building of the future: in themselves they cannot yet be regarded as a central force capable of moulding anew the life of the whole people. But a great educational institution in Palestine, which should attract Jews of learning and ability in large numbers to carry on their work on Jewish national lines in a true Jewish spirit, without constraint or undue influence from without, might even now rejuvenate the whole people and breathe new life into Judaism and Jewish literature.

I know full well that such is not the usual course of things. In every nation which develops in a healthy and natural way, the development starts from below and proceeds upwards. First of all, the economic and political foundations of the national life are consolidated; and it is only after creating such external conditions as are favorable to its survival that the nation

turns to less material things, and produces what it is
capable of producing in the domain of culture. That
is the course of development of a young nation, new
to the stage of history, which mounts the ladder of
progress rung by rung. But with the Jews it is different. They climbed the lower rungs of the ladder
thousands of years ago, and then, after they had attained to a high stage of culture, their natural progress
was forcibly arrested: the ground was cut away from
under their feet, and they were left hanging in mid-
air, burdened with a heavy pack of valuable spiritual
goods, but robbed of any basis for a healthy existence
and a free development. Generations came and went
—and still this wretched nation was left hanging in
mid-air, exerting all its remaining strength to preserve
its inheritance of culture, and to save itself from fall-
ing below the level which it had reached in its more
prosperous days. And now, when its life is illumined
by a spark of hope, when it dreams of a return to the
solid earth, of a national life based on secure and
natural foundations—can we now bid this nation throw
away its spiritual burden, so as to be able the more
easily to concentrate on the material work which should
come first in the natural order of things, and then
afterwards begin again from the bottom of the ladder,
in the customary way?

" There is nothing in the universal that is not in the
particulars." There is no nation so rich as ours in men
who combine a highly developed intellect with an elementary ignorance of the alphabet of culture, and are

forced to make up this deficiency after they have reached maturity and acquired a large stock of knowledge. Solomon Maimon, for example, went to school, and learned German and other subjects together with children, when he had arrived at middle age, and was known in Germany as a profound philosopher. Now what would he have said, and others like him (and there have been many Jews of this type in the past few generations), if some fatuous person had advised them to forget all that they had learned before, and to devote their whole mind to the elementary subjects, until they should attain once more, slowly and laboriously, to the rank of educated men, progressing from the simple to the difficult, as other mortals do? The Jews as a nation are in an analogous position, child and grown man in one. The Jewish nation emerged from childhood a hundred generations back, and now demands the food of grown men; but the conditions under which it lives compel it to go to kindergarten again, and to master the alphabet of national life. What then is it to do? " It is good that thou shouldst take hold of this; yea, also from that withdraw not thy hand ": build from below and from above at the same time! Of course, nation building in this style is something abnormal. But then our life altogether is abnormal; and build how we will, the building must be something quite without precedent. In this matter, therefore, we must not look for guidance to the history of other nations: we must do what our peculiar position forces us to do, relying on our nation's strength of will and power of endurance, which have preserved it miraculously to the present day, and will be its savior in the future.

But we must recognize at the outset that this programme of a *spiritual* " back to the land," if one may so call it, of the re-centralization of our spiritual potentialities, is not one which can be carried out easily, and as it were by the way. To lay the foundations of a spiritual " refuge " for our national culture demands perhaps preparations no less elaborate, and resources no less extensive, than to lay the foundations of a material refuge for persecuted Jews. And besides the work of preparation for the future, there is also a great deal of work to be done in the present. We are all familiar with the division in the Zionist camp on the question of the immediate programme. For my own part, I am of opinion that work for the improvement of the material and political position of the Jews in the Diaspora, though it is undoubtedly necessary and useful as a temporary measure of relief, however slight, and though it has, therefore, undeniable claims on all who have the opportunity of taking part in such work, is yet not properly to be included in the work essential to Zionism. Life in exile, at its best, will always remain life in exile; that is to say, it will always remain the opposite of that free national life which is the aim of the Zionist movement: and one movement cannot concern itself with two opposites. But it is different in the case of cultural work. Our national creative power, as I have said above, remains the same in all ages; and it has not ceased even in exile to work in its own specific fashion. Hence, every atom of that power which is severed from its original source, and floats away into a strange world, is an irreparable loss to the nation. To gather these atoms together, and keep them in our own world for the benefit of our own national culture, is essentially Zionist work, because it adds to our spiritual wealth in the present, and also prepares the way for the greater cultural work that is to come after the establishment of the centre in Palestine. That centre once established, Palestine will make use of the products of these forces, and will enable their activity to be carried on in a more complete and perfect manner.

This is a long and arduous task, and certainly demands a powerful and well-knit organization, the business of which will be to gather the necessary resources without delay, and to keep constant watch over these erring atoms of spiritual force, so that they may neither waste away unheard of, nor be attracted outside the confines of Judaism. The organization will have to support every achievement or creation of promise in any branch of culture, always with an eye to a gradual approach towards its real goal—the establishment of the spiritual centre in Palestine. Now the Zionist organization of to-day, with all its faults, is as yet the only Jewish institution brought into being for the sake of the national revival. But it cannot possibly be saddled also with the task of reviving the national culture. In the first place, it has enough to do in propagating the

idea, in educating people up to its aims, and strengthening its own institutions : indeed, these objects, which
lie nearest to its intention and aim, are already beyond
its strength.   Secondly, no single organization can
pursue two objects which, however closely connected,
are different in character, and demand different means
and different men.   The man who is able to collect
funds and sell shares is not necessarily able to recognize a budding literary talent, and to further its development.   The man with a gift for diplomacy
and political organization may not be the ideal leader
for a spiritual movement, or the man best able to
organize educational and literary effort.   Thirdly, there
is not as yet complete unanimity among nationalist
Jews as regards either the means or the end of the
national movement.   We have, on the one side, the
" political " Zionists, who regard the spiritual aspect
as subsidiary and not worth the trouble ; we have, at
the other extreme, the " spiritual " Zionists, who are
dissatisfied with all " political " work, at least in its
present form, and think it useless.   We have, further,
" nationalists " of different kinds, who do not believe
in Zionism at all, but have a regard for the national
culture, and think that the concentration of effort on
its promotion is a great national object, which deserves
the widest support.   This being so, if we wish not to
waste any of our strength, which is little enough as
it is, but to use it all in the service of the general
culture, finding for each individual his proper work,
we must establish a special organization for cultural

work. That organization will attract to itself all those who appreciate the value of the national culture, and make its extension and free development their aim, whether they are Zionists in the official sense, or not. All its machinery and its activities must be directed solely to its own end; it must neither subserve the political organization nor be dependent on its opinion. It is of course obvious that the two organizations, aiming, as they do after all aim, at the same end— that of the revival of Israel—and differing only in that they approach the goal from different sides, must be closely interconnected, and be in constant need of each other. But if only they both understand the ultimate object which they have in common, their relation will not be one of jealousy and competition, but one of peace and harmony and constant mutual assistance. There will perhaps be more unity than there is at present within the Zionist organization between the different elements which are mixed up together, and are pulling Zionism this way and that.

.   .   .   .

This brings us to the second branch of cultural work. This side of the question is in reality much simpler than the other aspect, and needs no long exposition.

Does the Jewish people as a whole stand in need of improvement from the point of view of culture?

Some months ago a Jewish writer in a Russian periodical tried to prove that the Jews ought not to complain, because they are on a higher level of culture than the nations among which they live. The Jews, he points out, can read and write, and are endowed with exceptional intellectual and psychological qualities, which enable them everywhere to adapt themselves to the surrounding conditions much more readily than other nations. Why, then, should they grumble? The whole cry has been raised by a few atrabilious scribblers on the lookout for a grievance; it is they who are responsible for the invention of the " Jewish tragedy."

This kind of reasoning is characteristic of slaves, whose highest ideal is to be entirely like their masters. The master is the criterion by which they measure themselves and their own worth. If they find that they come up to the standard and have no need to be ashamed before their master, they think themselves lucky, and do not dare to ask for anything more. But the free man measures himself and his standing by his own measure, not by other people's. His ideal is not to attain to the level of the men around him, but to rise as high as his own powers enable him to rise. If circumstances hinder his development, and do not allow him to put forth his powers to their full extent and realize all the possibilities of his individuality, he suffers untold agonies, and it is no comfort to him that even as things are he is superior to many other men. Take a young Jew in some benighted village, who is spending himself in the search after knowledge, and eating out his heart because he cannot burst the trammels and find free scope for his self-development, and ask him why he is discontented—point out to him that even as things are he has attained to a higher level of culture than many men in the big cities, and that he ought to be satisfied with that. He will tell you that the man must be utterly cramped in mind and devoid of sensibility who does not feel the enormous tragedy of the soul conscious of manifold powers that seek an outlet and find none.

If we estimate the cultural position of the Jewish people by this criterion, we shall have to admit that it is very unsatisfactory, and much worse than that of other nations. Every other nation is free to climb as high on the ladder of culture as its strength allows. If it stops at an early stage, that only proves, unfortunately for this particular nation, that it is not fit to mount higher. But we Jews are hemmed in by obstacles of all kinds. We are compelled to fight at every turn, with what strength we have left, for things which every other nation obtains without a struggle. When we see that, in spite of all, we are not inferior to other nations, and need not be ashamed of ourselves, this should not console us; on the contrary, it ought to be galling to us to see how much further we might rise, if we too could use our powers without hindrance, and if each of us could develop in the way best suited to him, as other men do. None but a slave could fail to feel or could deny the national tragedy involved in the inability to rise to the level of culture for which we are fitted by our inherent powers.

Beyond doubt, therefore, there is an urgent need for the improvement of our position from the point of

view of culture. But this is not *in itself* a task for
Zionism; it only becomes so because of its national
aspect. Zionism need not and cannot be a sort of
"Association for the Diffusion of Enlightenment,"[1]
because enlightenment as such has no necessary connection with the Zionist ideal, and many people are
engaged in "diffusing" it without the assistance of
Zionism. Modern life of its own accord forces Jews
to pursue enlightenment; and even the best minds of
the "upper ten" of Jewry have been accustomed
these three generations to work strenuously for
the enlightenment of the people, seeking in this way to
satisfy that national instinct which occasionally impels
them to demonstrate in some tangible fashion that there
is a link between them and their nation. Hence Zionism has no need to undertake this task; it would be
simply carrying coals to Newcastle. But, on the other
side, Zionism is bound to supply this work of enlightenment with the *nationalist* basis which it lacks at
present. We are all familiar with the inwardness of
that enlightenment which our philanthropic benefac-
tors are endeavoring to spread among the Jews. We
know that its growth is in inverse proportion to the
development of the national spirit, which dwindles
ever more and more as this enlightenment spreads.
Hence the improvement of our cultural position, which
should be, as with other nations, an elixir of life for
the people, inspiring it with new strength and vigor
in its struggle for existence, has become a poison, bring-

[1] [As to "Enlightenment" see note on p. 64.]

ing in its train nothing but death and disintegration. For this reason Zionism, which aims at the revival of the national spirit, cannot exclude popular enlightenment from the sphere of its proper work, and allow its opponents to use this force for their own ends. To exercise a wise guidance over the movement for the diffusion of enlightenment; to secure that it shall be conducted in the national spirit, and shall be productive of good to the nation; to wage incessant warfare against the alien spirit which is artificially introduced into our midst along with enlightenment, though the two have no essential connection—this is one of the most important branches of Zionist work. Zionism, we must all agree, has need not only of subscriptions and shares, but even more of souls. One Jewish soul saved from the snare of assimilation is worth never so many shares.

At one of the earlier Congresses the battle-cry went forth, " Win over the synagogue organization." Zionists everywhere responded obediently, and spent much time and effort in an unequal struggle with the communal leaders. But so far their labor has scarcely anywhere had any tangible results. Indeed, it would have been better, in my opinion, if the watchword had been, " Win over the educational organization." In the synagogue we have to deal with the parents, in the schools with the children. To conquer the parents, to infuse a new spirit into grown men who have already settled down into a certain way of life, whose opinions and feelings have already become, as it were, stereotyped, would be a matter of more labor than profit; the small results would not generally be worth the expenditure of energy. Surely, it were better for our purpose to lay out this energy on the conquest of the children. In them we have a clean sheet on which we may write what we will. If in course of time we can put into the field a large squadron of younger men to fight their elders, the products of the school against the leaders of the synagogue, where will the victory lie? History bears witness that in a war of parents and children it is always the children who win in the end; the future is theirs.

But the duty of Zionists in the sphere of education is not confined to schools of the "enlightened" type. We must remember that, side by side with the "improved" education of to-day, we have also the old traditional system, which is no doubt losing ground every year, but is still strong, is struggling hard for its existence, and will undoubtedly play an important part in our national life for many years to come, influencing by its method and its spirit the education and upbuilding of tens of thousands of Jewish children. This being so, we are bound to pay attention to this system of education also, and reform it too, in a manner suited to our purpose. We must not, indeed, set out with the idea that the traditional system is opposed, like the "improved" system as at present used, to our national spirit. It is well known that the atmosphere of the Heder is Jewish through and through. The picture of "the community of Israel," with its sorrows and its hopes, is placed in the foreground of the children's daily life in the Heder, and works itself ineradicably into the texture of their minds. There is not a book in the Heder but reminds its young readers of their people and its history in happiness and in exile. Even the Song of Songs, the only love-song left to our people from the days of its youth, is metamorphosed into a national hymn, wherein the community of Israel pours out her heart before her " Beloved," weeps and smiles, entreats and yearns; and the Song inspires in the hearts of the tender Heder children a love for their nation that passes all bounds. Yet it is obvious and undeniable, however extraordinary, that most orthodox Jews who have been trained in this system, for all their devotion to the *community* of Israel, are unable to understand the ideal of the regeneration of Israel as a *people*. The masses stand aloof, and regard the new movement with complete indifference; and their leaders are mostly opposed to it, and try, by every means that jealousy and hatred can suggest, to put obstacles in its path.

This is not the place for a lengthy explanation of the causes of this inconsistency. But I think it right to mention here an expression used by a well-known Rabbi in the course of the discussion on culture at the last Congress. " In my opinion," he said, with an allusion to his orthodox friends, " a Jew who is no Zionist is still a Jew; but he is not a logical Jew."[1] No doubt the Rabbi meant that the Jew who is con-

[1] Report of the Sixth Congress, p. 394.

cerned for his national possessions, and has been accustomed from the earliest years of childhood to mourn his people's ruin and dream of its restoration, must, if he were logical, be thrilled at the trumpet-call of the revival, and be one of the first to put hand and heart to the work. If he fails to do so, it is simply a mistake, due to lack of logic. This explanation cannot, indeed, be considered satisfactory to-day, when philosophers have taught us that there is no such thing as a " mistake," and that men's loves and hates are not dictated by logic. But for our present purpose we need not go deeply into the question. Even if we agree with the Rabbi that nothing but a lack of logic is responsible, we must still admit that, since these lack-logics are the majority of the products of the Heder, this fact cannot be a mere accident, but there must be some fault inherent in the educational system of the Heder, which perverts its pupils' sense of logic, and makes them unable to understand or feel the connection between the " community of Israel " of the Song of Songs, yearning after her " Beloved " in Heaven and waiting for Him to bring her redemption, and the actual people of Israel, yearning after its beloved land and striving to redeem that land by its own strength.

If this is so, whose business is it to reform this educational system, in order to straighten out the crookedness of its logic, if not that of the *orthodox Zionists,* who are themselves emancipated from this logical inconsistency, and at the same time recognize and acknowledge that it is rampant in their own camp?

I say " the *orthodox* Zionists " advisedly: for we have no need and no right to demand of any section that it shall entrust the education of its children to another section which is fundamentally opposed to its views on human life. Just as the " modernists " cannot sacrifice the education that they want in order to satisfy the orthodox, so the orthodox cannot give way a single inch in a matter so vital to the existence of the ancient stronghold for which they would give their lives. It is a natural desire, and therefore a natural and inviolable right, of every man to educate his children so that they will grow up to be of his own way of thinking. And since the two main sections of the Jewish people are united under the banner of Zionism, they must both recognize the points of union and of difference between them in every department of life, and especially in that of education. They must both obey the demands of the wider idea that unites them. Every inevitable outcome of that idea is common to both, and imposes on both an equally binding obligation. But outside the limits thus laid down they are once more separate sections, and each has the right to act as it thinks best, with absolute freedom, in all its affairs. If we take this criterion, we shall conclude that Zionism must demand from both sections— and both must obey implicitly and without reserve— that each shall make the ideal of the national revival, in the modern sense, the basis of education; but on this foundation each is at liberty to erect its own superstructure in its own way, without hindrance or interference from outside.

This solution of the problem is so natural and so simple, that one cannot help being surprised at the angry struggle which goes on incessantly within the camp on the question of education.

.   .   .   .

With this I think that I have fulfilled the promise made at the beginning of this paper: to clear up the "problem of culture" in the plain meaning of the term, without introducing startling new ideas or over-subtle refinements. It may be that many of my readers hoped for more practical suggestions as to the organization of the work of culture in its two aspects; for Zionists nowadays attach so much importance to questions of organization. But to my mind that is not the essential thing. The idea itself, if it is clearly understood and accepted with thorough conviction, will be the best organizer; it will always produce the necessary machinery in a form suited to its object. Wherever you find men worrying too much about their organization and continually patching it up, you may be sure that the underlying idea is not sufficiently understood.

Perhaps these words of mine will help to clear up the conceptions involved in the phrase "cultural work," and create a true appreciation of the nature and object of that work. If so, the practical results will follow.

MOSES

(1904)

The influence of great men on the history of the
human race is a subject of much discussion among
philosophers. Some maintain that the great men create
history, and the masses are nothing more than the
material on which they work. Others assert that the
masses are the moving force, and the great men of
every age are only inevitable products of that age and
its conditions. Such discussions make one reflect on
the tendency of philosophers to shut their eyes to what
lies in front of them, and to seek by roundabout paths
what is really so near. Surely it is obvious that the
real great men of history, the men, that is, who have
become forces in the life of humanity, are not actual,
concrete persons who existed in a certain age. There
is not a single great man in history of whom the popular fancy has not drawn a picture entirely different
from the actual man; and it is this imaginary conception, created by the masses to suit their needs and their
inclinations, that is the real great man, exerting an
influence which abides in some cases for thousands of
years—this, and not the concrete original, who lived
a short space in the actual world, and was never seen
by the masses in his true likeness.

And so it is when learned scholars burrow in the

dust of ancient books and manuscripts, in order to raise the great men of history from the grave in their true shapes; believing the while that they are sacrificing their eyesight for the sake of " historical truth." It is borne in on me that these scholars have a tendency to overestimate the value of their discoveries, and will not appreciate the simple fact that not every archeological truth is also an historical truth. Historical truth is that, and that alone, which reveals the forces that go to mould the social life of mankind. Every man who leaves a perceptible mark on that life, though he may be a purely imaginary figure, is a real historical force; his existence is an historical truth. And on the other hand, every man who has left no impress on the general course of life, be his concrete existence at a particular time never so indisputable, is only one of the million: and the truth contained in the statement that such an one existed is a merely literal truth, which makes absolutely no difference, and is therefore, in the historical sense, no truth at all. Goethe's Werther, for instance, was a pure fiction; but his influence on that generation was so immense as to cause a large number of suicides: and therefore he is, in the historical sense, much more truly a real person than this or that actual German of the same period, who lived an actual concrete life, and died, and was forgotten, and became as though he had never been. Hence I do not grow enthusiastic when the drag-net of scholarship hauls up some new " truth " about a great man of the past; when it is proved by the most convincing evidence that some national hero, who lives on in the hearts of his people, and influences their development, never existed, or was something absolutely unlike the popular picture of him. On such occasions I tell myself: all this is very fine and very good, and certainly this "truth" will erase or alter a paragraph of a chapter in the book of archeology; but it will not make history erase the name of its hero, or change its attitude towards him, because real history has no concern with so-and-so who is dead, and who was never seen in that form by the nation at large, but only by antiquarians; its concern is only with the living hero, whose image is graven in the hearts of men, who has become a force in human life. And what cares history whether this force was at one time a walking and talking biped, or whether it was never anything but a creature of the imagination, labelled with the name of some concrete man? In either case history is certain about his existence, because history feels his effects.

And so when I read the Haggadah on the eve of Passover, and the spirit of Moses the son of Amram, that supremest of heroes, who stands like a pillar of light on the threshold of our history, hovers before me and lifts me out of this nether world, I am quite oblivious of all the doubts and questions propounded by non-Jewish critics. I care not whether this man Moses really existed; whether his life and his activity really corresponded to our traditional account of him; whether he was really the savior of Israel and gave his people the Law in the form in which it is preserved among us; and so forth. I have one short and simple answer for all these conundrums. This Moses, I say, this man of old time, whose existence and character you are trying to elucidate, matters to nobody but scholars like you. We have another Moses of our own, whose image has been enshrined in the hearts of the Jewish people for generations, and whose influence on our national life has never ceased from ancient times till the present day. The existence of this Moses, as a historical fact, depends in no way on your investigations. For even if you succeeded in demonstrating conclusively that the man Moses never existed, or that he was not such a man as we supposed, you would not thereby detract one jot from the historical reality of the ideal Moses—the Moses who has been our leader not only for forty years in the wilderness of Sinai, but for thousands of years in all the wildernesses in which we have wandered since the Exodus.

And it is not only the existence of this Moses that is clear and indisputable to me. His character is equally plain, and is not liable to be altered by any archeological discovery. This ideal—I reason—has been created in the spirit of the Jewish people; and the creator creates in his own image. These ideal figures, into which a nation breathes its most intense aspirations, seem to be fashioned automatically, without conscious purpose; and therefore, though they cannot, of course, escape a certain superfluous and inharmonious embroidery, and though we cannot insist that every detail shall be organically related to the central idea, yet the picture as a whole, if we look at its broad outlines, does always represent that idea which is the cause of its existence, and as it were the seed from which the whole tree has grown.

I take, therefore, a comprehensive view of the whole range of tradition about Moses, and ask myself first of all: What essentially is Moses? In other words, what manner of thing is the national ideal which has its embodiment in Moses? There are heroes and heroes —heroes of war, heroes of thought, and so forth; and when we examine an ideal picture we must first be clear as to the essential nature of the ideal which the artist had in his mind and attempted to portray.

And as I look at the figure of Moses I go on to ask: Was he a military hero?

No! The whole canvas betrays no hint of physical force. We never find Moses at the head of an army, performing feats of valor against the enemy. Only once do we see him on the battlefield, in the battle with Amalek; and there he simply stands and watches the course of the fighting, helping the army of Israel by his *moral* strength, but taking no part in the actual battle.

Again: Was he a statesman?

Again, no! When he had to confront Pharaoh and discuss questions of politics with him, he was helpless without his brother Aaron, his mouthpiece.

Was he, then, a lawgiver?

Once more, no! Every lawgiver makes laws for

his own age, with a view to the particular needs of
that time and that place in which he and his people
live.   But Moses made laws for the future, for a
generation that did not yet exist, and a country not
yet conquered; and tradition has made no secret of
the fact that many laws attributed to Moses only came
into force after several generations, while others have
never been put into practice at all.

What, then, was Moses?

Tradition   answers   in   the   most   explicit   terms:
" There arose not a *Prophet* since in Israel like unto
Moses."   This, then, is what Moses was: a Prophet.
But he was different from the other Prophets, whose
appearance in our history, as a specific type, dates
only from the period of the monarchy.   He was,
as later generations learned to call him, " the lord of
the Prophets," that is, the ideal archetype of Hebrew
prophecy in the purest and most exalted sense of the
word.

Again I take a comprehensive glance at what read-
ing and reflection have taught me about the nature
of Hebrew prophecy, and try to define its essential
characteristics.

The Prophet has two fundamental qualities, which
distinguish him from the rest of mankind.   First, he
is *a man of truth*.   He sees life as it is, with a view
unwarped by subjective feelings; and he tells you what
he sees just as he sees it, unaffected by irrelevant considerations.   He tells the truth not because he wishes
to tell the truth, not because he has convinced him-

self, after inquiry, that such is his duty, but because
he needs must, because truth-telling is a special characteristic of his genius—a characteristic of which he
cannot rid himself, even if he would. It has been
well said by Carlyle that every man can attain to the
elevation of the Prophet by seeking truth; but whereas
the ordinary man is able to reach that plane by
strength of will and enormous effort, the Prophet can
stand on no other by reason of his very nature.

Secondly, the Prophet is an *extremist*. He concentrates his whole heart and mind on his ideal, in which
he finds the goal of life, and to which he is determined to make the whole world do service, without
the smallest exception. There is in his soul a complete,
ideal world; and on that pattern he labors to reform
the external world of reality. He has a clear conviction that so things *must* be, and no more is needed
to make him demand that so they *shall* be. He
can accept no excuse, can consent to no compromise,
can never cease thundering his passionate denunciations, even if the whole universe is against him.

From these two fundamental characteristics there
results a third, which is a combination of the other
two: namely, the supremacy of absolute *righteousness*
in the Prophet's soul, in his every word and action.
As a man of truth he cannot help being also a man
of justice or righteousness; for what is righteousness but truth in action? And as an extremist he cannot subordinate righteousness (any more than he can
subordinate truth) to any irrelevant end; he cannot

desert righteousness from motives of temporary ex-
pediency, even at the bidding of love or pity. Thus
the Prophet's righteousness is absolute, knowing no
restriction either on the side of social necessities or on
that of human feelings.

The Prophet, then, is in this position: on the one
hand, he cannot altogether reform the world according
to his desire; on the other hand, he cannot cheat himself
and shut his eyes to its defects. Hence it is impossible
for him ever to be at peace with the actual life in
which his days are spent. There is thus a grain of
truth in the popular idea of the Prophet as above all
a man who predicts the future; for, in truth, the whole
world of the Prophet consists of his heart's vision of
what is to come, of " the latter end of days." This is
his delight and his comfort whenever the cup of sorrows is full to the brim, and he has no strength left
to pour out his soul in bitter outcry against the evil
that he sees around him.

But just as the Prophet will not bow to the world,
so the world will not bow to him, will not accept his
influence immediately and directly. This influence
must first pass through certain channels in which it
becomes adapted to the conditions of life. Then only
can it affect mankind. These channels are human
channels. They are men who cannot rise to the
Prophet's elevation, and have no sympathy with his
extremism, but are none the less nearer to him in
spirit than the mass of men, and are capable of being
influenced by him up to a certain point. These men

are the *Priests* of the prophetic ideal. They stand between the Prophet and the world, and transmit his influence by devious ways, adapting their methods to
the needs of each particular time, and not insisting
that the message shall descend on the workaday world
in all its pristine purity.

Thus I picture the Prophet in his purest form.[1]
Such, in essentials, were all the true Prophets of
Israel, from Hosea and Amos to Jeremiah and Ezekiel;
but the type is most perfectly realized in the ideal
picture of " the lord of the Prophets."

When Moses first leaves the schoolroom and goes
out into the world, he is at once brought face to face
with a violation of justice, and unhesitatingly he takes
the side of the injured. Here at the outset is revealed
the eternal struggle between the Prophet and the
world.

" An Egyptian smiting a Hebrew," the strong tread-
ing scornfully on the weak—this every-day occurrence
is his first experience. The Prophet's indignation is
aroused, and he helps the weaker. Then " two
Hebrews strove together"—two brothers, both weak,
both slaves of Pharaoh: and yet they fight each other.
Once more the Prophet's sense of justice compels him,
and he meddles in a quarrel which is not his. But this
time he discovers that it is no easy matter to fight the
battle of justice; that the world is stronger than himself, and that he who stands against the world does
so at his peril. Yet this experience does not make

[1] See the essay " Priest and Prophet " [p. 125].

him prudent or cautious. His zeal for justice drives him from his country; and as soon as he reaches another haunt of men, while he is still sitting by the well outside the city, before he has had time to find a friend and shelter, he hears once more the cry of outraged justice, and runs immediately to its aid. This time the wranglers are not Hebrews, but foreigners and strangers. But what of that? The Prophet makes no distinction between man and man, only between right and wrong. He sees strong shepherds trampling on the rights of weak women—" and Moses stood up and helped them."

This is the sum of our knowledge about Moses' life till the time when he stood before Pharaoh—and he was then " eighty years old." Of all that long stretch of years, and what happened in them, tradition takes no account, because they were only the preface, only the preparation for the real work of the Prophet. If an exception was made in the case of these three events, which happened to the Prophet at the outset of his life's journey, and if we see that all three have the same characteristic, that of the Prophet standing up against the world in the name of righteousness, we may believe that the object of the tradition was to throw this conflict into relief, and to show how the Prophet displayed the essential qualities of his kind from the very first. We may therefore infer that throughout the whole of that period, in all his wanderings, he never ceased to fight the battle of justice, until the day came when he was to be the savior of his people, and teach the world justice, not for his own time merely, but for all eternity.

That great moment dawned in the wilderness, far away from the turmoil of the world. The Prophet's soul is weary of his ceaseless battle, and he would fain rest in peace. He turns his back on men for the shepherd's life, and takes his sheep into the wilderness. There " he came to the mountain of God, unto Horeb." But even here there is no rest for him. He feels that he has not yet fulfilled his mission; a secret force in his heart urges him on, saying, " What doest thou here? Go thou, work and fight: for to that end wast thou created." He would like to disregard this voice, but cannot. The Prophet hears " the voice of God " in his heart, whether he will or not: " and if I say, I will not make mention of him. . . . . then there is in mine heart as it were a *burning fire* shut up in my bones, and I am weary with forbearing, and I cannot contain."

And the Prophet remembers that in his youth, at his first encounter with life, the same fire burnt in his heart and gave him no rest. From that day to this he has done all in his power to make justice supreme in the world: and the fire is still burning. The best of his years, the flower of his strength, have been consumed in the battle; and victory is not his. Now old age has come upon him; yet a little, and he will be sapless as a withered and barren tree—even like this bush before him. Can he still find new means of reaching his goal? Can his old age succeed where his youth has failed?

What is there to do that he has not done? Why should the fire still burn within him, still disturb his soul's peace?

Suddenly he hears the inner " voice of God "—the voice that he knows so well—calling to him from some forgotten corner of his heart:

" I am the God of thy father . . . . I have surely seen the affliction of my people which are in Egypt . . . . Come now, therefore, and I will send thee unto Pharaoh, that thou mayest bring forth my people, the children of Israel, out of Egypt."

" The God of his father," " the affliction of his people "—how can he have forgotten all this till now? Faithfully has he served the God of the Universe, fighting a hero's battle for universal justice. In Midian, in every country in which he set foot, he has striven always to deliver the oppressed from the oppressor, has preached always truth and peace and charity. But the God of his father he has forgotten; his people he has not remembered; the affliction wherewith the Egyptians afflict his people—of that he has taken no thought.

Now a new hope springs up in the Prophet's heart, and grows stronger each moment. With this hope, he feels, his strength increases, and the days of his youth are renewed. Now he knows the right way to the goal which he has striven after all his life. Hitherto he has consumed his strength among strangers, who looked on him as an alien even after he had spent years among them; who took no account of him, and paid no heed to his teaching; who would not believe him even if he called on the name of their own gods. But now, now he will go to his own brethren, his own people, and will speak to them in the name of the God of his fathers and theirs. They will know and respect him; they will listen to all that he says, will listen and obey: and the sovereignty of righteousness, hitherto nothing more than his heart's ideal, will be established in the world by this his people, which he will bring forth out of the house of bondage.

Under the spell of this noble idea the Prophet forgets for a moment all the obstacles in his path, and in fancy sees himself already in Egypt among his people. To Pharaoh, indeed, he will not go alone. He knows beforehand that such a man as he, unskilled to speak smooth words, cannot bend the hearts of kings to his desire. But he will approach first of all his own people; he will assemble the " elders of Israel," men who are known in the royal house; to them first he will reveal the great tidings, that God has visited them. And these men, the flower of the people, will understand him and " hearken to his voice." They will go with him to Pharaoh, and give God's message to the king in a language which he understands.

But how if even they, the elders of Israel, " will not hearken to his voice," " will not believe " in his mission?

In that case he knows what to do. Not for nothing was he brought up in Pharaoh's house on the knees of the magicians. " Enchantments " are an abomina-

tion to him; but what can he do if the "elders of
Israel" believe only in such things, and are open to
no other appeal?

Even the "sons of God" have been known to fall
from Heaven to earth; and even the Prophet has his
moments of relapse, when the spirit of prophecy deserts
him, and his mortal elements drag him down into the
mire of the world. But only for a moment can the
Prophet cease to be what he ought to be, and needs
must be—a man of truth. Scarcely has Moses conceived this idea of gaining credence by means of magic
enchantments, when the Prophet in him rises up in
arms against this unclean thought. Never! Since first
he began to hear "the voice of God" his tongue has
been a holy instrument, the outer vesture of that
Divine voice within him; but "a man of words," a
man whose words are only means to the attainment of
his desires, not genuinely connected with his thought
—such a man he has never been "heretofore," nor
will ever be. That is a price which he will not pay
even for the redemption of his people. If there is no
way but through enchantments, then let the redemption be achieved by others, and let him alone in his
spotless truth, alone in the wilderness:

"Oh, Lord, send, I pray thee, by the hand of him
whom Thou wilt send."

But it is not easy for the Prophet to remain in the
wilderness. The burning fire which has just roused
all his spiritual forces to action has not yet been
quelled; it will give him no rest till he find some way
to carry out his thought.

So, at last, the Prophet finds the necessary " channel " through which his influence shall reach the
people. He has a brother in Egypt, a man of position,
a Levite, who knows how to shape his words to the
needs of the time and the place. His brother will need
no enchantments to gain him allegiance. He, the
" Priest " of the future, will go with the Prophet to
the elders and to the king himself. Nay, he will know
how to find a way into the hearts of all of them:

" And thou shalt speak unto him . . . . and he
shall be thy spokesman unto the people: and it shall
come to pass, that he shall be to thee a mouth, and
thou shalt be to him as God."

So the *immediate* goal is reached. Pharaoh and all
his host lie at the bottom of the Red Sea, and Moses
stands at the head of a free people, leading them to the
land of their ancestors.

" Then sang Moses . . . ." In this hour of happiness his heart overflows with emotion, and pours itself
out in song. He does not know that he is still at the
beginning of his journey; he does not know that the
real task, the most difficult task, has still to be com-
menced. Pharaoh is gone, but his work remains; the
master has ceased to be master, but the slaves have not
ceased to be slaves. A people trained for generations
in the house of bondage cannot cast off in an instant
the effects of that training and become truly free, even
when the chains have been struck off.

But the Prophet believes in the power of his ideal.
He **is** convinced that the ideal which he is destined to

give to his people will have sufficient force to expel the taint of slavery, and to imbue this slave-people with a new spirit of strength and upward striving, equal to all the demands of its lofty mission.

Then the Prophet gathers his people at the foot of the mountain, opens the innermost heavens before them, and shows them the God of their fathers in a new form, in all His universal grandeur.

"For all the earth is Mine," so speaks the voice of the God of Israel "out of the midst of the fire." Hitherto you have believed, in common with all other nations, that every people and every country has its own god, all-powerful within his boundaries, and that these gods wage war on one another and conquer one another, like the nations that serve them. But it is not so. There is no such thing as a God of Israel and a different God of Egypt; there is one God, who was, is, and shall be: He is Lord of *all* the earth, and Ruler over *all* the nations. And it is this universal God who is the God of your fathers. The whole world is His handiwork, and all men are created in His image; but you, the children of His chosen Abraham, He has singled out to be His peculiar people, to be " a kingdom of priests and an holy nation," to sanctify His name in the world and to be an example to mankind in your individual and in your corporate life, which are to be based on new foundations, on the spirit of Truth and Righteousness.

"Justice, justice shalt thou follow." "Keep thee far from a false matter." You shall not respect the

strong; " and a stranger shalt thou not wrong. . . . .
Ye shall not afflict any widow, or fatherless child."
But neither shall you wrest justice on the side of the
weak: " Neither shalt thou favor a poor man in his
cause." The guiding rule of your lives shall be neither
hatred and jealousy, nor yet love and pity, for all alike
pervert the view and bias the judgment. " Justice,
justice "—that alone shall be your rule.

" Did ever people hear the voice of God speaking
out of the midst of the fire " such lofty and majestic
words? And the nation that has heard this message,
though it may have been sunk for centuries in the
morass of slavery and degradation, how can it fail to
rise out of the depths, and feel in its innermost soul
the purifying light that streams in upon it?

So thinks the Prophet; and the people confirm his
belief, as they cry ecstatically, with one voice, " All
that the Lord hath spoken we will do."

So the Prophet leaves the camp in peace of mind,
and withdraws into solitude on the top of the mountain, there to perfect and complete the law of righteousness. But before he has been many days out of
sight the Egyptian bondman rears his head, and in
a moment overturns the dream-castle which the Prophet
has built on the foundation of his faith in the power of
the ideal. " The voice of God " is drowned by " the
noise of the people as they shouted "; and the Priest,
whom the Prophet trusted, who was his mouthpiece
before Pharaoh and the people, this very Priest is
carried away by the mob, and makes them " gods "

after their own heart, and builds an altar . . . . This, in his view, is what the hour demands: and the Priest is above all a man of the hour.

The Prophet's grief knows no bounds. All his work, all his visions of his people's glorious mission, all the hope which comforted him in his arduous path, all is vanished into nothing. He is seized by impotent despair. " The tablets of the Covenant " fall from his hand and are broken; his faith in himself and his work is shaken. Now he sees how hard it is to create a " peculiar people " out of such warped material, and for one moment he thinks of abandoning this " obstinate people," and entrusting his tablets to the remnant who are faithful to his covenant. They will observe his law, and win over little by little the best of mankind, till they become " a great nation "; and he will return to his shepherd's life in the wilderness.

But the Prophet is not a Priest: it is not for him to bow to circumstances without a struggle, and to change his way of thought at their bidding. The first impulse passes away, and the Prophet returns to his mission, and resolves to go forward, come what may. Now he realizes the hard task that lies before him. He no longer believes in a sudden revolution; he knows that signs and wonders and visions of God can arouse a momentary enthusiasm, but cannot create a new heart, cannot uproot and implant feelings and inclinations with any stability or permanence. So he summons all his patience to the task of bearing the troublesome burden of his people and training it by slow steps till it is fit for its mission.

Thus the first period passes away. The Prophet
teaches, trains, bears, and forgives, borne up by the
hope of seeing the fruits of his labor at no distant day,
when his people's mission will be fulfilled in their
own land.

And then comes the incident of the spies. Here is
a nation on its way to conquer a country by force,
and there build up its own distinctive national life,
which is to be an example to the world: and at the
first unfavorable report despair sets in, and the glorious
future is forgotten. Even the Prophet's heart fails
him at this evidence of utter, fathomless degradation.

Moses now sees, then, that his last hope is groundless. Not even education will avail to make this degraded mob capable of a lofty mission. Straightway
the Prophet decrees extinction on his generation, and
resolves to remain in the wilderness forty years, till all
that generation be consumed, and its place be taken
by a new generation, born and bred in freedom, and
trained from childhood under the influence of the
Law which it is to observe in the land of its future.

It requires unusual courage to go out boldly to meet
danger, to fall single-handed on an enemy of vastly
superior strength, to plunge into a stormy sea. But
far greater heroism is demanded of the man who goes
about consciously and deliberately to tear out of his
heart a splendid hope, which has been the very breath
of his life; to stop half-way when all his feelings
tumultuously impel him on towards the goal which
seemed so near. With such heroism has this Hebrew

tradition endowed its Superman, the prince of its Prophets. In vain do his followers, now conscious of their error, urge him to take up the work again, and lead them to their inheritance; in vain is their entreaty, " Lo, we be here, and will go up "! The Prophet has decreed, and will not, nay cannot, retract. He is convinced that " this evil congregation " can be of no use for his purpose, and no entreaty will induce the Prophet to act against his convictions. He mourns with them and makes their grief his own; but for their supplications he has one stern answer, " Go not up, for the Lord is not among you."

So the Prophet remains in the wilderness, buries his own generation and trains up a new one. Year after year passes, and he never grows weary of repeating to this growing generation the laws of righteousness that must guide its life in the land of its future; never tires of recalling the glorious past in which these laws were fashioned. The past and the future are the Prophet's whole life, each completing the other. In the present he sees nothing but a wilderness, a life far removed from his ideal; and therefore he looks before and after. He lives in the future world of his vision, and seeks strength in the past out of which that vision-world is quarried.

Forty years are gone, and the new generation is about to emerge from its vagabond life in the wilderness, and take up the broken thread of the national task, when the Prophet dies, and another man assumes the leadership, and brings the people to its land.

Why does the Prophet die? Why is it not vouch-safed to him to complete his work himself? Tradition, as we know, gives no sufficient reason. But tradition recognized, with unerring instinct, that so it needs must be. When the time comes for the ideal to be embodied in practice, the Prophet can no longer stand at the head; he must give place to another. The reason is that from that moment there begins a new period, a period in which prophecy is dumb, a period of those half-measures and compromises which are essential to the battle of life. In this period reality assumes gradually a form very different from that of the Prophet's vision; and so it is better for him to die than to witness this change. "He shall see the land before him, but he shall not go thither." He has brought his people to the border, fitted them for their future, and given them a noble ideal to be their lodestar in time of trouble, their comfort and their salvation; the rest is for other men, who are more skilled to compromise with life. Let them do what they will do and achieve what they will achieve, be it much or little. In any case they will not achieve all that the Prophet wished, and their way will not be his way.

As for him, the Prophet, he dies, as he has lived, in his faith. All the evil that he has seen has been powerless to quench his hope for the future, or dim the brightness of the ideal that illumined his path from afar. He dies with gladness on his face, and with words of comfort for the latter days on his lips: dies, as tradition says, "in a kiss," embracing, as it were, the ideal to which he has consecrated his life, and for which he has toiled and suffered till his last breath.

When Heine wanted to describe the greatness of the prince of Hebrew poets, Jehudah Halevi, he said that "he was born with a kiss." But that idea is foreign to the Jewish spirit. When the national tradition wishes to describe the greatness of the prince of Prophets, it makes him die, not come to life, with a kiss. That death-kiss is the crown of a work completed and a duty fulfilled to the uttermost, of a life whose burden has been borne from first to last with the steadfastness of a sea-girt rock, which flinches not nor bows, but bears unmoved the onset of the devouring waves.

"The creator," I have said, "creates in his own image." And in truth, our people has but expressed *itself,* at its highest, in this picture of Moses. Well have the Cabbalists said that "Moses is reincarnated in every age." Some hint of Moses has illumined the dark life of our people, like a spark, in every generation. This needs no lengthy proof. We have but to open our Prayer Book, and we shall see almost on every page how constant has been the striving after the realization of the prophetic ideal in all its world-embracing breadth, constant throughout the blackest periods of the Jew's history, when his life has been most precarious, and persecution has driven him from country to country. Israel has never lived in the present. The present, with its evil and its wickedness, has always filled us with anguish, indignation, and bitter-

ness. But just as constantly have we been inspired
with brilliant hopes for the future, and an ineradicable
faith in the coming triumph of the good and the right;
and for these hopes and that faith we have always
sought and found support in the history of our past,
whereon our imagination has brooded, weaving all
manner of fair dreams, so as to make the past a kind
of mirror of the future. Our very Hebrew language,
the garment of the Jewish spirit, has no present tense,
but only a past and a future. The question has been
much debated, whether the fundamental characteristic
of the Jewish spirit is optimism or pessimism; and extreme views have been propounded on both sides. But
all such discussion is futile. The Jew is both optimist
and pessimist; but his pessimism has reference to the
present, his optimism to the future. This was true of
the Prophets, and it is true of the people of the
Prophets.

There has, indeed, been one short period in modern
Jewish history when Israel grew utterly weary of toil
and trouble, and began to long for solace in the present,
taking pleasure in the fleeting hour, as other nations do,
and demanding no more of life than what it can give.
And when once this longing was aroused, and became
Israel's ideal (despite its fundamental opposition to the
prophetic outlook), the prophetic characteristic at once
manifested itself here also: the ideal was pursued to
extreme lengths, without any regard to the obstacles
that lay in the way of its attainment. The Jews of
that period had no pity on the vision of a great future,

to which their ancestors clung throughout history.
They wiped it out at a single stroke, as soon as its
abandonment seemed to be a necessary step to the
attainment of the ideal of to-day. And with the future
the past necessarily went, seeing that it had no meaning
except as a mirror of the future. But we all know the
end of the story. The ideal of to-day was not attained;
and all the labor of that period, its attempt to destroy
one world and build another, left nothing but ruin and
the bitterness that comes of wasted effort.

But this was a mere passing phase, a sort of faint-
ing-fit, a temporary loss of consciousness. The prophetic spirit cannot be crushed, except for a time. It
comes to life again, and masters the Prophet in his
own despite. So, too, the prophetic people regained
consciousness in its own despite, and we see once again
some beginning of the " reincarnation of Moses." The
Spirit which called Moses thousands of years ago and
sent him on his mission, against his own will, now
calls again the generation of to-day, saying,

" And that which cometh into your mind shall not
be at all; in that ye say, we will be as the nations . . .
as I live, saith the Lord God, surely with a mighty
hand . . . . will I be king over you."

INDEX

INDEX

seq.; loss to, through assimilation, 265 *et seq.;* revival of, antecedent to spiritual revival, 289-91; the work necessary for the revival of, 293-4; the revival of, requires a special organization, 296; the revival of national, the aim of Zionism, 299-300; see also *Hebrew Spirit, the;* and under *National,* etc.

Damascus blood-accusation, the, 195.

Darwin, Charles, alluded to, 44, 183, 190, 194; stigmatized by Nietzsche, 237.

David, king, alluded to, 124.

Death-kiss, the, in Jewish tradition, 326-7.

De Coulanges, cited, 163 (n.).

Deism, and Judaism, 184, 187-8.

Desire for life. See *Will-to-live, the.*

Despair, the philosophy of, 144.

Diaspora, the, the Hebrew spirit in, 35; regeneration in, aided by Palestine, 37; see also *Dispersion, the; Dissipation; Galut, the.*

Dictionnaire des sciences philosophiques, cited, 192 (n.).

Dietary laws, the, observance of, deprecated, 244-5; see also *Kashrut.*

Dispersion, the, of Israel, not a condition of his mission, 137; see also *Diaspora, the; Dissipation; Galut, the.*

Dissipation, national, antidote to, 123; see also *Diaspora, the; Dispersion, the; Galut, the.*

Dreyfus, alluded to, 171 (n.).

Dualism, the, of body and soul, 23-4; in later Judaism, 149-51; see also *Body, the, Flesh, the; Soul, the.*

East, the, the Jews of, criticised by S. Reinach, 243 *et seq.;*

the emancipation of, 245 *et seq.*

Ecclesiastes, quoted, 159.

Education, and Zionism, 301 *et seq.*

Ego. See *Self, the.*

Ego, the national. See *Self, the national.*

Egypt, the Jews of, averse from assimilation, 118.

Egyptians, the, use of stone vessels among, 41-2.

Election of Israel, the dogma of, 228 *et seq.*

Emancipation, the, of the Jew, fetters the Hebrew spirit, 30; effects of, 31-2; and the national restoration, 34-5; and the spirit of the age, 103-6; and the Jewish mission, 138-9; cost of, 182; demands religious changes, 183; demands denial of Jewish nationality, 191; Western Jews slaves to, 192; and the blood-accusation, 195-6; and S. Reinach, 245 *et seq.;* effect of, on Jewish creativeness, 265 *et seq.;* see also *Assimilation.*

Encyclopedia, a Hebrew, projected by Ahad .Ha-'Am, 36.

End, an, demanded by the moral individual, 143.

England, objective culture of, 260.

English literature, contrasted with American, 277-8.

" Enlightenment." See *Haskalah.*

Essenes, the, ascetics, 20; contrasted with the Pharisees, 20; and the modern mission theory, 39; on the dualism of body and soul, 150-1; hold ascetic view of national life, 153-4, 157.

" Eternal Ideals," article in Voschod, cited, 171 (n.).

European Morals, by Lecky, cited, 166 (n.).

Evil, the, distinguished from evildoers, 47-8, 50; in the life of

AHAD HA-'AM was the pseudonym of Asher Ginzberg, who was born in the Ukraine on August 18, 1856. He adopted his Hebrew pen name (which means "one of the people") when he began writing his influential essays on cultural and spiritual Zionism. Ahad Ha-'Am settled in Palestine in 1921 and died in Tel Aviv on January 2, 1927.

LEON SIMON, a noted British civil servant, was born on July 11, 1881. Sir Leon (he was knighted in 1944) was educated at Oxford and is known for his editions and translations of Ahad Ha-'Am, whose biography he has also published.

Atheneum Paperbacks

Atheneum Paperbacks

STUDIES IN AMERICAN NEGRO LIFE